In
Whose
Interest?

SOUTH AFRICA: BANTUSTANS

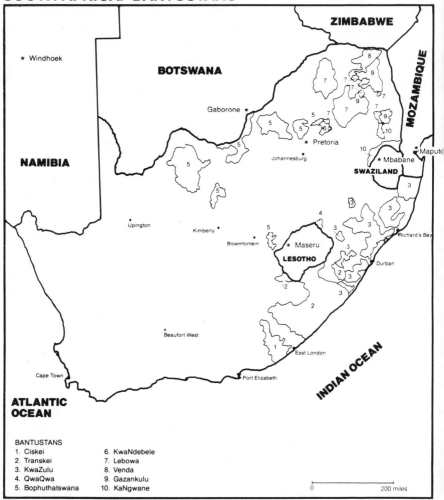

ZIMBABWE

MOZAMBIQUE

★ Windhoek

BOTSWANA

Gaborone ★

NAMIBIA

Johannesburg

★ Pretoria

★ Maputo

★ Mbabane

SWAZILAND

Upington

Kimberly

Bloemfontein

★ Maseru

LESOTHO

Richard's Bay

Durban

Beaufort West

East London

Cape Town

Port Elizabeth

INDIAN OCEAN

ATLANTIC
OCEAN

BANTUSTANS
1. Ciskei
2. Transkei
3. KwaZulu
4. QwaQwa
5. Bophuthatswana
6. KwaNdebele
7. Lebowa
8. Venda
9. Gazankulu
10. KaNgwane

0   200 miles

SOUTHERN AFRICA

South Africa in Relation to the United States

In Whose Interest?

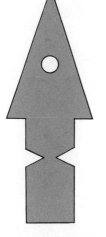

A Guide to U.S.-South Africa Relations

Kevin Danaher

Institute for Policy Studies
Washington, D.C.

First Edition

Library of Congress Cataloging in Publication Data

Danaher, Kevin.
  In whose interest?

  Bibliography: p.
  Includes index.
  1. United States—Foreign relations—South Africa. 2. South Africa—For-
eign relations—United States. 3. Blacks—South Africa—Segregation. 4.
South Africa—Race relations. I. Title.
E183.8.S6D36   1984   327.73068   84-19151
ISBN 0-89758-038-9

Institute for Policy Studies
1901 Q Street, N.W.
Washington, D.C.   20009

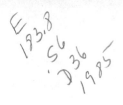
to my mother, Caroline Danaher

Contents

3. Peaceful Change
Law, Shame, and Violence
59

4. The "Communist Threat"
East-West Politics and African Independence
79

Conclusion
101

Abbreviations/Glossary
107

Country Profile
111

Chronology
113

Bibliography
191

Directory of Information Sources
257

Index
267

List of Illustrations and Tables

Maps

Figures

Tables

Acknowledgments

This work, like all books, benefited from the labor of many people. My deepest thanks to the following friends and colleagues who discussed the issues with me, edited the manuscript, provided moral support, searched out documentation, and guided the book through production: Lynn Barbee, Carol Barr, Medea Benjamin, Robert Borosage, Peter Evans, Guy Gran, Brigit Helms, Archie Hendrick, Mitchell Hinz, Robert Lawrence, Stewart Lawrence, Bernard Magubane, William Minter, Prexy Nesbitt, James O'Connor, Carolyne Pion, Andrew Schlosser, Elizabeth Schmidt, Bereket Selassie, Howard Takiff, Basker Vashee, and Lynn Whittemore. I am grateful to Carol Ferry for timely financial assistance. All errors and omissions are mine.

Introduction

Year by year, the crisis in South Africa deepens. The struggle between the white minority regime on one side and antiapartheid forces on the other can be likened to an immovable object confronting an irresistible force. As the government expands its military capacity, the opposition grows in size and intensity.

Since the 1976-77 Soweto rebellion,[1] South Africa's schools have been plagued by protests and police repression. Thousands of young Africans, frustrated by an inferior education system, and tired of trying to fight well-armed police with sticks and rocks, have fled the country to receive guerrilla training. Hundreds, perhaps thousands, have returned, intent on escalating the struggle against apartheid. Black trade unions have grown increasingly militant: worktime lost to strike activity has risen steadily since the early 1970s, and the unions have gained broad support from civic and church groups.

Since 1975, three neighboring white minority regimes—in Angola, Mozambique, and Rhodesia—have been replaced by leftist governments. Their support for antiapartheid forces, and Pretoria's attempts to destabilize the new regimes, have raised inter-regional conflict to a dangerously high level.

The United States is deeply involved in this cockpit of conflict. As the leading world power and South Africa's top trading partner, the United States has a strong impact on developments there. And of all areas of U.S. foreign policy few have as much potential for inciting conflict at home.

For over two decades, U.S. policy toward South Africa has been contradictory. U.S. leaders, in government and industry, have denounced the system of apartheid as abhorrent and antithetical to basic American principles. Yet the net effect of U.S. policy toward

South Africa has been to sustain the white minority regime militarily, economically, and diplomatically.

Over the years, U.S. corporate and government officials have utilized specific rationales for maintaining normal relations with the white minority regime. These state that:

1. fundamental change can come about via the existing political institutions;
2. U.S. corporations can be a force for democratic change;
3. only black groups that rely on peaceful methods of change deserve U.S. recognition and support;
4. communism is a greater danger than apartheid;
5. the United States is strategically dependent on the Cape sea route and South Africa's mineral exports, and therefore Washington has limited leverage over the white minority.

In leadership circles, these rationales have taken on the characteristics of dogma: often repeated to support policy decisions but seldom critically examined.

This essay subjects each of the themes in U.S.–South Africa relations to the tests of empirical evidence and logical plausibility. It illuminates the gulf between the rhetoric of policy-as-preached and the reality of policy-as-practiced. In doing so, it examines the ways in which U.S. policy has had an antidemocratic effect both at home and abroad: abroad, by sustaining white minority rule, and at home, by deceiving the American public.

The second section of the book is a profile of South Africa and a chronology of U.S.–South Africa relations during the period following the 1974-75 demise of Portuguese colonialism in Angola and Mozambique. Emphasis is placed on this period because the transfer of power from rightist white settlers to leftist black nationalists marked the key turning point of politics in the region and of U.S. policy there.

The third section is an annotated bibliography on U.S.–South Africa relations. It contains over three hundred entries, each briefly described and indexed by topic.

The final section is a select list of periodicals and organizations that provide information on U.S. involvement in southern Africa, with emphasis on sources most useful to those interested in influencing U.S. policy.

Note

1. Although the youth/worker revolt that rocked South Africa during 1976 and 1977 carries the name of South Africa's largest African township (over one million people) where the most intense disturbances took place, civil strife was rampant throughout the country. Government security forces and vigilantes murdered upwards of one thousand young Africans before the rebellion subsided. For details, see *Black South Africa Explodes* (London: Counter Information Services, 1977); Baruch Hirson, *Year of Fire, Year of Ash: The Soweto Revolt, Roots of a Revolution?* (London: Zed Press, 1979); John Kane-Berman, *South Africa: The Method in the Madness* (London: Pluto Press, 1978); Denis Herbstein, *White Man, We Want To Talk To You* (Harmondsworth, England: Penguin Books, 1978).

1. Reform in South Africa
Neo-Apartheid and U.S. Policy

Introduction

For many years, South African government officials have been telling the world that they are reforming their system of apartheid, and given more time, free from outside pressure, everything will work out for the better. These sentiments have been echoed by many in the West who either support white supremacy or sincerely believe that democratic reforms are underway. In 1978, when the current Prime Minister, P.W. Botha, took office, many liberal and conservative voices in the West hailed Botha as a genuine reformer. Many Americans were led to believe that apartheid was on its way out.

The reforms implemented by the Botha regime have been more than cosmetic. White South African leaders recognized the need to upgrade black° education: they began phasing in compulsory education for blacks and increased funding for the education of urban Africans. In September 1978, the government expanded opportunities for black businessmen by dropping regulations that 1) limited the size of black business sites to 350 square meters, 2) limited blacks to owning one business, 3) required black employers to hire only persons of their own race, and 4) required that black businessmen reside in the same area as their business.

Most significant are the labor reforms. Based on the 1979 findings of the Wiehahn Commission, the South African government took

°The complexity of South Africa's racial legislation makes precise reference to various groups difficult. Throughout this book the term "black" is used to refer to all non-whites, whereas "African," "Coloured," and "Indian" refer to those specific sub-groups.

steps to promote a skilled segment of the black working class: it dropped rules barring Africans from many higher-level jobs (job reservation); expanded training programs for African workers; and, most importantly, extended trade union rights to African workers. Although the new legislation placed numerous constraints on African unions, e.g., they are prevented from engaging in what the government considers to be political activity, membership has risen steadily and the unions have won some important concessions from management.

The Reagan administration used these changes to justify its policy of "constructive engagement." Led by Assistant Secretary of State for African Affairs Chester Crocker, administration officials portrayed South Africa as a dynamic society moving steadily toward racial equality. The reforms were "steps in the right direction."

> We recognize that a measure of change is already underway in South Africa. At such a time, when many South Africans of all races, in and out of government, are seeking to move away from apartheid, it is our task to be supportive of this process so that proponents of reform and nonviolent change can gain and hold the initiative.[1]

In a comprehensive mid-term restatement of Reagan policies in southern Africa, Under Secretary of State for Political Affairs Lawrence Eagleburger enumerated the concrete steps taken by the Administration, in cooperation with Congress, to support reform in South Africa.

- A $4 million-a-year scholarship program which brings approximately 100 black South African students a year to the United States for undergraduate and graduate degrees. The majority of these students are studying in the hard sciences. By 1985 there will be some 400 black South Africans enrolled in U.S. institutions of higher education, and we will begin graduating more black engineers, chemists, and computer engineers than now exist in South Africa.

- In cooperation with the AFL-CIO, programs of support are being initiated to train labor leaders in South Africa in skills which will improve the collective bargaining ability of black and mixed trade unions, and enhance the dialogue between the American and South African labor communities. The U.S. contribution to this program will increase from $190,000 this fiscal year to $875,000 next year.

- In cooperation with the National African Federated Chamber of Commerce of South Africa, we are beginning this year a project to support small business development in the black community. Over the next two years, some $3 million will be invested in this project designed to enhance the economic leverage of the black community.

- ...we have underway a tutorial program to assist black high school students preparing for the matriculation examination which will determine their professional futures. Over the next two years this $2 million project should significantly boost the number of blacks eligible for university admission.[2]

The Reagan administration reversed many long-standing restrictions on U.S.–South Africa relations and moved the United States into closer cooperation with the white minority regime. It authorized South Africa to open consular offices in several more American cities; granted U.S. entry to South African military intelligence officers to meet with high-ranking officials; and permitted South African military personnel to enroll in training courses at the U.S. Coast Guard school on Governor's Island, New York. South Africa and the United States increased the number of military attachés in each country.

In 1981, the Reagan administration pressured Congress (unsuccessfully) to repeal the 1976 Clark Amendment which prohibits U.S. covert aid to South African-backed UNITA rebels fighting against the Marxist government in Angola. UNITA's leader, Jonas Savimbi, was given a warm, semi-official reception in Washington, and also met secretly with Reagan officials abroad. A top-secret U.S. intelligence report revealed that the Reagan administration had advance knowledge, via satellite photographs, of an August 1982 South African invasion of Angola, yet chose to take no preventive action. Long-standing restrictions on the export of U.S. computer technology, nuclear materials, electric shock batons, and various goods for the South African military were overturned or circumvented. On several occasions when South Africa came up for condemnation in the United Nations for its continued occupation of Namibia and attacks on other neighbors, Reagan officials either failed to support the measures or vetoed them. The Reagan administration played a key role in securing a $1.1 billion loan for South Africa from the International Monetary Fund.

Change is taking place in South Africa. But questions remain regarding the true nature of the reform process, its ultimate goals, and the resulting policy implications for the United States. Do the reforms result from a change of heart by South Africa's white rulers or are these changes merely adaptations of apartheid to new political and economic circumstances? To what extent do the reforms lead South Africa away from minority domination toward peace and stability, and to what extent do they simply rearrange inequality and oppression, thus guaranteeing continued conflict? Will a friendly posture by the U.S. government encourage Pretoria to dismantle apartheid or will it give the white minority more time to consolidate its hold on power?

The reforms of the Botha regime are neither a dismantling of apartheid, as Pretoria's defenders claim, nor are they "cosmetic" changes, as some critics charge. The recent government reforms were designed to 1) gain better control over the African workforce, by cultivating more skilled workers while keeping the majority locked up in the rural labor reserves ('bantustans'), 2) create class cleavages in the African community, by giving black businessmen and industrial workers some economic and social privileges while keeping the black masses in a state of abject poverty, and 3) upgrade the state security apparatus, giving it a greater role in general policymaking.

Background to Recent Reforms

The reforms of the Botha regime can only be understood by placing them in the context of centuries of white minority rule regularly updated to meet new conditions. South Africa's integration into the world economy has continually forced the ruling whites to modernize their system of control over the African majority.[3]

When the development of diamond and gold mining in the late 1800s created the need for more African workers, the whites devised burdensome taxes and restrictive land tenure rights to force Africans from often prosperous farms into urban wage labor. When the industrial growth associated with World War II brought a large influx of Africans into the cities, white voters rallied behind the National Party's apartheid plan for extending and tightening control over the lives of Africans.

In the 1970s, a conjuncture of economic and political developments set the stage for changes in labor policy by the South African government. A succession of victories by black radicals in neighboring states, massive civil unrest by black South Africans, and growing guerrilla insurgency in Namibia and South Africa convinced officials of the South African Defence Force (SADF) that white privilege could not be preserved solely by military means. Top South African commanders argued that an effective defense against the "total onslaught" confronting white supremacy would consist primarily of political, not military, techniques.[4]

Moreover, by the late 1970s, many of the political groups representing big business in South Africa were pressing for changes in the system of black labor control. They complained that the strict regulations governing the mobility of African workers resulted in labor supply bottlenecks which impeded the profitable utilization of African labor. Big business sought to reorganize production more along lines of productivity than race. They also saw a need for greater discipline among African workers and therefore favored some form of trade union rights that would permit collective bargaining while maintaining government control. White business leaders pushed for reforms aimed at expanding the "black middle class," giving the black elite a greater stake in the capitalist system and creating a buffer against revolution. White corporate leaders were necessarily more sensitive to international criticism than were the white workers and small businessmen who supported the more conservative politicians.

The combination of economic recession and intensified black activism during the 1970s sparked a power struggle within the leadership of the ruling National Party (NP). A party of four, semi-autonomous provincial parties,° each with a different class composition and ideological emphasis, the NP is prone to factional disputes. By the latter half of the 1970s, a serious feud was brewing between NP members who favored the reforms backed by big business and the military (this faction having its strongest base in the Cape NP), and more conservative members, centered in the Transvaal branch, who favored the strict racial controls the NP had pioneered in the 1950s. In 1977, the Information Department scandal gave reform forces an edge.

Under the direction of Information Minister Connie Mulder, and with the knowledge of Prime Minister Vorster, the Information Department had been running dozens of secret propaganda and influence-buying schemes in foreign countries and within South Africa.[5] Government funds had been used to establish a pro-NP newspaper, *The Citizen*, and government officials were siphoning money from the secret slush fund into their personal accounts.

°The Cape and Transvaal branches of the NP dominate the smaller Orange Free State branch, which tends to align itself with the Transvaal, and the Natal branch which is the weakest of the four and relatively insignificant. The Cape NP traditionally has based its strength on an alliance of wealthy capitalist farmers and a small group of financiers in the SANLAM (and later, Rembrandt) companies. The Transvaal NP is based on a different class alliance. It brings together white farmers, workers, small businessmen, civil servants, and a small but growing group of commercial and finance capitalists. Hence, the Cape branch was more sympathetic to capitalist-oriented reforms.

When these and other revelations broke, they undermined the legitimacy of Vorster and his Information Minister Mulder, the strongest conservative NP leaders.

By 1978, Vorster was forced to step down as Prime Minister. After a brief succession struggle, he was replaced by Minister of Defence P.W. Botha. Leader of the Cape NP, Botha supported the reforms favored by the large financial interests that dominate that organization. During his fourteen years as Minister of Defence, Botha had developed strong backing in the military and was close to the generals who recognized that political and economic reforms were needed to help fend off revolution. Botha's personal career made him well-qualified for the attempt to hammer out an alliance between the reform-oriented elements in big business and the military. The nature of the reform alliance, combining military needs with those of large corporations, helps to explain the seemingly contradictory behavior of the Botha regime: at the same time the government trumpeted a new labor reform or expanded residential rights for some African workers, it also increased its arrests of union leaders and launched military assaults on neighboring states.

The Wiehahn Reforms

In 1979, a government-appointed study group, the Wiehahn Commission,[6] issued a series of six reports on legislation affecting African workers. Since that time, the government has implemented some of the Wiehahn recommendations.* It expanded training and employment opportunities for some Africans; relaxed its enforcement of laws requiring segregation in workplace cafeterias and restrooms (but this type of segregation is still widespread); and created two new institutions, the National Manpower Commission, which researches labor issues and advises the Minister of Manpower Utilisation, and the Industrial Court, designed to speed up the resolution of labor disputes by taking them away from the civil courts.

The most important change based on the Wiehahn proposals was the legalization of African trade unions. Prior to 1979, Africans were permitted to form unions but these were not officially recognized

---

*We are not concerned here with the differences between what the Wiehahn Commission recommended and what the government eventually enacted. For an evaluation of these differences see David Hauck, *Black Trade Unions in South Africa* (Washington, DC: Investor Responsibility Research Center, 1982).

by the government. This excluded Africans from participation in the industrial councils that establish working conditions and minimum wages in each industry. Africans were also barred from joining white, Coloured, or Indian unions that were already registered with the government. Hence, African workers, despite their numerical superiority, had a very weak bargaining position. It was illegal for Africans to go out on strike. Employers could simply refuse to negotiate with African workers and rely on the government to suppress worker militancy.

Despite these obstacles, African unions grew in size and militancy during the 1970s. Some companies, particularly foreign corporations under pressure at home from antiapartheid forces, found it expedient to grant *de facto* recognition to African unions. Responding to this trend and the growing dependence of the economy on skilled black labor, the Wiehahn Commission argued that it was time to bestow legal recognition on African unions. While granting unionized Africans greater bargaining power with their employers, legal recognition would bring them under the controlling mechanism of the government's industrial conciliation system. Under the Industrial Conciliation Amendment Act (1979) and the Labor Relations Amendment Act (1981), the government has numerous ways to circumscribe the behavior of unions.

- When an African union applies for registration, the government decides if and when it will grant registered status to that union.
- Registered status can be withdrawn at any time by administrative fiat.
- Industrial councils, the joint committees of management and white unions which negotiate for various industries, have the right to veto the entry of black unions into the industrial council system.
- Registered African unions are required to provide the government with detailed financial reports and lists of membership, officers, and activities.
- Upon registration, unions come under the Fund Raising Act (1976) which can be used to prohibit them from receiving funds raised internationally.
- And perhaps most importantly, the new legislation prohibits a registered union from engaging in political activity (as defined by the government).

In addition to these restrictions contained in the new labor laws, the government has utilized its broad police powers to harass militant unions with arrests, detentions, and bannings. In the few years since the new labor legislation was passed in 1979, well over three hundred black trade unionists have been jailed. In July 1980, a strike by some ten thousand black municipal workers in Johannesburg was broken when the city council had the strike leaders thrown in jail and hundreds of migrant workers forcibly removed to the bantustans. In February 1982, police announced the death in detention of Dr. Neil Aggett, a 28-year-old regional secretary of the Food and Canning Workers Union. During the inquest following Aggett's death, it was revealed that he had been tortured during interrogation. Nevertheless, the police were exonerated by the court.

The white government has been assisted in these anti-union activities by some bantustan leaders. Key among these has been the notoriously corrupt and repressive government of the Ciskei.[7] Because Ciskei is located near East London, a major industrial center, many African residents of Ciskei are active in the new trade unions. The Ciskei government views African trade unions such as the South African Allied Workers Union (SAAWU) as subversive, and goes to extreme lengths to harass the union. A case in point is the treatment of SAAWU President Thozamile Gqweta. In March 1981, Gqweta's home was set afire after the doors had been wired shut from the outside. Gqweta's house burned but he managed to escape. Later in 1981, Gqweta's mother and uncle were burned to death when their home was set ablaze with the doors tied shut. At the funeral for Gqweta's mother there was a large, militant crowd of SAAWU members and supporters. The police opened fire and shot just one person in the crowd, killing her. It was Gqweta's fiancee, Deliswa Roxisa. Next it was SAAWU lawyer Griffiths Mxenge who, after a number of political death threats, was found stabbed to death.

Despite this intimidation, Thozamile Gqweta and other African trade unionists continue to organize. As *Business Week* acknowledged, "despite restrictions on the new union reforms, disputes are beginning to occur that pose a severe test to Prime Minister Pieter W. Botha's plan to avoid revolution by gradually allowing a politically inactive black middle class to develop."[8] In recent years, the African unions have grown at a rapid pace. Dozens of new unions have formed and overall black membership has increased tenfold since the early 1970s. The roughly 400,000 African trade unionists are a small fraction of all African workers (8 million), but they have succeeded in organizing strategic sectors of the South African economy. Automobile worker unions in companies such as Ford and General Motors have been militant, and their strike actions have created diplomatic problems for these important companies.[9] In 1983, the Chamber of Mines, the management association of mining companies, agreed for the first time to bargain collectively with an African mineworkers' union. Although the union is young and has signed up less than 5 percent of all African miners, the potential power of these workers is great in an industry that accounts for "one-sixth of the gross domestic product and some 70% of foreign exchange earnings."[10]

The new wave of trade unionists seem to be growing more militant. By the government's own conservative figures there were 207 strikes in 1980, 342 in 1981, and 394 in 1982.[11] All of these strikes were illegal: as of 1983 there had been only two technically legal African strikes in South African history.[12] A more reliable indicator, worker-days lost due to strike activity, shows that African worker militancy has been steadily on the rise since the early 1970s. A study by the South African consulting firm, Andrew Levy and Associates, reveals that, "there has been a sharp and steady increase in man-days lost through strikes since 1971, despite occasional drops in individual years."[13] The study also found a general increase in the duration of strikes, and a correlation between the presence of a union and the longer duration of the strike. Eighty percent of the strikes studied were touched off by bread-and-butter issues such as wages and working conditions. In recent years, however, black workers have shown a willingness to conduct work stoppages in solidarity with workers in other workplaces. In addition, some unions chose not to register with the government, rejected the ban on political activity, and formed alliances with political and civic groups in the black community. African unions have been moving toward confederation and alliance with each other, greatly magnifying the power of each individual union.

If the African unions continue to grow in size and militancy as they have over the past decade, they may reach a point at which the government's traditional repression becomes ineffective. A strong African trade union movement capable of shutting down the economy could not be trifled with as were the small, isolated African unions of the past. African trade union rights are the only area of reform that hold potential for challenging apartheid. The government's powers of repression, however, should not be underestimated. In short, it is still an open question whether Pretoria's limited trade union reforms will succeed in coopting and controlling African industrial workers, or whether the reforms will be burst wide open by an organized sector of the black population that is vital to the white economy.

The Riekert Reforms

Another set of changes was based on the Riekert Commission report issued in May 1979.[14] Under the general rubric of improving "manpower utilisation," the Riekert report examined influx control (the system of state controls on the movement of African workers from rural to urban areas) and made suggestions for upgrading the effectiveness of this system. Although the reforms eventually implemented by the government were not as broad as those suggested by the Riekert report, the contents of the report itself were well within the bounds of apartheid as envisioned by its founders. Riekert made this explicit at the outset. Citing established government policy, the report set out strict boundaries for the inquiry.

> The first and foremost point of policy is...that every black person in South Africa, wherever he may find himself, is a member of his specific nation [meaning bantustan, K.D.].
> ...The second...The Bantu in the white area, whether they were born here or whether they were allowed to come here under our control laws, are here for the labour they are being allowed to perform.
> ...The third principle...is that the fundamental citizenship rights may only be enjoyed by a Bantu person within his own ethnic homeland...
> ...The fourth policy point...is that the maximum number of people must be present in their own homeland.[15]

The basic goal of the Riekert reforms is to strengthen government control over African migration to the urban areas by means of more systematic manipulation of two factors: housing and jobs. As the report stated, the goal was "more effective control over migration than in the past, and the avoidance of much of the friction that accompanied such control in the past, in that emphasis will be placed mainly on the *control of employment and control of accommodation.*"[16]

The existing system of labor bureaus, which had been established to allocate jobs and regulate the flow of African workers from the bantustans to the white economy, was proving unworkable. Many white employers simply neglected to register with the labor bureaus and hired their African workers illegally. Employers were not only put off by the cumbersome bureaucracy of the labor bureaus, they also found that African workers who were in the urban areas illegally were more docile than those employed legally. The penalties for circumventing the labor bureaus were mild for the employer (a small fine, seldom exacted), whereas the illegal African worker would lose his job and be "endorsed out" to the impoverished bantustans.

At no time were the proposed reforms intended to improve the lot of the African majority. Rather, the changes were designed to 1) meet the needs of the white business community for a more well-regulated African workforce, and 2) divide the African workers into several distinct strata with a hierarchy of rights and wealth, thus dividing Africans along class as well as ethnic lines.

The labor bureau system was strengthened to gain better control over migrant workers. Employers hiring outside the registration system can now receive stiffer fines than in the past. More effort has been put into coordinating job registration with the legal status of the worker. The goal is to make it impossible for an African worker to come into an urban area° and find work unless he has been recruited and signed a contract in his rural area.

Pass laws are more strictly enforced to separate the one-fourth of African workers who qualify for urban residential rights† from those who do not. In June 1983 *The Economist* reported that, "arrests for pass law offences have almost doubled in the past three years, and the government plans to tighten influx controls, imposing much heavier fines on employers of 'illegal' blacks."[17]

The privileged African workers with Section 10 rights are no

°There are three distinct residential areas: the bantustans, the white cities and suburbs, and the African townships near the white cities. The bantustans, 13.6 percent of South Africa, are the only place Africans can own land and ostensibly exercise their rights of citizenship. Africans are only permitted in the white cities and suburbs as laborers. The African townships are within the 86 percent of South Africa reserved for whites but Africans can qualify for limited residential rights in these areas.

†The main law governing African residential rights, Section 10(1) of the Bantu (Urban Areas) Consolidation Act, contains four sub-sections which describe the criteria Africans must meet to reside legally in the townships: Sub-section (a), those Africans who have lived in a township continuously since birth; Sub-section (b), those who have held the same job for ten years or more; Sub-section (c), dependents of men qualifying under (a) or (b); Sub-section (d), permanent residents of the bantustans who are temporarily in an urban area under a labor contract.

longer required to register with a labor bureau when taking a new job and they are allowed to move from one area to another if they have a job and housing in the new location. Section 10 Africans are also given preference in employment.

By linking the right to accommodation with legal job status, the government gained greater control over African migration to the cities. Only by being registered with and channeled through the labor bureau system can a rural African gain legal housing in urban areas. At the same time, the government cracked down on 'squatters', those coming to the urban areas illegally and setting up makeshift dwellings. The government's policy has been to demolish the squatter camps and forcibly to remove the residents to their assigned bantustans.

Residential conditions for Section 10 Africans were improved. The government for the first time allowed private contractors to build homes in African townships, and expanded the number of state-built homes. There is still a dire shortage of housing, however, and most urban Africans are living in overcrowded conditions.*
Basic services such as electricity, indoor plumbing, and schools are being expanded for the African workers who qualify under Section 10. These privileged Africans can now apply for 99-year leases on residential property (blacks can never own land in the white 86 percent of South Africa). But so few have the money and meet the legal requirements that only a very small percentage of Africans have been able to benefit from this provision.

At the same time, the government has implemented broad measures to raise the cost of living for urban Africans. This has made it more difficult for rural Africans to live illegally in urban areas while searching for work. The cost of living for urban Africans has outpaced most wage increases as the government raised rents and increased the cost of basic services such as transportation and utilities.

The government lifted some restrictions on the African business class. Africans can now run more than one business, employ people of other races, and are not limited to business sites under 350 square meters. White and black entrepreneurs can now do joint ventures in

---

*"...the 1979-1980 budget allocated only 73 million Rand to low-cost housing, enough for 12,500 units—though estimates of the likely backlog over the next two decades begin at 4 million units!" (John Saul and Stephen Gelb, "The Crisis in South Africa," *Monthly Review*, July-August 1981, p. 68). In mid-1983, South Africa's deputy minister for African affairs told parliament that the government will build no more houses for urban Africans.

the African townships on a 51 percent black/49 percent white basis. Although African business has grown in recent years, creating an elite group who may have a greater stake in the system, the government keeps a tight rein on black "free" enterprise. Blacks cannot do business in the white cities, suburbs, and industrial parks. In the neighboring African townships, it is impossible for African businessmen to gain freehold rights to property, making it difficult for them to come up with security for creditors. The Small Business Development Corporation, formed jointly by the government and white businessmen, provides low-interest loans but only one-fifth of these have gone to blacks, and the maximum amount of each loan is less than $1,000.

Another Riekert proposal, one that has gotten much publicity, involves a limited form of self-government for urban blacks. The Black Local Authorities Act (1982) provides for local self-government through the election of community councils in the African townships. These councils, however, are restricted to dealing with mundane infrastructural problems such as roads, sewage, and electricity. They cannot affect broad policy questions; they can be dissolved at any time by the white government; and they do nothing to change the fact that even this urban black elite can only participate in 'national' politics via the bantustan governments. But perhaps the most telling criticism is that the overwhelming majority of Africans reject these government-sponsored institutions. In council elections held in late 1983, less than one of every five Africans registered to vote bothered to do so. In Soweto, the largest and most politically significant African township, voter turnout in the thirty administrative wards ranged from 1.6 percent to a high of 13 percent.[18]

The main goal of the Riekert reforms was to weaken further the Africans by stratifying them according to wealth and social privilege, in addition to separating them ethnically. A detailed post-Riekert study of the labor control system found that it "helps foster a hierarchy of living standards, market opportunities and rights within the African population."[19]

Educational Reform

Like the other areas of reform, changes in the education system were sparked by the political protests and economic stagnation of the 1970s. The appallingly low standards of African education limited the supply of skilled African workers and presented a security problem due to the frequent protests against the education system.

To deal with these problems within the bounds of the "separate development" strategy, Pretoria has increased funding for African education but has targeted it to intensify the class divisions within the African population. While devolving African educational responsibility onto the bantustans—currently over two-thirds of African students are in the bantustan schools—the government has focused its upgrading measures on the minority of African students whose parents possess urban residential privileges. This reinforces the effort to create a black elite whose skilled labor is vital to the white economy, and whose political quiescence contributes to the survival of white supremacy.

Government spending on African education has risen substantially: from R27 million in 1972/73 to R369 million in 1981/82.[20] However, the key indicator of change—the gap between educational standards for whites and blacks—reveals continued discrimination. The government spends more than ten times as much on the average white student as on the average African student.[21] The pupil–teacher ratio in a bantustan such as KwaZulu runs 56–1, whereas the average for white schools is 18–1.[22] A 1982 U.S. Congressional study found that, "overall per capita spending and teacher–pupil ratios for South Africa remain less favorable to blacks than they were in 1949 shortly after the Nationalists took power."[23]

Another aspect of educational discrimination is the quality of teaching. Whereas only 3.36 percent of white teachers are underqualified, 85 percent of African teachers are underqualified.[24] African schools are forced to use a curriculum designed by the white government to be inferior to that used in white schools. The content of textbooks, examinations, and detailed lesson plans is rigidly controlled by the government. *The New York Times* described the contents of a typical textbook used in one of the better African schools.

> In Atteridgeville, a Pretoria township, 10-year-olds in a newly refurbished primary school were using an English reader called "Benny and Betty at Home and in Town" that situated its characters in a perfect apartheid society in which there were no whites.
>
> True to the old goals of Bantu education, the reader seemed to define a rural habitat as the natural one for black children. Thus these urban children read about black children their age who hunt rabbits with bows and arrows when they are not weaving baskets.[25]

Many courses are taught from a Eurocentric perspective; English courses are introduced late in the child's education; citizenship classes emphasize submissiveness; and the pedagogical style in African schools is based on rote learning.[26]

It is not surprising, therefore, that the overwhelming majority of African students do not survive the white-ruled educational gauntlet. *Less than 2 percent* of African students make it through high school and pass the nationwide matriculation exams.[27] According to the U.S. Embassy in Pretoria, as of 1980, of all economically-active Africans in the urban areas, 40 percent had no education and another 42 percent had less than five years of schooling. Among rural Africans, 65 percent had no education and 29 percent had less than five years.[28]

Similar patterns afflict the African colleges. Prior to 1959, South Africa's universities were segregated but the University of Witwatersrand and the University of Cape Town admitted some black students on the basis of merit. In 1959, the National Party passed the Orwellian-titled Extension of University Education Act. This law established a rigid separation of the races in higher education. It drove wedges into the black community by limiting each ethnic group to a particular university: Indians would attend the University of Durban–Westville; Coloureds, the University of Western Cape; Xhosa-speaking Africans, Fort Hare University; Zulu and Swazi speakers, University of Zululand; and Sotho, Tsonga and Venda speakers, the University of the North. In this way, even the few blacks who survived the inferior primary and secondary schools, would be forced into the government's divide-and-rule framework.

Although black college enrollment has increased in recent years, it still lags far behind that of whites. A 1982 study by a team of U.S. college administrators found many serious flaws in the African universities.[29] These colleges are staffed primarily by whites, mostly Afrikaners. As of 1980, out of 621 lecturers at African universities, 441 were white.[30] Afrikaner educators who are underqualified to teach at the more competitive white universities are able to find work in the African universities. Mirroring the situation in elementary and secondary schools, the African universities are poorly equipped and have a narrower curriculum than their white counterparts. Another similarity with pre-college education is that African universities are plagued by high dropout rates. For example, at the University of the North in Turfloop, 60 percent of the African students drop out in their first year, and there is no research to investigate why this is so.[31] Although some brilliant thinkers have

South African Universities (Residential), Student Enrollment by Racial Group (1954-1980)

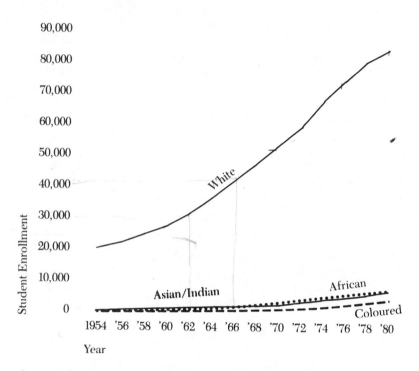

Source: John A. Marcum, *Education, Race, and Social Change in South Africa*
(Berkeley: University of California Press, 1982), p. 7.

survived South Africa's education system, and there are ongoing efforts in the black community to counteract the limitations placed on African universities, the white government shows no sign of releasing African higher education from the bonds of apartheid. The Congressional study summed it up: "Black universities in South Africa are rigidly controlled by government officials who approve the hiring of faculty and senior staff, limit academic freedom, and generally provide inferior faculties and facilities. They tend to be suffused with the demoralizing, and protest-inspiring atmosphere of apartheid."[32]

In June 1980, the government commissioned the Human Sciences Research Council, a state-funded body, to conduct a comprehensive study of the South African educational system. Led by the Rector of the Rand Afrikaans University, Professor J.P. de Lange, the committee put together a report that challenged some of the basic premises of apartheid schooling. The committee argued for opening up the education system and reducing inequalities. It called for a single department of education capable of unifying, at least administratively, the many strata of apartheid schooling, and moving the various ethnic school systems toward eventual parity. The committee recommended voluntary racial integration at the local and regional level. It also suggested that universities be given the freedom to admit students based on academic rather than racial standards.

The Botha regime rejected the key recommendations of the de Lange report, emphasizing the government's intent to retain the racial and ethnic divisions of the current school system. The regime reaffirmed its support for "the principles of Christian education" and the "national character of education," that "each population group should have its own schools," and that "each population group should also have its own education authority/department."[33] The combination of the government's vague pledges to work toward "equal opportunities" in education, and its insistence on retaining a segregated system, conjures up visions of the long-discredited notion of 'separate but equal'. When asked about the government's response to the de Lange Committee report, one of the committee members remarked: "this, in fact, reestablishes apartheid education and places us back where we started."[34]

The research team sponsored by the U.S.–South Africa Leader Exchange Program (USSALEP) pointed out that under South Africa's political structure there is no chance of the judiciary intervening to change the education system, as was the case in the United States: "Americans also need to be realistic. Neither the dominant ideology nor the constitutional law of white-ruled South Africa is conducive to social and political reform. There is no chance that a *Brown v. Board of Education* case will crack the wall of apartheid surrounding South African education."[35]

Educational programs comprise a large portion of U.S. involvement with black South Africans. The U.S. government, some U.S. corporations, and the AFL-CIO have programs to provide assistance in the training and education of South African citizens.[36] The programs cited by Under Secretary of State Eagleburger,[37] and projects such as the PACE school in Soweto funded by the American Chamber of Commerce,[38] provide several thousand South Africans with expanded educational opportunities. But these efforts, while benefiting a few, have little impact on blacks as a group.

The PACE Commercial High School charges tuition of $1,400 per year, so that only sixteen of the original 263 students could afford to pay their own way; the rest are on scholarships. Ultimately the school will enroll six hundred students, who will concentrate on developing commercial and administrative skills. The small number of students, and the narrow focus of their education, make the PACE school thoroughly consistent with the white government's efforts to cultivate a black labor aristocracy. In its own literature, the American Chamber of Commerce in South Africa explains that the PACE school "will provide a source of commercially well-trained blacks...and enhance the image of business, both here and overseas."[39]

None of the official U.S. programs challenge the apartheid regime's plans to create a small elite among urban Africans. It could be argued that these programs reinforce Pretoria's strategy by concentrating their assistance on a small number of Africans within that privileged one-fourth who qualify for urban residential rights. Most African students are in the bantustans, and because no government, including the United States, will recognize these bogus "nations," most educational assistance gets channeled into the African townships in 'white' South Africa. Given Pretoria's continuing bantustanization of the African majority, foreign educational assistance is forced into a no-win set of choices: give aid to urban Africans and thus contribute to the growing disparities between them and their impoverished brethren in the bantustans, recognize the bantustans by channeling aid there, or do nothing.

Underlying the U.S. choice of the first alternative is a vague belief in a trickle-down notion of educational benefits: the relatively few Africans who receive advanced training will ostensibly devote themselves to raising the living standards of their less-privileged compatriots. Hard data to support or refute this thesis is not available. However, judging from the evidence of other countries where a section of the working class experienced upward mobility, it would be reasonable to expect that a large percentage of these upwardly-mobile individuals will focus on improving their own lot in life and not jeopardize their economic progress by being 'too active' politically. Yet, the percentage of black South Africans educated by U.S. programs is so small—less than one-tenth of 1 percent—that even if they all became active reformers the impact would be negligible.

The Constitutional Reforms

In the early 1980s, the Botha regime developed a detailed plan for restructuring the legislative and executive branches of government. This constitutional reform plan was approved by white voters on 2 November 1983.* Because the new structure involves some non-white participation in the central government, the reforms have gained considerable attention in the western press and have caused some people to conclude that South Africa is moving toward democratic rule. However, a detailed examination of the plan reveals that an opposite conclusion would be closer to the truth.

The most important part of the plan—other than its exclusion of the African majority—is the concentration of power in the new chief executive. Under the new system, the President is head of the Republic and chairman of the cabinet, combining the powers of the offices of Prime Minister and President. He has veto power over legislation. He can pass laws by means of plebiscite, and has the power to dissolve parliament. The President is not elected directly by the people. Rather, he is chosen indirectly by an electoral college composed of fifty whites, twenty-five Coloureds, and thirteen Indians. In selecting his cabinet, the President can appoint members from outside the ranks of parliament, again circumventing popular control. The cabinet, in turn, will feed legislative proposals to parliament.

The pre-existing white chamber of parliament (178 members) is supplemented by a Coloured chamber (85 members), and an Indian chamber (45 members). Each of the three chambers legislates separately on "group affairs" but the three can collaborate on "matters of common interest." The President holds the crucial power of deciding whether any particular issue should be defined as a matter of common or ethnic interest. On matters of common interest, in the event of a deadlock—unlikely due to the preponderance of white members—a final determination is made by another body, the President's Council. Like the cabinet, electoral college, and parliament, the President's Council has a majority of white members.

Ever aware of the need to mollify foreign criticism, South African government officials have portrayed the constitutional reforms merely as a move away from the British model of parliamentary

---

*Seventy-six percent of the 2.7 million eligible white voters cast ballots. Some 1,360,223 (nearly 66 percent) voted in favor and 691,577 voted against the new plan.

Schematic Presentation of New Executive/Legislative Structure

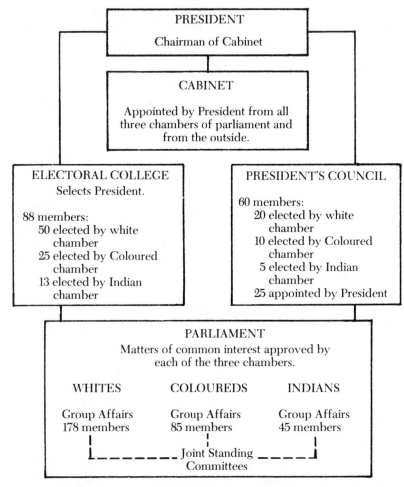

democracy, toward an executive presidential model along the lines of the U.S. government. But, as *The Washington Post* pointed out, the analogy is incorrect. The new plan...

...has none of the checks and balances of the U.S. system. There is no judicial role limiting executive power, and the legislature is given no constraining authority.

There is no suggested mechanism for impeachment of the president, who would be elected for a seven year term and be eligible for reelection.

The South African constitution contains no bill of rights or clauses protecting individual freedoms. It is a simple act of parliament, changeable at any time by a majority of one.[40]

The dictatorial aspects of the new reform package are clear. Yet Botha's supporters argue that this concentration of power in the executive is necessary to circumvent the power of National Party right-wingers, and to implement more reforms. A Johannesburg banker defended the strategy, arguing that, "we may be creating a dictator, but it's a risk we have to take. It's the only way to get round the right wing of the Afrikaners, who have enough power under the present system to prevent any change."[41] In a 1981 speech in South Africa, Professor Samuel Huntington of Harvard's Center for International Relations gave an American imprimatur to this line of reasoning, stating that, "it is not inconceivable that narrowing the scope of political participation may be indispensable to eventually broadening that participation. The route from a limited uni-racial democracy to a broader multi-racial democracy could run through some form of autocracy."[42]

Top officials in Pretoria, however, have made it clear that the constitutional proposals are not a step toward one-person-one-vote democracy. Prime Minister Botha explained that, aside from the community councils, the exercise of African political rights "will have to be done by means of independent and national states,"[43] i.e., the bantustans which have not been recognized as "independent and national states" by any government in the world except Pretoria. Ambassador to the United States Brand Fourie and National Education Minister Gerrit Viljoen elaborated Pretoria's opposition to universal suffrage:

> The notion that the diverse cultures of South Africa can be forced into a unitary society on the basis of a one man, one vote formula is ruled out because, like single-group supremacy, it promises only conflict.[44]

> White South Africans, therefore, simply are not prepared to submit to universal suffrage in a unitary state under conditions in which they would be swamped by a vast black majority and be reduced to political impotence.[45]

Aside from its inherent weaknesses, the constitutional reform plan is opposed by a broad spectrum of interests within South Africa and internationally. The far-rightists within Botha's National Party and the parties to the right of the NP[46] denounce the reforms as the thin end of a wedge that will lead to the destruction of white power. The strong electoral showing of far-right parties in recent years indicates that a significant number of whites agree with this position.[47]

Representatives of international business are critical of the constitutional reforms for not going far enough. *The Economist* criticized Botha because...

> ...his proposals are not really reformist at all. They purport to breach the political colour bar by extending parliamentary representation to the coloured (mixed race) and Indian minorities. In fact the proposals are aimed at strengthening the position of whites by co-opting the coloureds and Indians as allies but in such a way that Afrikaners still dominate the system. Other regulations would further distance the blacks from power...[48]

The Financial Times complained that under the new constitution the President "would be a dictator in all but name."[49] *The Wall Street Journal* noted that "Prime Minister Pieter Botha's attempts to liberalize South Africa's racial laws seem to have slowed to a crawl," and "Mr. Botha also has steadfastly refused to grant blacks the right to vote."[50]

Opposition from South Africa's non-white majority has been extremely broad-based and vehement in its denunciation of the constitutional reforms. In what *The Economist* described as "the broadest alliance of anti-government groups since the Congress movement of the 1950s," the United Democratic Front (UDF) brought together some four hundred trade unions, churches, civic, and student groups to oppose the new constitutional plan.[51] With a collective membership of more than one million, and actions such as naming imprisoned ANC leader Nelson Mandela a patron, the UDF could pose a serious challenge to the regime. *The New York Times* reported that the UDF "demonstrated a mass appeal that contrasted sharply with that of political parties that have agreed to go along with the new system."[52]

When some leaders of the (Coloured) Labor Party agreed to participate in the new tricameral parliament, the party was split down the middle and the collaborating faction was immediately denounced by some sixty civic associations, trade unions, and student groups in the Coloured community. Opposition to the collaborationist Coloured leaders was so intense that they were no longer able to hold open meetings in Cape Town.

Those members of the Indian community willing to collaborate with the new plan were previously associated with the South African Indian Council (SAIC), a body established by the white government to solicit advice from the Indian elite. Like the Coloured collaborators, the popular base of these Indian leaders is dubious. In the 1981 SAIC elections only 10.5 percent of registered Indian voters bothered to cast a ballot.[53]

Among Africans, not only the more militant groups denounced the plan and campaigned against it, but even more conservative voices such as Bishop Desmond Tutu and six bantustan leaders spoke out forcefully against the constitutional reforms.[54] Chief Gatsha Buthelezi, head of the KwaZulu bantustan, has always been careful to cultivate support in U.S. ruling circles. But when the Reagan administration praised the Coloured leaders who decided to collaborate with the new constitutional plan, the Zulu leader complained of being "slapped in the face" by the U.S. government.[55]

The most important effect of the constitutional reforms will be to contribute to the growing polarization of South African society. State power will be concentrated in the hands of the chief executive, and a small percentage of the Indian and Coloured elites will be incorporated into the white establishment, but the most important group—the African majority—will intensify its opposition due to its total exclusion from the political process.

Hidden Reforms

Given the limitations of Botha's reforms and the broad opposition they have engendered, it is difficult to imagine that they will succeed in coopting enough non-white leaders to stem the growing polarization of forces in South Africa. In preparing itself for the confrontation which seems inexorably to be approaching, the Botha regime has instituted another set of reforms, far more significant than anything hitherto discussed, but scarcely heeded in the West.

In tandem with the changes in racial laws, P.W. Botha has orchestrated sweeping changes in the structure of government. Since the late 1970s, the regime has intensified the militarization of the state and society, and has concentrated power in the office of the Prime Minister.

In response to the drastic change in Pretoria's security situation following the overthrow of Portuguese colonialism, leaders of the South African Defence Force (SADF) evolved a new "total strategy" to meet the "total onslaught" now confronting the white redoubt. The 1977 Defence White Paper explained that the regime was threatened with a coordinated assault on all fronts—military, political, economic, and psychological.[56] With a steadily shrinking perimeter of white buffer states, and with growing internal unrest, it became necessary for white strategists to elevate the role of the military, and extend security concerns into all sectors of South African life. Then-head of the SADF, General Magnus Malan,* a key figure in elaborating the new, total strategy, remarked, "South Africa is today...involved in total war. The war is not only an area for the soldier. Everyone is involved and has a role to play."[57]

Under P.W. Botha's fourteen-year leadership as Defence Minister, the South African military began evolving its new total strategy for preserving white rule, and underwent its greatest physical expansion in history. Under Botha the defense budget increased by nearly 1,000 percent.[58] The size of the Defence Force increased several times over.[59] The age-range of conscriptable men and the duration of their required military service steadily increased. Botha also played a key role in the expansion of ARMSCOR, the state corporation responsible for producing a wide assortment of weaponry.[60]

Given these trends, it is not surprising that following Botha's 1978 accession to the office of Prime Minister he engineered a sweeping militarization and centralization of state power. During his first two years as Prime Minister, Botha retained his Defence Minister portfolio. In 1980, this post was given to General Malan, one of Botha's closest aides. Other top military men were brought into key positions as Botha oversaw the restructuring of the executive branch.[61]

The Cabinet was thoroughly revamped in a way that concentrated power in the Prime Minister's office. Under the previous system, the Cabinet comprised National Party members of Parliament and therefore reflected the range of views in the NP. Within just a few years of coming to power, Botha managed to circumvent this restraint by gutting the Cabinet of real power. Most of its functions were taken over by six "Cabinet Committees," each headed by the Prime Minister or his designee, with overall coordina-

*Malan has stated his belief that the war against SWAPO and the ANC is 80 percent political and 20 percent military. Malan received training from the U.S. Army at Fort Leavenworth, Kansas in 1963 when U.S. counterinsurgency doctrine stressed the need to combat leftist rebellions with economic and social, as well as military, programs.

tion by the Department of the Prime Minister. The members of these committees can be selected from outside the Parliament, and Botha has used this to bring in military and business leaders who share his views.

Botha also acted quickly in militarizing South Africa's intelligence service.[62] Traditional rivalries between the military intelligence service and civilian intelligence under the Bureau of State Security (BOSS)° were stifled by placing new limits on BOSS's power. Botha appointed a 30-year-old academic with no political base as BOSS's chief. He also appointed top military men to BOSS's leadership, and instituted a new system whereby all intelligence operations would be integrated and brought under tighter control by the Prime Minister's most important agency: the State Security Council (SSC).[63]

It is here, in the expansion of the SSC's powers, that Botha has carried out his most significant act of reform. A mere advisory body established in 1972, the SSC remained moribund during Vorster's reign. But under Botha's leadership the SSC "has emerged as perhaps the most influential decision-taking political institution in the country and is the main forum for formulating and planning the implementation of the much-trumpeted total strategy."[64] With a preponderance of top military personnel, the SSC coordinates fifteen interdepartmental committees which extend security planning into all areas of South African life. Chaired by the Prime Minister, with its secretariat staffed by military officers, the SSC is the highest, most powerful policymaking body in the government. Even by 1980, before the SSC's full consolidation of power, *The Washington Post* noted that, "in many ways it [the State Security Council] is already an alternative cabinet by virtue of decisions it makes."[65]

The militarization of the state apparatus, and the concentration of power in the hands of the Prime Minister and his military advisors have no doubt assisted them in implementing some racial reforms despite opposition from right-wing whites. But these limited reforms do not come close to appeasing the majority of blacks, who reject 'neo-apartheid' as vehemently as they did the old variety.

More important than their role in circumventing anti-reform pressure from the Right, the moves to militarize and de-democratize the state are in preparation to resist pressure for radical change from

°Preceded by an agency called Republican Intelligence formed in 1960, BOSS was created in 1969 to conduct foreign and domestic espionage and covert operations. Under Botha, BOSS has undergone two name changes—Directorate of National Security (DONS) and National Intelligence Service (NIS)—in addition to its reduction in power.

Key Members of the State Security Council

Prime Minister	P.W. Botha	Minister of Defence (1966-80)
Minister of Defence	Gen. Magnus Malan	Chief of SADF (1978-80)
Chief of SADF	Gen. C.L. Viljoen	
Minister of Police	L. le Grange	
Commissioner of Police	Gen. M. Geldenhuys	
Minister of Justice	H.J. Coetsee	Deputy Defence Minister (1978-80)
Head of National Intelligence Service	N. Barnard	
Minister of Foreign Affairs	R.F. Botha	
Secretary of the SSC	Lt. Gen. A. van Deventer	(transferred from the SADF)

the black majority. With active guerrilla insurgencies in Namibia and at home, and the threat of student and labor unrest always looming, South Africa's rulers are preparing to go down fighting in defense of white minority rule.

The Basic Strategy: Denationalization and Retribalization

The core feature of 'grand apartheid', the systematic denationalization of the African population via the bantustan program, continues unabated. The government claims that each African ethnic group must have its own area, to "develop separately." Although the government uses *ethnic* criteria to divide the African population, all whites—including Portuguese, Polish emigrés, white Rhodesians, Afrikaners, and British descendants—are judged by *racial* criteria and officially lumped together as one group.

Through the creation of so-called independent states—Transkei (1976), Bophuthatswana (1977), Venda (1979), and Ciskei (1981)—

the white government has officially deprived some *eight million* Africans of their South African nationality.[66] This denationalization applies not only to Africans forced to live in the rural areas but to the Section 10, urban Africans as well. Under the provisions of the National States Citizenship Act, any African with genetic, cultural, linguistic, familial, or residential ties to a particular bantustan is automatically deprived of South African citizenship on the day that bantustan is declared independent.° Although the statutes are carefully worded to avoid withdrawing citizenship on racial grounds, no whites, Coloureds, or Asians have been denationalized under the bantustan program.[67] In a 1978 speech to parliament, the Minister of Bantu Administration and Development explained the central goal of the denationalization program: "if our policy is taken to its full logical conclusion as far as the black people are concerned, there will be not one black man with South African citizenship."[68]

Even under the leadership of the so-called reformer Botha, the government has pressed forward with its denationalization/retribalization strategy. This is in spite of unanimous international refusal to recognize the independence of these mini-states. It is also in spite of generalized opposition to the plan from black South Africans. For example, in the 1982 elections for the Bophuthatswana National Assembly, of the estimated 300,000 Tswana nationals living in the Johannesburg area, only 135 voted.[69] A telling rejection is the fact that millions of Africans "vote with their feet" to escape the abysmal conditions of these labor reservoirs. The most complete study on the subject found that, not counting pass law removals, the government since 1960 has forcibly resettled some *3.5 million* Africans from 'white South Africa' to the bantustans.[70]

The program also proceeds in spite of the well-known fact that these bantustans do not possess the economic resources to achieve true independence from South Africa.[71] The government's own figures show that as of 1982, "only 13 percent of the total income of blacks in the national states is self-generated."[72] *The Christian Science Monitor* described the homelands as "economic disaster areas."[73] Only one of the bantustans—Bophuthatswana—has advanced economically, but this has been achieved by erecting casinos and flesh houses catering to South African tourists.

°The clearest historical precedent for the bantustan/denationalization program was the 1941 Nazi law denationalizing German Jews. It is more than mere coincidence that the National Party supported the Nazi cause in World War II and now implements a similar policy.

Despite the lack of economic viability or international recognition, Pretoria will persevere with its bantustan strategy. Not only does the program lower the number of Africans officially considered citizens of South Africa, and divide the majority by forcibly retribalizing them, it also creates an administrative elite who cooperate in the suppression of trade unions, guerrilla groups, and other opponents of the regime. As part of Botha's "constellation of states" idea,[74] the SADF is creating surrogate security forces in the bantustans.

> It would appear that the South African government would ideally like to transform the homelands...into an "inner ring of buffer states" to replace what had been a defence in depth prior to the fall of the Portuguese holdings in Africa and the Zimbabwe resolution. As a first and rather ineffectual line of defence against insurgents, the bantustan armies do little more than pose token resistance. Still they are important. They are the triphammer that sets into motion emergency plans in which the homeland governments invite in the SADF. The security of the two regimes, Pretoria's and the homelands', are inextricably interwoven...[75]

Some bantustan authorities have done important work for Pretoria by suppressing African trade unions and student groups. For example, security forces and vigilantes in Ciskei and KwaZulu have carried out mass detentions, torture, and even mass murder against antiapartheid students and trade unionists.[76]

The bantustan program, like many other programs of the white minority regime, increases the polarization of South African society. The bantustans serve as labor reservoirs where 'surplus' African workers can be dumped at will, but they are also breeding grounds of discontent, ripe for the appeals of revolutionaries. Bantustanization has been used to cultivate an African elite willing to collaborate with the white minority regime, but these so-called black leaders are denounced around the world and detested by the people they are supposed to govern. When Pretoria declares a bantustan independent, it conveniently denationalizes millions of African citizens, no longer counting them in its statistics on unemployment, malnutrition, and the like. But the bantustan farce is universally condemned and fools only those with some interest in being deceived. The bantustan program sows seeds of suffering and bitterness. The longer it continues, the more prolonged and difficult will be the struggle for justice and peace.

Conclusion

What has changed under 'neo-apartheid' is the strategy of control: the government is more actively seeking Coloured, Indian, and African middle class allies to strengthen its resistance to the democratic demands of the African majority. The labor control system has been updated and streamlined. The security forces have been greatly expanded and given a central role in formulating general policy.

Although some blacks have benefited from recent reforms, the overwhelming majority has not. This is precisely the government's intent. By increasing economic and political opportunities for a select minority of blacks, the government hopes to coopt the better-educated strata, driving a wedge between them and the black masses. Although some government reforms tend to create a popular momentum for more change, the regime is prepared to repress that momentum.

The South African government has made it clear, for anyone who cares to see the truth, that it will continue forcibly to divide the black majority, and to deny full citizenship to all in a unified South Africa. The reforms of the recent past and foreseeable future are designed to provide a better-controlled African workforce for white industry, create class cleavages in the black community, and placate foreign criticism.

The central premise of the Reagan administration's "constructive engagement" policy is that by catering to Pretoria the United States can strengthen reform-minded elements of the white elite and thereby facilitate gradual movement away from apartheid. But the recent reforms have neither democratized nor liberalized South African society. Instead, they have served to reinforce minority rule and to ensure control of the black majority.

Not only has the National Party intensified the repression of its own population, it has also mounted a systematic campaign of terror against its regional neighbors. By carrying out economic, political, and military destabilization against neighboring black-ruled states, Pretoria seeks to reduce or eliminate regional support for the African National Congress.[77] This policy of blatant aggression forced Angola and Mozambique to sign non-aggression agreements with Pretoria in 1984, cutting back their assistance to SWAPO and the ANC.[78] But Pretoria's destabilization policy has also highlighted South Africa's outlaw status in the world community. And the Reagan administration, in refusing to condemn Pretoria's acts of

aggression, has caused considerable deterioration in America's standing internationally. Even conservative NATO allies in Britain and
West Germany distanced themselves from Reagan's open collaboration with Pretoria.

Neither the government in Pretoria nor the government in Washington has seen fit to press for democratic reform in South Africa. In
the other white settler colonies of southern Africa, the white minority rigidly opposed reforms that could foster majority rule, and the
United States did precious little to ease that rigidity.[79]

Even if top South African leaders wanted to dismantle apartheid,
democratic reform would be obstructed by the state bureaucracy.
The South African civil service, dominated by right-wing Afrikaners
whose livelihood comes from administering apartheid, has a vested
interest in the status quo and an important voice in National Party
politics. The Prime Minister cannot ignore their staunch opposition
to reform.[80]

The white minority has skillfully developed new techniques of
control, and, in the "reforms," has entrenched the most oppressive
aspects of minority domination.

Notes

1. Assistant Secretary of State for African Affairs, Chester A. Crocker,
   addressing the American Legion, 29 August 1981 (Current Policy Paper
   no. 308, U.S. Department of State, Bureau of Public Affairs). Also see
   Chester A. Crocker, "South Africa: Strategy for Change," *Foreign
   Affairs*, Winter 1980/81.
2. Under Secretary of State for Political Affairs, Lawrence Eagleburger,
   "Southern Africa: America's Responsibility for Peace and Change," an
   address to the National Conference of Editorial Writers, San Francisco,
   23 June 1983, pp. 18-20.
3. See "South African Far Right Appears to Gain Ground in Elections,"
   The New York Times, 1 July 1984; Martin Murray, ed., *South African
   Capitalism and Black Political Opposition* (Cambridge, MA: Schenk-
   man, 1982); Stanley Greenberg, *Race and State in Capitalist Develop-
   ment* (New Haven and London: Yale University Press, 1980); Bernard
   Makhosezwe Magubane, *The Political Economy of Race and Class in
   South Africa* (New York: Monthly Review Press, 1979); Frederick A.
   Johnstone, *Class, Race and Gold* (London: Routledge and Kegan Paul,
   1976); Kevin Danaher, "The Political Economy of U.S. Policy Toward
   South Africa," Dissertation, University of California/Santa Cruz, 1982;
   John W. Cell, *The Highest Stage of White Supremacy* (Cambridge:
   Cambridge University Press, 1982; George M. Frederickson, *White*

Supremacy: A Comparative Study in American and South African History (New York: Oxford University Press, 1981).
4. For background, see Kenneth W. Grundy, *The Rise of the South African Security Establishment* (Braamfontein: South African Institute of International Affairs, 1983); and International Defence and Aid Fund, *The Apartheid War Machine* (London: IDAF, 1980), especially Chapter 2: " 'Total War' and the Military State."
5. The largest volume of material on the Information Department scandal is contained in various South African newspapers. However, a comprehensive, insider account is "Muldergate: The Eschel Rhoodie Story," *Elseviers Magazine* (Neth.), August 1979. Also see Gordon Winter, *Inside BOSS* (Harmondsworth, England: Penguin, 1981); "South Africa: The Muldergate Saga," *Africa*, no. 94, June 1979; "Ruling party apartheid split underlies 'Infogate' scandal," *In These Times*, 10-16 January 1979; "Rhoodie Tells of 'Collaborators in West'," *The Washington Post*, 26 September 1979; "South Africa Scandal and U.S. Politics," *The San Francisco Chronicle*, 19 March 1979.
6. For background on the Wiehahn Commission and its recommendations, see David Hauck, *Black Trade Unions in South Africa* (Washington, DC: Investor Responsibility Research Center, 1982); Ken Luckhardt and Brenda Wall, *Working for Freedom: Black Trade Union Development in South Africa Throughout the 1970s* (Geneva: World Council of Churches, 1981); D. Michael Shafer, *The Wiehahn Report and the Industrial Conciliation Amendment Act: A New Attack on the Trade Union Movement in South Africa* (New York: U.N. Centre Against Apartheid, 1979); Moeletsi Mbeki, "Capital and Labor in South Africa: Preliminary Remarks on the Wiehahn Commission Report," *Monthly Review*, March 1980; Jud Cornell and Alide Kooy, "Wiehahn Part 5 and the White Paper," *South African Labour Bulletin*, vol. 7, no. 3, November 1981; John S. Saul and Stephen Gelb, "The Crisis in South Africa," *Monthly Review*, July-August 1981.
7. Joseph Lelyveld, "Misery In A South African 'Homeland'," *The New York Times* (magazine), 25 September 1983.
8. "Blacks grab for political action," *Business Week*, 25 February 1980, pp. 160, 165.
9. For background, see "Working for Ford?" special issue of *South African Labour Bulletin*, vol. 6, no. 2/3, September 1980; U.S. Congress, House, *Labor Situation in South Africa: Fall 1980* (Washington, DC: GPO, 1981); "South Africa's black workers strike at Ford, GM, and VW," *Multinational Monitor*, September 1982; "South Africa: Black Workers Take the Lead: The Ford Strike in Port Elizabeth," *Intercontinental Press*, 26 May 1980; "Cape car workers lead campaign for wage rise," *The Financial Times*, 8 July 1980; and "Labor Relations Turn Volatile in South Africa," *The Washington Post*, 10 February 1980.
10. "More Unions for Black Workers," *Africa News*, 2 May 1983.
11. "Black workers stand up to apartheid," *Intercontinental Press*, 11 July 1983.
12. *The Sowetan*, 29 June 1983.
13. *Rand Daily Mail*, 16 June 1983.

14. For background on the Riekert reforms, see Doug Hinson, "The New Black Labour Regulations: limited reform, intensified control," *South African Labour Bulletin*, vol. 6, no. 1, July 1980; Hauck, *Black Trade Unions in South Africa;* Luckhardt and Wall, *Working for Freedom. . .;* Saul and Gelb, "The Crisis in South Africa."
15. Quoted in Judy Seidman, *Facelift Apartheid* (London: International Defence and Aid Fund, 1980), p. 53.
16. Ibid.
17. *The Economist*, 4 June 1983, p. 54.
18. "Few Turn Out in Soweto to Elect a Council with Increased Power," *The New York Times*, 4 December 1983, p. 18. The actual rejection of the town council elections was greater than the government reported. The authorities failed to make clear that they were reporting the percentage of *registered* voters who actually voted, not the percentage of those eligible (Africans over 18 years of age). So, for example, in Kagiso where 1,016 people voted, the government reported a turnout of 36.6 percent. But the voting-aged population (based on a 1980 census) is 34,000. Thus, the correct poll percentage is roughly 3 percent, not 36.6 percent. See *The Star* (SA), 14 December 1983.
19. Stanley B. Greenberg and Hermann Giliomee, "Labour Bureaucracies and the African Reserves," *South African Labour Bulletin*, vol. 8, no. 4, February 1983, p. 43.
20. John A. Marcum, *Education, Race, and Social Change in South Africa* (Berkeley: University of California Press, 1982), p. 22.
21. U.S. Congress, House, *U.S. Educational Assistance in South Africa: Critical Policy Issues* (Washington, DC: Government Printing Office, 1982), p. 8.
22. Ibid., p. 9.
23. Ibid., p. 11.
24. Ibid., p. 9.
25. Joseph Lelyveld, "Pretoria and Black Education: Static Change?" *The New York Times*, 19 December 1982.
26. U.S. Congress, House, *U.S. Educational Assistance. . .*, p. 9.
27. Ibid.
28. Marcum, *Education, Race, and Social Change. . .*, p. 15.
29. See ibid.
30. Ibid., p. 4.
31. Ibid., p. 40.
32. U.S. Congress, House, *U.S. Educational Assistance. . .*, p. 10.
33. Marcum, p. 133.
34. Ibid., p. 130. Also see "South Africa: Reforms bite the gold dust," *The Economist*, 17 October 1981.
35. Marcum, p. 70.
36. Some of South Africa's militant trade unions view the AFL-CIO as an imperialist institution and have refused to cooperate. See "A rebuff abroad for the AFL-CIO," *Business Week*, 25 October 1982, p. 123; Jeremy Baskin, "AFL-CIO-AALC-CIA," *South African Labour Bulletin*, vol. 8, no. 3, December 1982; "New Western Strategies for Africa's Trade Unions," *New African*, January 1981; Michael Weber, "The AFL-CIO's rightist foreign policy," *The Guardian* (NY) 2

December 1981; *Work in Progress*, no. 24, 1982 (several articles on AFL-CIO involvement in South Africa). Also see the African-American Labor Center's *South Africa Labor News*.

37. Eagleburger's speech lauding the Reagan administration for its efforts to assist in the education of black South Africans was somewhat deceptive. Much of the impetus for the educational aid came from liberal Democrats in Congress. As Rep. Stephen J. Solarz pointed out:
> ...throughout 1981, as Congress considered and eventually passed legislation that provides $4 million a year for undergraduate and graduate scholarships in the United States for black South Africans, the administration repeatedly refused to endorse this proposal. (Stephen J. Solarz, "A Rapprochement with Racism," *Orbis*, Winter 1982, p. 878)

38. The PACE Commercial High School (PACE is an acronym for Project for the Advancement of Community Education) is funded by some 70 U.S. companies operating in South Africa. See "New S. African School Funded by U.S. Firms Trains Black Managers," *The Los Angeles Times*, 12 February 1982.

39. Quoted in U.S. Congress, House, *U.S. Educational Assistance...*, p. 13.

40. "S. African Panel Unveils New Plan for Charter Reform," *The Washington Post*, 13 May 1982.

41. Quoted in Thomas J. Bray, "South Africa: Repression and Political Reform," *The Wall Street Journal*, 14 September 1982.

42. Quoted in ibid. Also see Samuel P. Huntington, "Reform and Stability in a Modernizing, Multi-Ethnic Society," *Politikon*, vol. 8, no. 2, December 1981.

43. "South Africa's Political Options," *Backgrounder* by the Minister (Information), South African Embassy, Washington, DC, January 1983, p. 4.

44. "American Comments on South Africa," *Backgrounder* by the Minister (Information), South African Embassy, Washington, DC, April 1982, p. 2.

45. "South Africa's Political Options," p. 7.

46. For background on the far-right, see "South Africa: Botha's March," *Africa Confidential*, vol. 23, no. 6, 17 March 1982; "South Africa: Towards English Realignment," *Africa Confidential*, vol. 24, no. 8, 13 April 1983; "South Africa: Crack in the White Monolith," *Time*, 26 April 1982; "South Africa: Challenge from the Right," *Newsweek*, 7 December 1981; "South Africa's Ruling Party Split by Conservatives' Revolt," *The Washington Post*, 25 February 1982; "Afrikaner Founds Right-Wing Party," *The New York Times*, 21 March 1982.

47. See "South African Vote Seen as Rebuff to Ruling Party," *The New York Times*, 20 August 1982; "Afrikaners take bite out of Botha's power base and 'reform plan'," *The Christian Science Monitor*, 12 May 1983; "Secret Society's Reformist Shift May Be Costly Victory for Botha," *The Washington Post*, 16 July 1983.

48. "South Africa: The New Boer War," *The Economist*, 4 September 1982, pp. 30, 33.

49. "South Africa catalyst...," *The Financial Times*, 15 May 1982, reprinted in *Facts and Reports*, vol. 12, no. K, 28 May 1982, p. 9.

50. "South Africa's Move to Relax Race Laws Stymied by Botha's Conservative Critics," *The Wall Street Journal*, 4 January 1982.

51. "South Africa: A New Opposition," *The Economist*, 27 August 1983. Also see John Matisonn, "The UDF: Resurgence of Resistance," *Africa Report*, January-February 1984.
52. "Foes of Apartheid Hold Large Rally," *The New York Times*, 22 August 1983.
53. "Reject Dummy Institutions," *Sechaba*, April 1983, p. 16.
54. "Whites and blacks denounce 'reforms'," *South Africa/Namibia Update*, 16 June 1982.
55. Gatsha Buthelezi, "An Ally's Act of Betrayal," *The Washington Post*, 3 February 1983.
56. International Defence and Aid Fund, *The Apartheid War Machine*, p. 5.
57. Quoted in ibid., p. 5.
58. Ibid., see table on p. 10.
59. Ibid., p. 41.
60. For background on the Armaments Development and Production Corporation (ARMSCOR), see International Defence and Aid Fund, *The Apartheid War Machine*, pp. 13-17; "Embargo Spurs S. Africa to Build Weapons Industry," *The Washington Post*, 7 July 1981; "South Africa selling weapons developed under arms embargo," *The Christian Science Monitor*, 13 September 1982; "South Africa Promotes Sale of Modern Arms," *The Washington Post*, 27 September 1982.
61. Robert Jaster, *South Africa's Narrowing Security Options* (London: International Institute for Strategic Studies, 1980), p. 29. Also see John Fullerton, "South Africa: Day of the Generals," *Now*, 5-11 October 1979.
62. Andy Weir and Jonathan Bloch, "The Militarization of BOSS," *Covert Action Information Bulletin*, no. 13, July/August 1981.
63. For further details on the State Security Council, see Dan O'Meara, "Muldergate and the Politics of Afrikaner Nationalism," Work In Progress (Supplement to WIP 22), April 1982; "South African Military Exerts Greater Influence on Policy," *The Washington Post*, 30 May 1980; Kenneth W. Grundy, "South Africa's Domestic Strategy," *Current History*, March 1983; "South Africa: Entrenchment of White Domination," *Focus*, November 1981; "South Africa's generals in the corridors of power," *The Times* (UK), 1 September 1980.
64. O'Meara, "Muldergate...," p. 17.
65. "South African Military Exerts Greater Influence..."
66. John Dugard, "Denationalization: Apartheid's Ultimate Aim," *Africa Report*, July/August 1983, p. 43.
67. Ibid., p. 45.
68. Quoted in ibid., p. 44.
69. Ibid., p. 46.
70. "The Uprooting of blacks goes on," *The Star* (SA), 20 June 1983; "Removals and Apartheid" (International Defence and Aid Fund) *Briefing Paper*, no. 5, July 1982; "How Apartheid Uproots and Transplants Millions," *The New York Times*, 13 January 1984, p. A2.
71. See Barbara Rogers, *Divide and Rule* (London: International Defence and Aid Fund, 1980); Frank Molteno, "The Historical Significance of the Bantustan Strategy," in Martin Murray, ed., *South African Capital-*

ism and Black Political Opposition; Donald Moerdijk, *Anti-Development: South Africa and Its Bantustans* (Paris: UNESCO, 1981); "Government forced to think again: Homelands," *The Financial Times,* 26 May 1981; Roger Southall, *South Africa's Transkei: The Political Economy of an "Independent" Bantustan* (New York: Monthly Review Press, 1983).

72. "South Africa's Political Options," *Backgrounder* by the Minister (Information) South African Embassy, Washington, DC, April 1982, p. 3.

73. "South Africa's black 'homelands' sink deeper into poverty, instability," *The Christian Science Monitor,* 21 July 1983.

74. First announced publicly at a November 1979 conference with businessmen, P.W. Botha's plan for a "constellation of states" has fallen into disrepair. Conceived as a neocolonial model for granting "independence" to the bantustans but retaining control over them and South Africa's weak neighbors such as Lesotho and Swaziland, the plan was too fraught with contradictions to prove successful. Any black leader who cooperates too closely with Pretoria runs a distinct risk of losing legitimacy with the people he is trying to lead. Most leaders in the area cooperate with Pretoria out of economic and military necessity, not free choice. For useful details on the constellation of states idea, see Kenneth W. Grundy, *The Rise of the South African Security Establishment,* pp. 22-28; Saul and Gelb, "The Crisis in South Africa...," pp. 53-54; Deon Geldenhuys, "South Africa's Regional Policy," in Michael Clough, ed., *Changing Realities in Southern Africa* (Berkeley: University of California Press, 1982), pp. 148-159. For the government's view, see *Economic Co-operation in Southern Africa* (Pretoria: Department of Foreign Affairs and Information, 1981); "Southern African Constellation: A Progress Report," supplement to *South Africa Digest,* 28 August 1981.

75. Grundy, *Rise of the South African Security Establishment,* p. 24.

76. Nicholas Haysom, *Ruling with the Whip: A Report on the Violation of Human Rights in the Ciskei* (Yeoville: Southern African Research Service, 1983); "Zulu University closes campus," *Rand Daily Mail,* 2 November 1983; Gerhard Mare, "Repression In/Through the Bantustans," *DSG/SARS Information Publication no. 6* (Johannesburg: Southern African Research Service/Development Studies Group, 1982); Ernest Harsch, "South Africa: Terror in the Bantustans," *Intercontinental Press,* 26 December 1983; "Homeland Labour Laws," *South African Labour Bulletin,* vol. 8, no. 8/vol. 9, no. 1, September/October 1983.

77. For background on Pretoria's policy of regional destabilization, see U.S. Congress, House, *Regional Destabilization in Southern Africa* (Washington, DC: GPO, 1983); Simon Jenkins, "Destabilizing southern Africa," *The Economist,* 16 July 1983; "Destabilization in Southern Africa," *TransAfrica Forum Issue Brief,* January 1983; "South African Aggression" (International Defence and Aid Fund) *Briefing Paper,* no. 7, March 1983; Joe Molefi, "Few Safe Havens for Apartheid's Exiles," *Africa Report,* January-February 1984.

78. Glenn Frankel, "Mozambique, S. Africa Sign Detente Accord," *The Washington Post,* 17 March 1984, p. A1; Allister Sparks, "Angola, South Africa Reach Quick Accord On Truce Procedures," *The Washington*

Post, 29 February 1984, p. A17; James Khatami, "Strained relations between Mozambique and ANC," *The Guardian* (NY), 4 April 1984, p. 17.

79. For useful theoretical formulations on the question of settler colonialism, especially with regard to its differences from the predominant variety of colonialism, the rigidity of white settler rule, and its ability to foster economic growth, see Kenneth Good, "Settler Colonialism: Economic Development and Class Formation," *The Journal of Modern African Studies*, vol. 14, no. 4, 1976; and Arghiri Emmanuel, "White-Settler Colonialism and the Myth of Investment Imperialism," *New Left Review*, no. 73, May/June 1972. For background on traditional U.S. support for the white minority regimes of southern Africa, see Rene Lemarchand, ed., *American Policy in Southern Africa* (Washington, DC: University Press of America, 1981); Danaher, "The Political Economy of U.S. Policy Toward South Africa"; Robert M. Price, "U.S. Policy Toward Southern Africa," in Gwendolen Carter and Patrick O'Meara, eds., *International Politics in Southern Africa* (Bloomington: Indiana University Press, 1982).

80. U.S. Congress, House, *South Africa: Change and Confrontation* (Washington, DC: GPO, 1981), p. 13.

2. The "Progressive Force"
U.S. Corporations and Apartheid

Introduction

U.S. corporate and government leaders claim that American investment is a "progressive force" for change in South Africa. The
argument generally includes the following elements:

- Race prejudice is anachronistic, an irrational holdover from
  pre-industrial society that will be dissolved gradually by
  market forces. This assumption finds support in the social
  science literature on "modernization."[1]

- American corporate involvement will help spur growth in
  the South African economy, creating more jobs and income
  for blacks.

- As the economic situation of blacks improves, they will be
  better equipped to press for full social equality. With a
  greater stake in the system, they will be more likely to rely
  on peaceful, orderly methods of social change.

U.S. officials invoke the progressive force theme to fend off U.N.
initiatives for economic sanctions against South Africa. They argue
that a break in economic ties would be deleterious because it would
decrease black job opportunities and cut off the liberalizing influence of western democracies.* Defenders of continued U.S. investment in South Africa argue that divestment would not seriously

---

*Note, however, that this purported liberalizing influence of contact with the West
has not prevented the U.S. government from implementing economic sanctions
against the Soviet Union, China, Cuba, Vietnam, Nicaragua, Uganda, Grenada, and
others.

undermine apartheid because U.S. properties "could readily be taken over by South Africa or by other foreign countries."[2]

The argument that American business involvement in South Africa will help abolish apartheid was given its greatest boost during the Carter administration. In 1976, candidate Carter ruled out the use of an economic embargo against the white minority regime, saying "I think such sanctions could be counter-productive."[3] Carter posited that, "economic development, investment commitment and the use of economic leverage...seems to me the only way to achieve racial justice there."[4] This was no blind belief in the impersonal forces of the market. Carter recognized that the dependence of the South African economy on western capital conferred political leverage on U.S. corporations: "our American businessmen can be a constructive force for achieving racial justice within South Africa. I think the weight of our investments there, the value the South Africans place on access to American capital and technology can be used as a positive force in settling regional problems."[5]

Although many of Carter's top officials echoed this theme, its most outspoken proponent was U.N. Ambassador Andrew Young. The former civil rights activist told a South African audience that "the free market system can be the greatest force for constructive change now operating anywhere in the world."[6] He drew analogies to the gains won by blacks in the southern United States and gave most of the credit to capital as a political force, noting, "when in Atlanta, Georgia, five banks decided that it was bad for business to have racial turmoil, racial turmoil ceased....they put up four million dollars to develop a public relations campaign for our city, a city too busy to hate."[7]

Several years before Ronald Reagan appointed him U.S. Ambassador to South Africa, Herman Nickel gave the following rendition of the progressive force thesis in *Fortune* magazine.

> ...there is little doubt that, however erratic and confused, an evolutionary process is at work. The striking mark of this process is that the forces for change in the political sector receive their strongest thrust from progress in the economic sector. In the light of this fact, it hardly seems sensible to argue that political redemption can be accelerated by a full-scale American retreat from the economic arena.[8]

The Reagan administration's chief architect of Africa policy, Chester Crocker, reaffirmed a core assumption of the progressive force thesis.

...if helped through this crisis period with the right mix of aid, policy reform, and a strongly reinvigorated role for the private sector, African peoples will opt for the growth and the freedom—the personal, economic, and political freedom—that is inherent in the free world's international economic system.[9]

This argument has also been propagated by the South African government and cooperative members of the black elite. One of Pretoria's propaganda sheets aimed at American businessmen claims that, "participation in the economic expansion of South Africa is not only profitable for the participants but also desirable from the humanitarian point of view by improving the quality of life of all South Africans."[10] Another, arguing that withdrawal of foreign investment will hurt more blacks than just those in South Africa, warned that, "curbs on foreign investment will seriously harm the fragile economies of neighboring and other black African countries on the sub-continent."[11] Under sponsorship of the white government, conservative blacks have propagated similar views. The following statement by Chief Gatsha Buthelezi, head of the KwaZulu bantustan, appeared in expensive ads in major American newspapers such as *The New York Times* and *The Washington Post*.

> Those who advocate trade sanctions and economic withdrawal to help my people and punish the whites in South Africa may be killing us with kindness. What we need is not disengagement, but full foreign participation in South Africa's overall economic development to create more jobs, higher wages and better training opportunities.[12]

Lucy Mvubelo, General Secretary of the National Union of Clothing Workers, lamented the high unemployment rate among blacks, stating that, "disinvestment would only make it worse. These are people without skills and education. All they can do is use their hands. What they need is more opportunity to work, and that means more investments in South Africa by multinational companies, not less."[13]

Historical Background

Corporate and government leaders began relying on the progressive force theme in the late 1960s and have intensified their use of it since the mid-1970s.[14] This ideological development coincided with two political trends, one foreign and one domestic. The antiapartheid movement in the United States had for many years concentrated its efforts on the federal government, hoping to influence U.S. policy by putting pressure on the Executive and Congress. As that strategy proved relatively ineffective, and as the movement incorporated an increasing number of young leftists, antiapartheid forces turned their sights on American corporate ties to South Africa. The Polaroid Revolutionary Workers' Movement and its successful efforts to force the photography giant out of South Africa, was one of the earliest and best-known cases of this direct attack on U.S. investment in South Africa.[15] College students, trade unions, and church groups increasingly challenged the "right" of American companies to profit from the exploitation of workers under apartheid.[16]

This domestic shift in antiapartheid strategy was related to international developments. The 1971-72 general strike in Namibia, the Natal strikes of 1973-74, the anticolonial struggles in Angola and Mozambique, the Soweto uprising of 1976-77, and the growing support in the United Nations for economic sanctions against South Africa, all were characterized to some degree by anticapitalist and anti-imperialist sentiment. This trend was strengthened by a new generation of black leaders in southern Africa who were pressing the claim that western trade and investment acted to solidify the class domination of the white minorities.

The combined impact of popular struggles domestically and internationally prompted U.S. elites to elaborate a more detailed ideological program for defending U.S. corporate involvement in South Africa. As the extensive research of P.H. Martin concludes, "the activity against American business aimed at disengagement... further stimulated efforts to produce more favorable images of South Africa, or at least of American business activity in South Africa."[17]

Apartheid: A Racist System of Labor Control

A fundamental misconception underlying the progressive force theme is that apartheid is a system of racial separation or segregation. Government officials and the media consistently describe apartheid as separation of the races.* The apartheid system, however, is

*A random selection from major periodicals and government statements reveals a consistent definition of apartheid: "...racially separatist policies..." *The Wall*

designed not for separation, but domination. And this distinction is at the center of the debate over U.S. policy toward South Africa. The racist system of labor control in South Africa serves to incorporate major sections of western ruling classes into the South African status quo, but also secures the support of the majority of nations for the revolutionary struggle against that status quo.

The major components of South Africa's racial system—the bantustans, pass laws, labor bureaus, residency rules—were instituted, not primarily to keep blacks and whites separate, but to secure white control over black workers. The history of South African development shows that modifications in the system of white supremacy were brought about by changing needs for black labor, not by white attitudes toward racial segregation.[18] The uniqueness of South Africa's racial system stems from the way that society was incorporated into the world capitalist economy: a white settler minority, with assistance from foreign capital, industrializing via the rigid control of a black majority workforce. In other white settler colonies (e.g., the United States) where the indigenous people were decimated, this problem of harnessing the natives as a labor force did not arise. But the economic development of South Africa was predicated on creating institutional structures and cultural rationales designed to keep black labor disciplined and inexpensive.

The considerable overlap of race and class—whites as bosses, blacks as workers—accounts for much misunderstanding by outsiders. American opinion makers emphasize the racial element, rather than the class dimension of apartheid: U.S. companies profiting from apartheid, as well as the U.S. government, refrain from any reference to apartheid as a system of exploitation rooted in the class structure of a capitalist economy, lest American working people make troublesome analogies to other areas of the world, not least the United States.

Viewing the problem in strictly racial terms makes some Americans receptive to testimonials by wealthy South African blacks to the effect that their society is not all that bad, even though this 'black' evidence is not representative of the South African majority.

The goal of the apartheid government is not so much to separate the races, as it is to divide the black population in as many ways as possible. Africans, Asians, and Coloureds are separated. Africans are

---

Street Journal; "...racial segregation..." *Foreign Affairs;* "...racial separation..." *The Washington Post;* "...separation of the races..." Henry Kissinger; "...legally entrenched racial separation..." Chester Crocker.

divided into ten ethnic groups, with the divisions institutionalized in the bantustans. The state purposefully breaks up many African families via its migratory labor system and residency rules. In recent years, the government has also developed new methods for developing class cleavages in the African community: permanent bantustan residents are the worst off, agricultural workers on white farms have it slightly better, migrant workers temporarily benefit from the greater wealth of the urban areas, Africans with permanent residential rights in the townships come next, and at the top of the ladder are the black businessmen and bantustan leaders who play an openly collaborationist role. The primary objective of all this divide-and-rule manipulation is not to foster racial purity but to maintain political domination by controlling the African workforce.

Those who draw parallels between the struggle of blacks in South Africa and the Civil Rights movement in the United States display a racial bias: while racial separation characterizes both societies, the two cases are otherwise very different.

- Black Americans were constitutionally guaranteed formal political equality and took to the streets in the 1950s and 1960s to have the law enforced. In South Africa blacks are constitutionally deprived of formal equality and take to the streets to protest that status.
- Black Americans have always been a minority, so white leaders could afford to support formal political equality without posing an immediate threat to their power. Blacks in South Africa are an overwhelming majority and formal political equality would result in a rapid overthrow of white power.

Because of these vastly different conditions, the tactics utilized by the Civil Rights movement in the United States are often inappropriate against the repressive powers of the South African state. For example, in response to a 1983 bus boycott in Ciskei to protest increased fares, police *forced* protestors to ride the buses, killing five and wounding forty-five in the process.[19]

Capitalist Growth and Racial Oppression

Ever since the mining boom of the late nineteenth century formed the basis of South African industrialization, Americans have exerted an influence disproportionate to their numbers.[20] Based on their experience in the California gold rush, American engineers and managers played a key role in the development of South Africa's most important industry. As early as 1896 roughly half of South Africa's mines were run by American engineers.[21]

Influential Americans such as John Hays Hammond not only played an important role in South Africa's economic development but also helped shape early U.S. government policy.[22] Hammond's position as Cecil Rhodes' personal engineering consultant, at a salary of $75,000 a year and a share of the profits, helped him become "the virtual czar of South African mining by 1894."[23]

Although the mines required large numbers of laborers, they were also capital-intensive, using significant amounts of construction materials, chemicals, and machinery. Hammond and other American engineers were partial to American equipment and were keen to get U.S. companies a better foothold in the South African economy. Their influence helped the United States become the largest supplier of equipment to the mines.[24]

The gold mining industry was the leading edge of South African industrialization in more than a technical or financial sense. It was in the mining sector that South Africa pioneered its unique system of labor control. The same mining boom that was causing important sectors of the U.S. ruling class to sink roots in the South African economy, was also creating a society dependent on the unfree labor of the black majority. As U.S. companies became more deeply involved in South Africa's industrialization, their profits grew more dependent on the institutions of white minority rule.

Building on early involvement in mining, U.S. companies developed an important role in key sectors such as petrochemicals, metals, the motor industry, agricultural equipment, and other manufactured goods. Major U.S. firms that later gained prominence in the U.S. and world economies got an early start in South Africa. These included Singer Sewing Machine (1870s), Kidder, Peabody Co. (1870), Mobil (1897), General Electric (1899), Ford (1905), and Kodak (1913).[25] By 1929 the following corporations had opened branches: National Cash Register, Armour and Co., National City Bank of New York, Prentice-Hall, Colgate-Palmolive, Firestone, B.F. Goodrich, American Cyanimid, General Motors, and International Harvester.[26]

Today, U.S. corporations are dominant in key strategic sectors of the South African economy. American electronics firms provide computers and other advanced technology to the police, military,

Table 2.1: Real Wages of African Miners in South Africa, 1905–1969

Year	Wage (Rand)	Index (wages corrected for inflation)
1905	54	—
1911	57	100
1921	66	69
1936	68	100
1946	87	92
1961	146	89
1969	199	99

Source: Francis Wilson, *Labour in the South African Gold Mines, 1911-1969* (Cambridge, 1972), pp. 45-46.

and various sections of the labor control system.[27] Because South Africa does not have its own supply of petroleum, U.S. firms such as Mobil and Caltex play a key role in keeping industry and the military supplied with oil, gas, and chemicals.[28] Large American firms such as General Electric, Honeywell, and Allis-Chalmers have helped South Africa build its nuclear industry even though Pretoria has refused to sign the Non-Proliferation Treaty and is suspected of developing its own nuclear bombs.[29] There is no denying that American capital and technology have helped South Africa's white minority, not only in controlling its own population but in dominating the entire region as well.[30]

But what of the black population during this hundred years of industrialization? Did the forces of economic growth help undermine racial oppression? Although a small minority of South African blacks have attained some affluence, capitalist growth has been quite compatible with white supremacy. The African miners who were the backbone of South Africa's development received no real increase in wages during most of the twentieth century. And this stagnation in income was true for the African majority as a whole: "the historical record on African living standards is reasonably clear: nearly a century of capitalist development between 1870 and 1960 brought almost no gains to the African majority."[31]

As recently as the early 1900s many Africans were successful commercial farmers with large tracts of land. But the 1913 Land Act and subsequent white encroachment have restricted Africans to the least fertile 13 percent of the country. Now most rural Africans are reduced to scraping a bare subsistence from eroded, overgrazed land.[32]

> ...the development of the capitalist sector depended upon the conscious underdevelopment of African peasant communities—the creation of labour control mechanisms, labour surpluses, and wage elasticities that did not previously exist. Entry into the 'modern' sector did not represent some advance on peasant life but the culmination of processes that disintegrated and impoverished it.[33]

Had Africans been allowed to retain their productive farms, it would have been difficult to lure them to work in the dirty and dangerous mines. Mineowners would have been forced to pay much higher wages to secure the labor of successful African farmers. But through a combination of onerous taxes and deprivation of land, the whites forced the Africans to seek the meager wages of the mines.

In pre-industrial South Africa the whites had needs for African labor but not on the scale that manufacturing later required. As the nation industrialized, more Africans moved to the urban areas. The increasing urbanization of Africans created among key white groups a material interest in controlling the lives of Africans. White mineowners and industrialists wanted sufficient numbers of Africans to be driven off the land and forced into wage labor. White farmers wanted African urbanization controlled so as to ensure sufficient low-cost labor in rural areas. White workers in the cities, threatened by competition from Africans willing to work for less pay, had their own interest in tight controls on the African workforce. And later, white civil servants who ran the many programs of the apartheid state also developed an interest in controlling the Africans.

The economic boom of the World War II period and its accompanying mass urbanization of Africans led white South Africans to vote the National Party (NP) into power in 1948. The NP had a plan for dealing with an urbanized African workforce—apartheid. As the white minority implemented ever-tighter restrictions on the black majority, U.S. investment continued to pour into the country (see graph on next page).

When popular rebellion and savage government repression threatened international investor confidence in South Africa, U.S. capital played a key role in restoring that confidence. The March 1960 massacre at Sharpeville frightened holders of short term debt and investors in the Johannesburg stock exchange so deeply that "South Africa faced a balance-of-payments crisis more severe than any

U.S. Direct Investment in South Africa

(in millions of dollars)

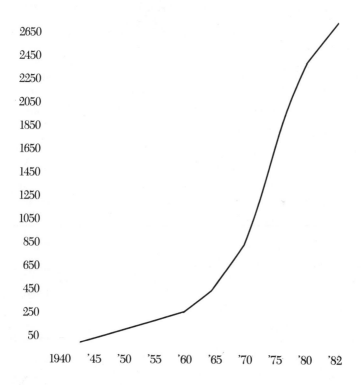

Sources: Elizabeth Schmidt, *Decoding Corporate Camouflage*, p. 5; and Commerce Department data.

experienced since 1932."[34] In just six weeks following the massacre, the Johannesburg stock exchange registered a decline of nearly one billion dollars.[35] American corporations and financial agencies such as the International Monetary Fund made large infusions of capital into the embattled South African economy, so that, "by 1962, South Africa's economic crisis was over."[36]

In 1976 and 1977 when South African police shot down hundreds of children in the streets of Soweto and other cities, it again shook investor confidence. Both the Ford and Carter administrations supported Pretoria's emergency request for infusions of cash from the International Monetary Fund.[37] The amount eventually granted to South Africa, $464 million, was greater than IMF loans to all other African countries combined during those same years.

Throughout South African history, economic growth and racial oppression have been remarkably compatible.* The editors of *The Wall Street Journal* acknowledged that, "South Africa itself is the best argument against the notion that economic growth necessarily brings political liberalization. Official repression coexisted quite nicely with economic growth during much of the past 50 years or longer."[39]

The Sullivan Principles

In 1977, the Rev. Leon Sullivan, a black member of General Motors' board of directors, devised a corporate code of conduct for U.S. firms operating in South Africa. The Sullivan principles are voluntary and call for signatory companies to strive for equal pay for equal work, fair employment practices, more training for blacks, integrated worksite amenities, and greater corporate attention to black workers' non-work problems such as housing, health-care, and transportation.

Many corporate and government leaders have claimed that these affirmative action guidelines are the most practical way for U.S. companies to play a progressive role in South Africa. But this code of conduct actually does more harm than good.[40]

The most important constraint on the Sullivan principles is something too great for any code of conduct to change. American investment in South Africa is concentrated in capital-intensive sectors such as petrochemicals, computers, nuclear power, and transportation equipment. These sectors expand primarily through tech-

---

*The direct relationship between foreign investment and repression is not unique to South Africa. In the global market economy, investment is attracted by political 'stability' and high rates of return, not democracy and racial equality. Capital has always been a political opportunist. Many U.S. firms did business with Nazi Germany.[38] Right-wing dictatorships in Chile, South Korea, the Philippines, Indonesia, Thailand, and Zaire are favorite spots for international capital. These nations, like South Africa, are attractive because their labor-repressive policies provide an environment conducive to 'labor peace' and high profits.

nological innovation, not greater employment. They tend, therefore, to contribute to structural unemployment. In addition to the human suffering brought on by high levels of unemployment...

> ...the labour surplus problem also has important political implications. With estimates of current African unemployment ranging between 13 and 22 per cent, and 10-year projections that stretch upwards from 19 to 26 per cent and higher, there is growing potential for social and political instability.[41]

There is no chance whatsoever of U.S. investment alleviating this massive unemployment: it is more likely to exacerbate it.

The capital-intensive nature of U.S. firms also means that they employ a higher ratio of skilled to unskilled workers than the rest of the economy, that is, a disproportionate share of whites.* White workers comprise 36 percent of those employed by Sullivan signatory firms, but only 20 percent of the South African workforce nationwide; whereas Africans comprise only 44 percent of the Sullivan companies' workforce, but 68 percent of all South African workers.[42]

Despite their nearly $3 billion in direct investment in South Africa,† U.S. companies employ less than 1 percent of all African workers. Whatever pay and perquisites these companies give to their black employees will only reinforce the white government's strategy of cultivating a small, affluent black elite.

Allowing for these serious limitations, what has been the record of the Sullivan principles? The code is voluntary, and roughly half of the more than three hundred U.S. subsidiaries have refused to sign it. Leon Sullivan himself has deplored this record and called for

---

*Whites are also concentrated at the upper end of the wage scale in these firms. This is important to keep in mind when Pretoria's defenders argue against economic sanctions and divestment by claiming that these actions would hurt blacks more than whites. It is true that if all U.S. firms were shut down, there would be a greater number of blacks losing jobs than whites. But proportionately, white wages and white income (from stocks, etc.) would suffer most. As some black South Africans say: those higher up on the social ladder have further to fall than those near the bottom.

†A classified document leaked from the State Department in late 1983 reports that the figure traditionally given for U.S. direct investment in South African ($2.6 billion in 1983) grossly understates the real extent of U.S. holdings. The study titled *U.S. Investment in South Africa: The Hidden Pieces*, found that in addition to direct investment Americans had extended $3.6 billion in short-term loans and owned over $8 billion in South African stocks, giving a total for all U.S. investment of $14.6 billion. (See James Cason and Michael Fleshman, "Dollars for Apartheid," *Multinational Monitor*, November 1983).

stockholders and the U.S. government to take action against these firms. His reasoning is straightforward. Because multinational corporations "have been the main beneficiaries of cheap labor and profits from this evil and unjust system and among its main supporters," if they don't now work to change that system "they have no moral justification for remaining in South Africa, and should be compelled to leave the country."[43]

The Arthur D. Little Company prepares annual reports on the performance of the Sullivan signatory companies. The Sixth Report on the Signatory Companies to the Sullivan Principles, published in late 1982, reveals the following:

- fewer companies were willing to report on their activities than in the preceding three years (nearly one-fourth failed to file the required compliance questionnaires);
- of those who filed reports, more than one-third received "failing grades" for non-compliance with the affirmative action principles;
- twenty-nine signatory companies (more than in any previous year) dropped out of the program;
- the proportion of blacks in supervisory and skilled positions declined since the last reporting period;
- and due to continued inequality in training and pay scales, the already wide wage gap between white and black employees is growing.[44]

While U.S. corporations gain public relations benefits from their efforts at workplace integration and better pay for blacks, they are making a bad situation worse by driving wedges into the black community. The key issue is not at the micro level—the working conditions of a hundred thousand—it is at the macro level—the disenfranchisement and destitution of over twenty million.

Conclusion

As banks came under increasing pressure to halt their lending to South Africa, the financiers defended themselves by earmarking some of their credit for black housing and hospitals. However, like most U.S. educational aid and direct investment, these loans only reinforce the structure of apartheid. A 1981 Congressional study found:

As long as American banks finance major housing and hospital projects which are established exclusively for blacks and are confined to black areas, they only perpetuate rather than ameliorate South Africa's oppressive system of apartheid. Moreover, most blacks with whom we spoke said they would prefer to see the U.S. Government ban all loans—even those benefiting blacks in black areas—until South Africa changes its overall policy of apartheid. To support additional loans to South Africa to construct segregated housing and health facilities only entrenches apartheid.[45]

Even if corporate leaders genuinely desired to reform the system, the white minority government has put strict limits on what the private sector can accomplish. As part of the growing militarization of state and society, Pretoria has created a web of laws to tie corporations into the defense of the system.

...the government has co-opted many foreign firms into security collaboration. The National Key Points Act of 1980, the Atomic Energy Act as amended, the National Supplies Procurement Act as amended, and the Petroleum Products Amendment Act, among other pieces of legislation, implicate private firms in a secrecy about their production levels, sources of supply, trading partners and so forth that contribute to the siege mentality.

One could also surmise that in this atmosphere there is a good deal of planning and implementation of secret stockpiles, strategic reserves and contingency plans entangling the private sector and the strategic planners.[46]

Given Pretoria's ability to prevent the private sector from challenging fundamental aspects of apartheid, and given the strategic importance of U.S. firms to the survival of the regime, Washington's tolerance for U.S. corporate operations in South Africa amounts to support for white minority rule. The U.S. government position that "we neither encourage nor discourage" investment in South Africa is a flimsy defense. For decades, the United States has provided corporations with free information and support services to facilitate their penetration of the South African economy.[47]

This is why all but a few nations in the world have supported efforts at the United Nations to impose economic sanctions against South Africa.[48] The U.S. government, on the other hand, has expended considerable political capital by blocking proposals for an economic embargo.[49] Those supporting sanctions have argued, correctly, that centuries of western investment in South Africa have made matters worse, and the only sure way to pressure the white minority is to cut it off from its international supporters.

A growing number of South Africans agree with this line of reasoning. As far back as 1977, a confidential cable from the U.S. Ambassador in South Africa reported that "with radicalization of black attitudes, tendency to call for disinvestment grows stronger" and it "must be expected that [the] role of American firms here will become increasingly controversial and [the] rationale for continued presence will seem less and less persuasive to [a] growing number of blacks."[50] As Bishop Desmond Tutu, General Secretary of the South African Council of Churches, pleaded:

> We ask our friends to apply economic pressure...Our last chance for peaceful change lies in the international community applying political, diplomatic and especially economic pressure... Any black leader who calls for economic sanctions is already guilty of treason under the Terrorism Act, and subject to five years of prison or death. We said as much as we can possibly say. We hope we have... reasonably intelligent friends overseas who will know what we are saying.[51]

With a growing number of black South Africans willing to take up arms, and the apartheid state intensifying its military preparations, Bishop Tutu is probably correct in his assertion that economic sanctions are the only way to terminate apartheid nonviolently.

Notes

1. A representative sample of the modernization school includes Samuel Huntington, *Political Order in Changing Societies* (New Haven: Yale University Press, 1968); David Apter, *The Politics of Modernization* (Chicago: University of Chicago Press, 1965); and S.N. Eisenstadt, *Modernization: Protest and Change* (Englewood Cliffs, NJ: Prentice-Hall, 1966). For useful critiques of the modernization literature, see Dean C. Tipps, "Modernization Theory and the Comparative Study of Societies: A Critical Perspective," *Comparative Studies in Society and History*, vol. 15, no. 2, March 1973; and C.D. Lummis, "On the Uses of History: The Case of Modernization Theory," *Berkeley Journal of Sociology*, XXI, 1976-77.
2. William A. Hance, "Selected Arguments Against United States Economic Disengagement from South Africa," *Issue*, vol. III, no. 4, Winter 1973, p. 3.
3. "Carter Speaks on SA," *The Financial Mail* (SA), 5 November 1976, p. 501.
4. Ibid.
5. Ibid.
6. *Sevendays*, 20 June 1977, p. 10.

7. Andrew Young, quoted in Stanley B. Greenberg, *Race and State in Capitalist Development* (New Haven and London: Yale University Press, 1980), p. 443.
8. Herman Nickel, "The Case for Doing Business in South Africa," *Fortune*, 19 June 1978, p. 68.
9. Chester Crocker, "Regional Strategy for Southern Africa," address before the American Legion in Honolulu, Hawaii, on August 29, 1981; U.S. Department of State, Bureau of Public Affairs, Current Policy no. 308.
10. "South Africa: Time to Invest," *Backgrounder* from the Information Minister, South African Embassy, Washington, DC, June 1980.
11. "USA/South Africa: The Trade Connection," *Backgrounder* from the Information Minister, South African Embassy, Washington, DC, no. 6, 1978.
12. *A New Face for Apartheid* (New York: The Africa Fund, 1974), p. 1.
13. Quoted by William Raspberry, "Investing in the Fight Against Apartheid," *The Washington Post*, 8 October 1979.
14. The article by Norman MacRae ("The Green Bay Tree") that caught the eye of Richard Nixon was published in *The Economist*, 29 June 1968. Another version of the progressive force thesis, by Anglo-American Corporation executive M.C. O'Dowd, which takes its cue from the work of W.W. Rostow, is found in Lawrence Schlemmer and Eddie Webster, eds., *Change, Reform and Economic Growth in South Africa* (Johannesburg: Ravan Press, 1978). This volume also contains several critiques of O'Dowd's argument.
15. See Alan Booth, "Polaroid's Experiment in the Disengagement from South Africa," in Charles Harvey, et al., *The Policy Debate* (Uppsala: Africa Publications Trust, 1975).
16. Alfred O. Hero and John Barratt, eds., *The American People and South Africa* (Lexington, MA: Lexington Books, 1981). See Chapters 2, 6, 7, and 8.
17. Patrick Henry Martin, "American Views of South Africa, 1948-1972," Dissertation, Louisiana State University, 1974, p. 164.
18. See sources cited in Chapter 1, note 3.
19. *Africa Report*, September/October 1983, pp. 40-41.
20. Thomas J. Noer, *Briton, Boer and Yankee: The United States and South Africa, 1870-1914* (Kent, OH: Kent State University Press, 1978), p. 44.
21. Ibid., p. 31.
22. Ibid.
23. Ibid.
24. Ibid.
25. Ward Anthony Spooner, "United States Policy Toward South Africa, 1919-1941: Political and Economic Aspects," Dissertation, St. Johns University, 1979, p. 215; and Ann and Neva Seidman, *South Africa and U.S. Multinational Corporations* (Westport, CT: Lawrence Hill, 1977), p. 109.
26. Mira Wilkins, *The Maturing of Multinational Enterprise* (Cambridge, MA: Harvard University Press, 1974), pp. 143-4; and Spooner, pp. 215, 219, 220, 221.

27. NARMIC/American Friends Service Committee, *Automating Apart-heid: U.S. Computer Exports to South Africa and the Arms Embargo* (Philadelphia: AFSC, 1982).
28. Ann Seidman and Neva Seidman Makgetla, Chapter 8: "The Oil Majors" in *Outposts of Monopoly Capitalism* (Westport, CT: Lawrence Hill, 1980); Desaix Myers III, et al., *U.S. Business in South Africa* (Bloomington and London: Indiana University Press, 1980), pp. 153-188; Martin Bailey and Bernard Rivers, *Oil Sanctions Against South Africa* (New York: U.N. Centre Against Apartheid, 1978); "Fueling Apartheid: American Oil Interests in South Africa," *Newsletter*, Council on Economic Priorities, 4 December 1978.
29. Barbara Rogers and Zdenek Cervenka, *The Nuclear Axis* (New York: Times Books, 1978); U.S. Congress, House, *United States-South Africa Relations: Nuclear Cooperation*, Hearings Before the Subcommittee on Africa (Washington, DC: GPO, 1978); "Stop the Apartheid Bomb" (Washington, DC: Washington Office on Africa, 1982); Samuel Day Jr., "The Afrikaner Bomb," *The Progressive*, September 1982.
30. Seidman and Makgetla, *Outposts. . .*
31. Stanley B. Greenberg, "Economic Growth and Political Change: the South African Case," *The Journal of Modern African Studies*, vol. 19, no. 4, 1981, p. 678.
32. On the land question, see Francis Wilson, Chapter 2: "Farming, 1866-1966" in Monica Wilson and Leonard Thompson, eds., *The Oxford History of South Africa* (New York and Oxford: Oxford University Press, 1971); and Part III: "The Development of Capitalist Production Processes: The Mining Industry, the Demand for Labour, and the Transformation of the Countryside, 1870-1910" in Martin J. Murray, ed., *South African Capitalism and Black Political Opposition* (Cambridge, MA: Schenkman, 1982).
33. Greenberg, "Economic Growth. . .," p. 674.
34. D. Hobart Houghton, *The South African Economy* (Cape Town: Oxford University Press, 1976), p. 186.
35. Jonathan Wouk, "United States Policy Toward South Africa, 1960-1967: Foreign Policy in a Relatively Permissive Environment," Dissertation, University of Pittsburgh, 1972, p. 82.
36. Anthony Lake, "Caution and Concern: The Making of American Policy Toward South Africa, 1946-1971," Dissertation, Princeton University, 1974, pp. 82-83.
37. James Morrell and David Gisselquist, "How the IMF Slipped $464 Million to South Africa" (Washington, DC: Center for International Policy, 1978).
38. Charles Higham, *Trading with the Enemy* (New York: Delacorte Press, 1983); James Pool and Suzanne Pool, *Who Financed Hitler* (New York: Dial Press, 1978); Antony C. Sutton, *Wall Street and the Rise of Hitler* (Seal Beach, CA: '76 Press, 1976).
39. Thomas J. Bray, "South Africa: Growth and Political Reform," *The Wall Street Journal*, 9 September 1982.
40. For the full text of the Sullivan Principles and a detailed critique, see Elizabeth Schmidt, *Decoding Corporate Camouflage* (Washington, DC: Institute for Policy Studies, 1980).

41. Greenberg, "Economic Growth. . . ," pp. 690-691.
42. Elizabeth Schmidt, *One Step in the Wrong Direction* (New York: Episcopal Churchmen for South Africa, 1983), pp. 4-5.
43. Leon Sullivan, "It's Time to Step Up the Pressure on South Africa," *The Washington Post*, 10 May 1983.
44. Schmidt, *One Step. . . .* For additional data on the black/white wage gap in U.S. firms, see Investor Responsibility Research Center, South Africa Review Service, *Reporter*, vol. I, no. 3, September 1983.
45. U.S. Congress, House, *South Africa: Change and Confrontation* (Washington, DC: GPO, 1981), p. 27.
46. Kenneth W. Grundy, *The Rise of the South African Security Establishment* (Braamfontein: South African Institute of International Affairs, 1983), p. 21. Also see "Fortressing Industry, Fortressing Apartheid," *Resister*, no. 28, October/November 1983.
47. A review of U.S. government publications dealing with South Africa shows that nearly 100 percent of this literature is designed to facilitate U.S. business involvement. See Julian W. Witherell, *The United States and Africa: Guide to U.S. Official Documents and Government-Sponsored Publications on Africa, 1785-1975* (Washington, DC: GPO, 1978).
48. The most comprehensive examination of the sanctions issue was published in 1980 by the now-defunct International University Exchange Fund. The multi-volume study—"Economic Sanctions Against South Africa"—covered various aspects of this issue. For a comprehensive discussion of the literature, see D.G. Clarke, *Policy Issues and Economic Sanctions on South Africa*, vol. 1, (Geneva: IUEF, 1980). For a useful list of resources, see *Sanctions Against South Africa: A Selective Bibliography* (New York: United Nations, 1981). For a detailed discussion of U.N. sanctions from a legal standpoint, see David Lawther Johnson, "Sanctions and South Africa," *Harvard International Law Journal*, vol. 19, no. 3, Fall 1978.
49. Kevin Danaher, "The U.S. and South Africa: Building the Base for Sanctions," *Freedomways*, vol. 21, no. 1, 1981; Camille A. Bratton, "A Matter of Record: The History of the United States Voting Pattern in the United Nations Regarding Racism, Colonialism and Apartheid, 1946-1976," *Freedomways*, vol. 17, no. 3, 1977.
50. "Confidential Diplomatic Cable Reveals Black Hostility to US Investment in South Africa," *Southern Africa*, April 1978, p. 6.
51. Quoted in *Namibia: The Strength of the Powerless* (Rome: IDOC International, 1980), p. 37.

3. Peaceful Change
Law, Shame, and Violence

Introduction

The United States has been an insistent advocate of peaceful change in South Africa, urging blacks to further their goals through nonviolent political means, not armed struggle. The official reasoning behind this assertion has three components.

- the military/police apparatus of the white government is so powerful as to make any black armed struggle futile, only bringing on more repression;
- armed struggle by blacks opens the door to "foreign intervention" (i.e., military aid from socialist countries);
- a full-scale civil war in South Africa would do so much damage to economic installations and race relations that the eventual 'prize' would not be worth the cost of the struggle.

The peaceful change theme has been given much greater emphasis by U.S. policymakers since the overthrow of Portuguese colonialism in 1974-75. The successful guerrilla movements in neighboring Mozambique and Angola provided evidence to black South Africans that white minority rule was not invincible. It is no mere coincidence that black South Africa erupted in the so-called Soweto rebellion within a year of black nationalists seizing power in Angola and Mozambique.

One consequence of the Soweto rebellion was that thousands of black youths fled from police violence to neighboring black-ruled states. Many of them joined the nationalist organizations, particularly the African National Congress of South Africa (ANC), which were training cadres to return to South Africa to wage guerrilla war.[1]

Prior to the regional victories by black guerrilla forces, U.S. policymakers discounted the ability of blacks to seize power militarily. A key Nixon/Kissinger document from 1969, displaying open disregard for black military capabilities in the white-ruled states of southern Africa, states that, "the whites are here to stay and the only way that constructive change can come about is through them. There is no hope for the blacks to gain the political rights they seek through violence."[2]

In the mid-1970s, following the black military victories in Angola and Mozambique, and a related increase in black militancy in the other white-ruled states, Washington's statements lost their smug tone. After the failure of his 1975 CIA/South African intervention in Angola, Henry Kissinger resorted to diplomacy in an effort to halt the advance of leftist forces in the region. He argued that it was "essential to provide responsible African leaders with a moderate alternative to the grim prospects of violence so rapidly taking shape before them."[3] Kissinger told African and Afro-American leaders that Washington's newfound interest in southern Africa "was designed to demonstrate that there is a positive and peaceful road open to fulfill African aspirations."[4]

The Carter administration continued this emphasis on the need for peaceful change. Many of Carter's top aides had been deeply affected by the U.S. defeat in Vietnam. They had concluded that in attempting to stop the spread of revolutionary nationalism in the Third World, the United States should rely more on diplomacy and economic leverage than on military might. Opinion polls showed that a majority of Americans were opposed to military interventions abroad.[5] Clearly, U.S. military intervention against black revolutionaries attacking white minority rule would be very difficult, if not impossible, to carry out. Hence, U.S. officials sought to avert an escalation of armed conflict that could force on them a choice between an embattled, pro-capitalist (but racist) ally, and a black, anticapitalist (but popular) insurgency. Thus, Washington hoped to convince black South Africans to rely solely on nonviolent methods.

The Carter team espoused nonviolent methods to South African blacks but, unlike Republican administrations, acknowledged that, given continued repression and intransigence by the white government, blacks could not be expected to eschew armed struggle indefinitely. Carter's top expert on southern Africa° criticized the white minority by quoting John F. Kennedy: "those who make peaceful evolution impossible will make violent revolution inevitable."[6]

Perhaps more than any other official, Carter's Ambassador to the United Nations, Andrew Young, personified the contradictions of a liberal U.S. government confronting the question of violence in South Africa. In addition to his official responsibility to favor peaceful change, Young's personal politics were steeped in the nonviolent strategies of the civil rights movement. Yet he recognized the legitimacy of the guerrilla wars being waged against white minority regimes. Referring to southern Africa, he stated: "I don't believe in violence. I fought violence in my own country. I am determined that the United Nations continue as one institution that is devoted to peaceful change. And yet, I have never condemned another man's right to take up arms in pursuit of his freedom."[7]

In contrast to the Carter team, the Reagan administration was not encumbered by thoughts about the legitimacy of armed struggle by the black majority. Prior to his election as President, Ronald Reagan referred to the ANC, SWAPO of Namibia, and ZANU and ZAPU of Zimbabwe as terrorist organizations.[8] As part of the shift from defending human rights to combatting "international terrorism," the Reagan administration attempted to downgrade the internationally-recognized nationalist movements of southern Africa to the status of terrorist groups.

The Reagan administration's most comprehensive policy statement on South Africa came in June 1983 when Under Secretary of State Lawrence Eagleburger touched on the theme of violence/peaceful change no less than twenty-five times.[9] The speech summarized key assumptions underlying U.S. advocacy of nonviolent tactics to South Africa's black majority: blacks cannot achieve their goals through violence; even if they could win, the struggle would cause unacceptable damage; and armed struggle is undesirable because it opens the door to Soviet influence.

°Anthony Lake, Carter's Director of Policy Planning at the State Department, had written his doctoral dissertation on U.S. policy toward South Africa (*Caution and Concern: The Making of American Policy Toward South Africa, 1946-1971*, Princeton University, 1974) and a book on U.S. policy toward Rhodesia (*The "Tar Baby" Option: American Policy Toward Southern Rhodesia*, New York: Columbia University Press, 1976).

The problem is not that these predictions are wrong. History will test their accuracy. The problem is drawing the wrong conclusion from these predictions. It is true that the white minority has a large repressive apparatus. It is true that civil war will take a terrible toll in lives and resources, and open avenues for Soviet assistance. It does not necessarily follow that the United States should therefore pursue a policy that repudiates blacks who resort to violence. This U.S. stance is rejected by the United Nations, the Organization of African Unity, the Frontline States, and all of the most successful nationalist movements in southern Africa.

Any government can issue moralistic policy statements advocating peaceful change, but if its policy *actions* do nothing to bring about the conditions for peace, then critics are justified in labeling that policy hypocritical. The intent of the following section is to 1) compare U.S. policy-as-preached with U.S. policy-as-practiced on the question of violence, and 2) examine the sources of violence in South Africa, and the decision of black South Africans, after decades of strict nonviolence, to engage in armed struggle.

Violence as a Tool of U.S. Policy

Many Africans are quick to point out that the United States gained its freedom from colonial oppression by military means. American revolutionary fighters often dressed in green and hid in the bushes while the red-coated British marched in the open, just as contemporary guerrillas utilize stealth and popular support to combat the might of conventional armies. The U.S. government erected monuments in front of the White House to honor Lafayette and other foreign 'meddlers' who assisted us in our war for liberation.

Eight years elapsed between the U.S. military victory over British colonial forces (1781) and the first elected president taking office (1789). Eighty years after the formation of the republic, Americans fought one of the bloodiest civil wars in history. Having coerced a working unity between North and South, the U.S. government oversaw the decimation and forced removal of Native Americans. With the completion of continental expansion, the United States violently seized territory in the Pacific, Caribbean, and Central America. The record of U.S. foreign policy reveals a willingness by Washington to use violence in various forms, including assassination plots against foreign leaders, sponsorship of coups d'état, and full-scale military interventions.

With regard to guerrilla insurgency, the United States has a mixed record. If the guerrillas are Afghan tribesmen battling the Soviets, or former Nicaraguan National Guardsmen harassing the Sandinista government, Washington supports the "freedom fighters." If the guerrillas are labeled Marxist and/or receive aid from socialist countries, Washington calls them terrorists. In other words, it is not a *principled* opposition to violence that guides U.S. policy, but a question of who is using that violence against whom.

This selective opposition to guerrilla war is explained in a declassified 1962 document of the National Security Council, approved by President Kennedy:

> The U.S. does not wish to assume a stance against revolution, *per se*, as an historical means of change. The right of peoples to change their governments, economic systems and social structures by revolution is recognized in international law. Moreover, the use of force to overthrow certain types of government is not always contrary to U.S. interests. A change brought about through force by non-communist elements may be preferable to prolonged deterioriation of governmental effectiveness or to a continuation of a situation where increasing discontent and repression interact, thus building toward a more dangerous climax. Each case of latent, incipient, or active non-communist insurgency must therefore be examined on its merits in the light of U.S. interests.[10]

In southern Africa, the U.S. government has provided support to insurgents fighting the MPLA regime in Angola.[11] This is in spite of the fact that most African states have denounced Washington's refusal to recognize the MPLA, and even businessmen such as David Rockefeller have urged the U.S. government to recognize the government in Angola.*[12] Secret State Department documents reveal that U.S. policymakers do not believe UNITA can win a military victory,[13] but by sabotaging economic targets and attacking villages, UNITA forces not only make it difficult for the MPLA government to set an example of socialist development, they also impede the operations of SWAPO guerrillas fighting in Namibia.

These factors have tarnished the credibility of Washington's advocacy of peaceful change in South Africa. The most damning fact, however, is that the United States and its NATO allies have provided the white minority regimes, including South Africa, with large amounts of sophisticated weaponry.[14] Despite over twenty years of

---

*The U.S. government is the only government in the world that does not recognize the MPLA.

a U.N. arms embargo against South Africa, the United States continues military cooperation with Pretoria. A congressional staff report on the arms embargo found that, "while there has been an official U.S. *policy* of embargoing arms to South Africa since 1963 ...the relevant U.S. Government agencies have thus far failed to adopt *procedures* to effectively implement the embargo."[15]

Although no U.S. president has fully enforced the arms embargo, the Reagan administration set new records for military collaboration with Pretoria. In its first three years, the Reagan administration authorized twenty-nine separate exports of Munitions List commodities to South Africa, worth more than $28.3 million. This was one and a half times greater than the total value of commercial military goods exported to South Africa during the preceding *thirty years*.[16]

Military hardware and training supplied by the NATO countries and Israel[17] have been used by Pretoria to commit recurring acts of violence against its own black population and eight other countries in the region.[18] The U.S. response to South African government aggression has been to deplore the violence or even to cast a U.N. vote criticizing Pretoria, but to oppose substantive measures aimed at punishing the apartheid regime.[19]

The "constructive engagement" policy devised by Assistant Secretary of State for Africa Chester Crocker was seen by Pretoria as a green light for aggression throughout southern Africa. During the Reagan years, the apartheid regime has mounted more numerous, more diverse, and more destructive acts of violence than ever before. The White House responded with silence, not even the customary perfunctory condemnation. When the issue was forced, as in the case of South Africa's summer 1981 invasion of Angola which prompted calls for retaliation in the United Nations, the Reagan administration vetoed efforts to punish Pretoria. Administration officials claimed neutrality and issued statements deploring violence on both sides.

The Reagan administration's rhetoric decrying an alleged "cycle of violence," and refusing to "take sides," implies a balance of coercive forces, when in fact the combined armed forces of all the neighboring states and guerrilla movements would not be a match for the destructive power of the apartheid regime.[20] The phrases of neutrality also imply equal legitimacy for both sides of the struggle, as if Pretoria had not initiated the violence against each of its neighbors and its own black population.

The African National Congress and the National Party

American advocacy of peaceful change seeks to delegitimize the organization most capable of posing a military challenge to apartheid—the African National Congress of South Africa (ANC). U.S. policy statements ignore the fact that the ANC took up arms reluctantly, after fifty years of strict nonviolence proved fruitless.

Formed in 1912 as the South African Native National Congress, the ANC was a predominantly middle-class organization made up of teachers, lawyers, tribal chiefs, journalists, and ministers. The group sought to overcome the ethnic and language differences among black South Africans in order to forge a working political unity. Their goals were non-revolutionary: they sought the *extension* of white political and property rights, not the overthrow of white power. Their tactics were impeccably nonviolent: they petitioned and pleaded but never resorted to force. Over the course of several decades, this quiet diplomacy met with repeated failure. The white government passed dozens of new restrictive laws, continued to expropriate African lands, and did not hesitate to use force in putting down opposition. Yet the ANC maintained its peaceful approach until after World War II.

In the post-war period, a new wave of nationalist aspiration spread through Africa and most of the Third World. The European colonial powers had made sweeping promises during the war in order to gain the active support of colonized peoples. These promises of greater freedom, coupled with the principles of self-determination embodied in the Atlantic Charter, led many black South Africans to believe that the time had come to push forward with their demands for sovereignty. In addition, the war-induced growth of the South African economy had brought a great influx of blacks into the urban areas and into more skilled lines of work, thus increasing the white economy's dependence on black labor.

Given these changes in the political-economic climate, it is not surprising that the ANC became more activist. Younger, more militant members of the ANC Youth League such as Oliver Tambo, Walter Sisulu, and Nelson Mandela argued that the ANC should replace its emphasis on petitioning a recalcitrant white government with a strategy of mass mobilization and active non-cooperation. While criticizing the mother organization for being too tame, the

Youth League still supported the policy of strict nonviolence in all mass actions.

The militant position of the young radicals was given a boost in 1948. In the parliamentary elections of that year, the United Party lost its majority of seats to the far-right National Party (NP). The NP was a tenuous grouping of regional Afrikaner parties united by a belief in the God-given nature of white supremacy over blacks. Opposed to humanist notions of the state as a device created by humans for their own use, Afrikaner Calvinism viewed the state's monopoly of force and authority over the individual as a divine gift. The emphasis was on discipline and obedience to this higher author-ity. The parallels to Nazism in Germany and fascism in Italy were direct and explicit.°

Militant supporters of Nazism later achieved prominence under National Party rule. Dr. H.F. Verwoerd, who as an editor during the war openly propagandized for the Nazi cause, later became Prime Minister and is considered the main architect of apartheid. Future presidents under NP rule such as Swart and Diederichs were Nazi supporters. B.J. Vorster, Prime Minister from 1966 to 1978, was a commandant in the Ossewabrandwag. In 1942 he declared: "we stand for Christian Nationalism, which is an ally of Nazism."[22]

Although its initial hold on state power was somewhat tenuous, the NP moved quickly to implement a wide range of measures aimed at breaking African resistance to the apartheid system of labor control. Africans were prohibited from leaving jobs without the permission of their white employers. Africans could not get employment or even move about without a "pass" (or "reference book") which contained vital information about them and was required to be shown to the police on demand. Going anywhere without one's pass or being in an area without proper authorization were, and still are, criminal offenses. The movement of Africans from rural to urban areas ("influx control") was tightened. A system of labor bureaus was established to ensure that labor needs of the white farms were met before releasing Africans to the city.

In its most far-reaching program, the NP began denationalizing the black population by transforming the rural areas reserved for

---

°During World War II, the extreme Afrikaner nationalists opposed South African entry on the side of the Allies. To block South African participation in the war against Nazism, the most militant Afrikaner groups (New Order and Ossewabrand-wag) carried out terrorist actions such as dynamiting railway lines, telegraph poles and theatres, and assaulting the police and military.[21]

Africans ("native reserves") into what are today known as bantustans or homelands. The strategy underlying the bantustan system was older than colonialism itself: divide and rule. Not only were Indians, Coloureds, and Africans segregated, but the Africans were divided into ten ethnic "nations," each with its own territory and administrative apparatus.

The harsh and intransigent rule of the National Party caused even the ANC's conservative members to accept militant action. The ANC's 1949 Programme of Action "transformed the A.N.C. from a cautious body into a dynamic mass movement. It urged noncollaboration and refusal to cooperate in oppressive measures. But non-collaboration was not thought of negatively, as mere withdrawal, it was a positive attitude involving coercion of the government."[23]

In 1949, as the new NP government was rapidly tightening its grip on South African society, the ANC organized a work stoppage and mass demonstrations for May Day. Although all the demonstrations were peaceful, the police broke them up with clubs and guns. Eighteen Africans were killed and more than thirty wounded. In 1952, the ANC again tried nonviolent mass resistance in the Defiance Campaign which brought out thousands of volunteers purposely to disobey many of the new apartheid laws. Much like the sit-down tactics used by the U.S. civil rights movement, the Defiance Campaign was based on a simple strategy: if enough people would openly disobey the racist laws, the government would not be able to enforce them, and the hated legislation would be dropped. Throughout the Defiance Campaign the ANC stressed the need for nonviolence. As thousands of blacks and their white sympathizers went to jail for minor crimes such as violating curfew and using public facilities reserved for another race group, the Defiance Campaign attracted publicity overseas, particularly in Britain and the United States.

The government moved quickly to stop the spread of the protest, using more police brutality against the demonstrators and passing new repressive legislation (the Criminal Law Amendment Act and the Public Safety Act) which imposed severe penalties for breaking any law as an act of political protest. For example, a black person sitting on a park bench reserved for whites would normally be fined a few dollars and given a few days in jail. Under the new laws, that person could be fined up to $1,000, imprisoned for up to ten years, lashed ten times with a whip, and have all his/her property confiscated. Although thousands of ANC followers were prepared to go to jail for weeks and even months, few were willing to risk ruining their lives. The protests died out.

The NP government steadily restricted the realm of legal protest. Laws such as the Suppression of Communism Act, which defined "communism" very broadly, were used to jail dissidents and break up acts of nonviolent protest.[24] Members of the ANC and other antiapartheid groups began to realize that protest actions made little sense if they only served as occasions for the regime to commit violence against the protestors. Despite decades of nonviolent tactics by blacks, the system was getting worse, not better.

The turning point came in 1960. In one of South Africa's most infamous massacres, police at Sharpeville and Langa fired on unarmed crowds of protestors, killing sixty-seven and wounding 186, many of them women and children and most shot in the back. This violence incited protests around the country. A massive crackdown followed. The ANC and other political groups were declared illegal, and thousands of activists were rounded up and jailed. The ANC was forced to go underground.

Only then, when other avenues of resistance had been closed, did the ANC decide to use force. And even then, it decided to target physical installations, e.g., electric power lines, not people. At the 1964 Rivonia trial where Nelson Mandela and seven other ANC leaders were sentenced to life imprisonment, Albert Luthuli, winner of a 1961 Nobel Peace Prize, gave the following defense of the prisoners.

> Over the long years these leaders advocated a policy of racial cooperation, of goodwill, and of peaceful struggle that made the South African liberation movement one of the most ethical and responsible of our time. In the face of the most bitter racial persecution, they resolutely set themselves against racialism; in the face of continued provocation, they consistently chose the path of reason. The African National Congress, with allied organisations representing all racial sections, sought every possible means of redress for intolerable conditions, and held consistently to a policy of using militant, non-violent means of struggle. Their common aim was to create a South Africa in which all South Africans would live and work together as fellow-citizens, enjoying equal rights without discrimination on grounds of race, colour or creed.
>
> To this end they used every accepted method: propaganda, public meetings and rallies, petitions, stay-at-home-strikes, appeals, boycotts. So carefully did they educate the people that in the four-year-long Treason Trial, one police witness after another voluntarily testified to this emphasis on non-violent methods of struggle in all aspects of their activities.

...However, in the face of the uncompromising white refusal to abandon a policy which denies the African and other oppressed South Africans their rightful heritage—freedom—no one can blame brave, just men for seeking justice by the use of violent methods; nor could they be blamed if they tried to create an organised force in order to ultimately establish peace and racial harmony.[25]

The ANC's guerrilla campaign remained relatively dormant until the mid-1970s. The downfall of Portuguese colonialism in Angola and Mozambique provided safe havens within striking distance of South Africa. The successes of neighboring blacks in overthrowing white rule inspired young black South Africans to launch the Soweto rebellion. The brutality of police repression during 1976-77 convinced many Africans of the need for armed struggle. Government violence also forced thousands of young blacks into exile, "and some three quarters of these joined the ranks of the ANC."[26]

These developments led to a marked increase in guerrilla activity. A leading academic expert reports that between 1976 and 1982 the ANC's military wing—Umkhonto we Sizwe (MK)—carried out 150 armed actions against police, military, and economic targets.[27] The ANC has focused on "hard targets" (physical symbols of white power) rather than "soft targets" (less secure sites where white civilians could easily be terrorized, e.g., shopping malls and theaters). A U.S. Central Intelligence Agency evaluation concluded that the ANC "could have inflicted a large number of white casualties if it had chosen to do so."[28]

A Johannesburg *Star* opinion poll (shown in Table 3.1) found the ANC to be the most popular opposition group among all categories of black South Africans. Recent reports by U.S. foreign policy experts testify to the ANC's growing popularity and a steady increase in the number of blacks who accept the necessity of armed opposition.[29] A 1981 Congressional study found that, "as a result of the slow pace of change, younger blacks in urban areas are adopting a much more radical and militant approach...they are increasingly of the persuasion that violence and massive strikes are the only way South African whites and government officials will undertake the changes which blacks seek."[30]

Following a 1982 trip to South Africa, former U.S. Secretary of Defense, Robert McNamara, corroborated this trend.

Already one sees signs of a growing, though reluctant, acceptance among both South African blacks and outside observers that fundamental changes will come only through revolutionary violence...

Table 3.1: African Party Preferences

"If you could vote for Parliament today, who would you vote for?"

	All	CITY			OCCUPATION			AGE			LANGUAGE		
		Jhb.	Dbn.	CT	Unskilled	Clerical skilled	Prof. self-empl.	16-25	26-39	40+	Zulu	Other Nguni	Sotho
ANC	40%	47%	37%	28%	29%	48%	59%	46%	40%	37%	39%	33%	56%
Inkatha*	21	29	31	5	28	16	8	14	17	31	31	13	8
AZAPO†	11	17	6	4	9	14	10	21	10	4	11	8	17
PAC‡	10	8	12	13	8	12	16	6	10	12	12	12	4

Source: *Africa News*, 2 November 1981, p. 5.

Inkatha is a largely Zulu organization, led by Chief Gatsha Buthelezi, and espousing less revolutionary positions than the other three groups (e.g., favoring more foreign investment, and cooperating with the government in various ways).

†AZAPO, the Azanian Peoples Organization, is a black consciousness group that is still active.

‡PAC, the Pan Africanist Congress, is a black nationalist faction that broke away from the ANC in the late 1950s, had a few years of successful organizing, was banned along with the ANC in the early 1960s, and has been racked by factionalism and leadership problems.

Because the South African Government continues to refuse to make any fundamental change in its racial policies, a violent explosion appears inevitable.[31]

In May 1983, ANC guerrillas detonated a car-bomb in front of Air Force headquarters in downtown Pretoria. Of the nineteen people killed and roughly two hundred wounded many were white armed forces personnel but some were black civilians. Some commentators hailed this as marking a new stage in the struggle, asserting that the ANC had broken with its tradition of avoiding civilian casualties.° The white press and government spokesmen laid great emphasis on the black casualties. Yet *New York Times* correspondent Joseph Lelyveld and others reported that even though passersby were injured, blacks supported the bombing of Air Force headquarters.

Those questioned all appeared to subscribe to the general view that whites have relied on violence to maintain their power and that blacks had no choice but to respond in kind.

. . . the immediate effect of the Pretoria bombing has apparently been to bolster support for the African National Congress, the sources all agreed.[32]

The Christian Science Monitor confirmed mass approval for the ANC's actions: "attacks by guerrilla insurgents are on the rise in South Africa. And while government security efforts are growing in step, the attacks are largely succeeding in earning publicity and a sense of legitimacy for the black nationalists responsible."[33]

In their growing acceptance of armed struggle as a political tactic, opponents of apartheid are reacting, not solely to the armed violence of the police and military, but also to the structural violence† of everyday life under apartheid. While there are no recorded cases

---

°The South African government later announced that the bomb had been defective and exploded prematurely. This raises the possibility that the ANC never intended for the bomb to explode during the afternoon rush hour, endangering passersby. See "S. Africa Identifies Bombers," *The Washington Post*, 3 August 1983.

†" 'Structural violence' is a term used in contemporary peace research and is to be distinguished from armed violence. While armed violence is violence exerted by persons against persons with the use of arms, structural violence is violence exerted by situations, institutions, social, political and economic structures. Thus, when a person dies because he/she has no access to food, the effect is violent as far as that person is concerned, yet there is no individual actor who could be identified as the source of this violence. It is the system of food production and distribution that is to blame. The violence is thus exerted by an anonymous 'structure'." Gernot Kohler, *Global Apartheid* (New York: Institute for World Order, 1978), p. 7.

of white children suffering from malnutrition, an average of ninety-six black children die every day from the effects of malnutrition.[34] Hundreds of thousands of African families are broken up by the migrant labor system.[35] In the course of forcibly removing 3.5 million Africans to their assigned bantustans, the government has bulldozed homes, demolished churches and schools, beaten and even killed individuals.[36] South Africa's mines, so important to the economy, lead the world with a record eight thousand miners killed in the past decade.[37] South Africa has the highest per capita prison population in the world, the highest rate of state executions (129 blacks in 1980), and prison conditions among the worst in the world.[38] The legal system, which intrudes into every corner of South African life, perpetuates a racially skewed sense of justice: two black reggae singers were sentenced to four years in jail for singing freedom songs, while a white man who killed a black man on a whim was sentenced to two years to be served on weekends; a black man was sentenced to eight years for having clothes in the colors of the ANC, while two leaders of a far-right paramilitary group convicted of possessing an arsenal of weapons were given suspended sentences; two black men were sentenced to a total of four years in prison for possessing a cassette tape of a pro-ANC song, while a member of the Air Force who kicked an innocent man to death was given a choice between six months in jail or a $500 fine.[39] After two watchdogs mauled an innocent black woman to death, the kennel holding the dogs was flooded with calls from security-minded whites wanting to purchase the animals.[40]

In a 1983 interview, Oliver Tambo, President of the ANC, summed up his organization's attitude toward this structural violence.

We are dying under the system. We are treated like foreigners in our own country. At best, we are sent to small little barren areas, and we die there. The system itself is an act of violence. . . .

And we say we can't allow this. We say: End that system. We will fight, and we will sacrifice to that end. We want to live in our country—we want to govern our country. It's true we have various racial groups and must govern together. We don't want anybody to leave—everybody's welcome here. But let's learn to regard ourselves as human beings. And until we have reached that position there will be no peace. There can be no peace.[41]

Conclusion

> ...when a long train of abuses and usurpations, pursuing invariably the same Object, evinces a design to reduce them under absolute Despotism, it is their right, it is their duty to throw off such Government...
>
> U.S. Declaration of Independence

Defenders of absolute nonviolence often point to the successes of Mohandes Gandhi and Martin Luther King, Jr. as notable exceptions to the historical rule that force is necessary to change the basic structures of society.

> It is no accident, however, that these two exceptions, the movements of Gandhi and Martin Luther King, took place within the political and moral boundaries of liberal democratic politics steeped in constitutional values, and thus susceptible to the constraint of law and the power of shame. Where law and shame are less easily mobilized, nonviolence has not fared well.[42]

In each of the white settler regimes of southern Africa, law and shame have not been easily mobilized, and the white minorities have blocked peaceful change toward a more just society. Black South Africans are aware of another historical fact: in each of the formerly white-ruled states, independence and majority rule required the development of military skills among blacks. Unless political avenues are opened, South African blacks will inevitably resort to force. Eventually, they will develop enough military power to threaten the regime, and whites will be forced to negotiate with black leaders. In the process, however, many lives will be lost on both sides, making the eventual accommodation more difficult.

If U.S. leaders sincerely desire to play a mediating role in reaching a political (not military) settlement in South Africa, they must have credibility with both sides in that conflict. Currently, Washington has some credibility with the white minority but very little with the main forces of change in the black community. This lack of leverage will not be improved by U.S. officials continuing to recite platitudes about peaceful change while refusing even to recognize the ANC, one of the two main protagonists in the conflict.

The only way to ensure peaceful change is through international pressure on Pretoria. Without it, whites will remain intransigent and a conflagration is inevitable. If the United States holds to its traditional course of advocating nonviolence to blacks while arming the white minority, the situation will continue to polarize, violence will escalate, and the U.S. government will once again find itself isolated, supporting an embattled right-wing minority regime.

Notes

1. See Carole A. Douglis and Stephen M. Davis, "Revolt on the Veldt," *Harper's*, December 1983; and Wilfred Burchett, *Southern Africa Stands Up* (New York: Urizen Books, 1978).
2. Mohamed A. El-Khawas and Barry Cohen, eds., *The Kissinger Study of Southern Africa* (Westport, CT: Lawrence Hill, 1976), p. 105.
3. Henry Kissinger, "An American Perspective," *Africa Report*, September/October 1976, p. 17.
4. Ibid.
5. John E. Rielly, "The American Mood: A Foreign Policy of Self-Interest," *Foreign Policy*, no. 34, Spring 1979; William J. Foltz, *Elite Opinion on United States Policy Toward Africa* (New York: Council on Foreign Relations, 1979); James E. Baker, J. Daniel O'Flaherty, and John de St. Jorre, *Public Opinion Poll on American Attitudes Toward South Africa* (Washington, DC: Carnegie Endowment, 1979).
6. John F. Kennedy quoted in Anthony Lake, "Africa in a Global Perspective," *Department of State Bulletin*, 12 December 1977, p. 843.
7. Andrew Young, "Developments Concerning Apartheid," *Department of State Bulletin*, 30 October 1977, p. 447.
8. U.S. Congress, Senate, Executive Report no. 97-8, *Nomination of Chester A. Crocker* (Washington, DC: GPO, 1981).
9. Under Secretary of State for Political Affairs, Lawrence S. Eagleburger, "Southern Africa: America's Responsibility for Peace and Change," an address before the National Conference of Editorial Writers, San Francisco, 23 June 1983.
10. National Security Action Memorandum no. 182, 24 August 1962, National Archives, Modern Military Section.
11. John Stockwell, *In Search of Enemies* (New York: W.W. Norton, 1978); Center for National Security Studies, "CIA's Secret War in Angola," *Intelligence Report*, vol. 1, no. 1 (1975); U.S. Congress, House, Subcommittee on Africa of the Committee on Foreign Affairs, *United States Policy Toward Angola—Update*, 96th Cong., 2nd sess. (Washington, DC: GPO, 1980); James Khatami, "U.S.–S. Africa objective: A partitioned Angola," *The Guardian* (NY), 16 February 1983.
12. Jay Ross, "David Rockefeller Cites 'Advantage' to U.S. of Normal Ties with Angola," *The Washington Post*, 3 March 1982.
13. The documents were published in *TransAfrica News Report* (special edition), August 1981.
14. Western Massachusetts Association of Concerned African Scholars, *U.S. Military Involvement in Southern Africa* (Boston: South End Press, 1978); Sean Gervasi, *The United States and the Arms Embargo*

Against South Africa: Evidence, Denial, and Refutation (Binghampton: State University of New York, 1978); Michael Klare, "South Africa's U.S. Weapons Connections," *The Nation*, 28 July-4 August 1979; U.S. Congress, House, Committee on Foreign Affairs, *Enforcement of the United States Arms Embargo Against South Africa*, 97th Cong., 2nd sess. (Washington, DC: GPO, 1982).

15. U.S. Congress, House, Committee on Foreign Affairs, *Enforcement of the United States Arms Embargo...*, p. 54.

16. Thomas Conrad, "Legal Arms for South Africa," *The Nation*, 21 January 1984, p. 42. Also see Richard Leonard, "A Review of Current U.S. Actions on Enforcement of the Arms Embargo Against South Africa," (New York: American Committee on Africa, 1983); and NARMIC/American Friends Service Committee, "Military Exports to South Africa: A Research Report on the Arms Embargo" (Philadelphia: AFSC, 1984).

17. See Israel Shahak, *Israel's Global Role: Weapons for Repression* (Belmont, MA: Association of Arab-American University Graduates, 1982); Esther Howard, "Israel: The Sorcerer's Apprentice," *MERIP Reports*, February 1983; Jack Anderson, "3 Nations to Begin Cruise Missile Project," *The Washington Post*, 8 December 1980, p. B15.

18. Each of the 8 countries in the region—Lesotho, Swaziland, Botswana, Namibia, Angola, Zimbabwe, Zambia, Mozambique—has been coerced in one way or another by Pretoria. See Chapter 1, note 77.

19. Kevin Danaher, "The Political Economy of U.S. Policy Toward South Africa," Dissertation, University of California/Santa Cruz, 1982.

20. International Defense and Aid Fund, *Apartheid: The Facts* (London: IDAF, 1983), p. 75.

21. Brian Bunting, *The Rise of the South African Reich* (Harmondsworth, England: Penguin, 1964).

22. Quoted in John C. Laurence, *Race Propaganda and South Africa* (London: Victor Gollancz Ltd., 1979), p. 141.

23. Ben Turok, "South Africa: The Violent Alternative," in Ralph Miliband and John Seville, eds., *The Socialist Register, 1972* (London: Merlin Press, 1972), p. 268.

24. The Suppression of Communism Act, later incorporated into the Internal Security Act (1976), not only outlawed Marxian socialism, Leninism and Trotskyism, it also made illegal any doctrine which "aims at bringing about any political, industrial, social or economic change within the Republic by the promotion of disturbance or disorder, by unlawful acts or omissions" or which "aims at the encouragement of feelings of hostility between European and non-European races of the Republic." See John Dugard, *Human Rights and the South African Legal Order* (Princeton: Princeton University Press, 1978), pp. 155-157.

25. Aquino de Braganca and Immanuel Wallerstein, eds., *The African Liberation Reader* (London: Zed Press, 1982), vol. 2, pp. 40-41.

26. Douglis and Davis, p. 34.

27. Tom Lodge, "The African National Congress in South Africa, 1976-1982: Guerrilla War and Armed Propaganda," paper presented at the Twenty-Fifth Annual Meeting of the African Studies Association, Washington, DC, 4-7 November 1982. Also see Thomas Karis, "Revolution in

the Making: Black Politics in South Africa," *Foreign Affairs*, Winter 1983/84; Mark Uhlig, "The Coming Struggle for Power," *The New York Review of Books*, 2 February 1984; Alfred Kagan, "The African National Congress of South Africa: A Bibliography" (New York: U.N. Centre Against Apartheid, 1982); Elaine A. Friedland, "The South African Freedom Movement: Factors Influencing Its Ideological Development, 1912-1980s," *Journal of Black Studies*, vol. 13, no. 3, March 1983.

28. Quoted in Glenn Frankel, "S. African Rebels Make Comeback," *The Washington Post*, 1 January 1984, p. A20.

29. See Karis, "Revolution in the Making..."; and Uhlig, "The Coming Struggle..." Polarization of political attitudes is reflected in the fact that, whereas more and more blacks accept the use of armed force, a 1982 survey of white opinion found that over 70 percent felt blacks had no legitimate reason to take up arms against the government. See Deon Geldenhuys, "What Do We Think?: A Survey of White Opinion on Foreign Policy Issues" (Braamfontein: South African Institute of International Affairs, 1982).

30. U.S. Congress, House, Committee on Foreign Affairs, *South Africa: Change and Confrontation* (Washington, DC: GPO, 1981), p. 16.

31. Robert S. McNamara, "South Africa: The Middle East of the 1990s?" *The New York Times*, 24 October 1982.

32. Joseph Lelyveld, "Blast in Pretoria: Blacks Appear to Applaud Act," *The New York Times*, 25 May 1983.

33. Paul van Slambrouck, "Guerrilla raids aim at gaining legitimacy," *The Christian Science Monitor*, 17 December 1981.

34. *The Sunday Times* (SA), 30 January 1983. A reputable British journal reported that "some 50,000 children die of hunger every year in South Africa." This averages over 136 malnutrition-related deaths per day. See *The Economist*, 2 June 1984, p. 73.

35. "On The Family," *Work In Progress*, no. 27, June 1983; and Colin Murray, *Families Divided: The Impact of Migrant Labour in Lesotho* (London: Cambridge University Press, 1981).

36. "Millions have been violently relocated in South Africa," *The Guardian* (UK), 10 June 1983.

37. "Black Unions Critical," *The Washington Post*, 17 September 1983, p. A14.

38. Frederick Johnstone, "State Terror in South Africa," *Telos*, no. 54, Winter 1982-83, p. 120; and "S. African Trial Gives Glimpse of Prison Conditions," *The Washington Post*, 28 September 1983. For background on state violence against political prisoners, see Amnesty International, *Detention Without Trial and Torture in South Africa* (Washington, DC: Amnesty International, 1982); Lawyers' Committee for Civil Rights Under Law, *Deaths in Detention and South Africa's Security Laws* (Washington, DC: Lawyers' Committee, 1983); *Torture in South Africa: Recent Documents* (London: Catholic Institute for International Relations, 1982); Gail Hovey, "Human Rights Violations in Apartheid South Africa" (New York: The Africa Fund, 1983); Paul van Slambrouck, "New light on S. African police interrogations," *The Christian Science Monitor*, 4 October 1982; Amnesty International,

Political Imprisonment in South Africa (New York: Amnesty International/USA, 1979).
39. *Sunday Express* (SA), 27 July 1983; and "Increase in Arrests Indicates New South African Security Tactic," *The Washington Post*, 11 December 1983, p. A35.
40. *The Guardian* (UK), 16 September 1983.
41. Quoted in Mark Uhlig, "The Coming Struggle...," p. 31.
42. Charles Krauthammer, "Pacifism's Invisible Current," *Time*, 30 May 1983, pp. 87-88.

4. The "Communist Threat"
East-West Politics and African Independence

The central element of U.S. foreign policy in the post-war period has been anticommunism. Until the 1960s, most African countries were controlled by European colonial powers. As Africans won political independence, the continent became an arena for Cold War competition. U.S. policymakers, in every administration during the past two decades, ignored the issues deemed important by Africans, and instead lectured African leaders on the communist threat.[1]

Until 1975, all countries in southern Africa remained under the control of pro-western regimes. But the overthrow of Portuguese colonialism by leftist forces in Angola and Mozambique made southern Africa a focus of U.S. anticommunism and precipitated a sharp increase in official U.S. statements opposing communism and "foreign intervention" in the region.

Henry Kissinger's fixation on competing with the Soviets led to one of Washington's worst policy debacles in Africa: the 1975-76 covert intervention in Angola's civil war.[2] With little personal knowledge of Africa, and against the recommendation of his own Africa experts, Kissinger authorized a CIA operation to cooperate with South Africa and Zaire in an attempt to prevent leftist forces from coming to power. John Stockwell, the CIA officer in charge of the Angola operation, reports that Kissinger's perspective was clouded by an obsession with Soviet competition.

> Uncomfortable with recent historic events, and frustrated by our humiliation in Vietnam, Kissinger was seeking opportunities to challenge the Soviets... Kissinger saw the Angolan conflict solely in terms of global politics and was determined the Soviets should not be permitted to make a move in any remote part of the world without being confronted militarily by the United States.[3]

Kissinger's policy failed. American complicity with South Africa's invasion of Angola damaged Washington's credibility in Africa; the war caused extensive human and material damage in a country already suffering from severe underdevelopment; and Angola ended up with an explicitly socialist regime supported by Cuban and Soviet military personnel whose presence was endorsed by the Organization of African Unity.

The Carter Administration

As more African nations gained independence, some U.S. policy makers—particularly Africa specialists in the State Department—recognized the political costs of sustaining white minority regimes. This "regionalist" or "Africanist" policy faction argued that any perceived U.S. friendliness toward the apartheid regime was a political windfall for the communist powers. Like the hardline "globalists," the regionalists gave high priority to checking communism, but sought to reconcile U.S. economic and military interests in the white minority regime with our international reputation on the race question. This straddle, however, became more difficult as black Africans and Afro-Americans gained greater political and economic power.

The regionalists gained ascendancy in the policy apparatus only once: during the first year of the Carter administration. Carter's advisors on Africa—Anthony Lake, Andrew Young, Donald McHenry, Goler Butcher, Ruth Schacter Morgenthau—had considerable experience with southern Africa and recognized that the roots of the conflict were more regional than global. The regionalists of the Carter administration favored "an Africa-centered policy, and not a corollary of the kind of anti-Soviet strategy that produced the Angola fiasco."[4]

The regionalists held sway for only a year, however, and a Cold War perspective returned to dominate U.S. policy toward southern Africa. The reasons for this shift are detailed elsewhere.[5] Briefly, developments in three arenas of conflict caused the policy to revert to the Cold War paradigm. First, within South Africa, Prime Minister Vorster took a hard line against Carter's antiapartheid rhetoric, cracked down on internal opposition in late 1977, and, running mainly on an anti-Washington plank, won the special parliamentary election of November 1977 with the National Party's biggest margin in history. Second, elsewhere on the African continent, the Soviets and Cubans mounted a massive intervention into Ethiopia in 1977-78, and Angolan-based rebels threatened Mobutu Sese Seko's pro-western regime in Zaire. These developments strengthened conservative elements in the third arena of conflict: Washington. By the beginning of Carter's second year in office, globalists in Congress and the executive branch stepped up their attacks on an Africa policy that downplayed East-West rivalry. By mid-1978, National Security Advisor Zbigniew Brzezinski and other globalists gained the intitiative on Africa, and the Administration's policy returned to the Cold War paradigm.[6]

The Reagan Administration

With the election of Ronald Reagan, the anticommunist content of U.S. policy reached its most extreme version yet. The Africa policy paper by Reagan's transition team at the State Department accused the Carter administration of suffering from a "severe case of regionalitis," i.e., being too closely attuned to African politics and not focusing sufficient attention on competition with the Soviets.[7] With little knowledge of African affairs,* Reagan made known his belief that "the African problem is a Russian weapon aimed at us."[8] As he told *The Wall Street Journal*, "the Soviet Union underlies all the unrest that is going on. If they weren't engaged in this game of dominos there wouldn't be any hotspots in the world."[9]

Anticommunism is a major theme in seminal policy documents of the Reagan administration that were leaked to the press in early 1981. One document reports on a meeting between Chester Crocker and top South African officials in which Crocker "stressed that top US priority is to stop Soviet encroachment in Africa."[10] Another confidential memo discusses the shared perception of South African leaders and the Reagan administration that "the chief threat to the realization...of stability and cooperation in the region...is the presence and influence in the region of the Soviet Union and its allies."[11] Indeed, Reagan's planners worry about Pretoria's regional aggression not because of the human suffering it causes, but because it may backfire and boost the communists: "we cannot afford to give them [the South African government] a blank check regionally

---

*In a 1980 off-the-record interview, one of Reagan's top Africa advisors told the author: "The problem with Reagan is that all he knows about southern Africa is he's on the side of the whites."

...SAG intransigence and violent adventures will expand Soviet opportunities and reduce Western leverage in Africa."[12]

The Reagan team has relied on the Soviet threat motif more than any administration in recent memory. Reagan spokesmen have shielded their southern Africa policy from domestic criticism by harping on anti-Soviet/anti-Cuban rationales to justify friendly relations with Pretoria. But this strategy has costs for U.S. foreign policy.

The National Party's View of the Communist Threat

A key problem with Washington's Cold War perspective on southern Africa is the way it reinforces the South African government's anticommunist views, and distances U.S. policy from African opinion. The ruling National Party has a much more extreme view of communism than even the most conservative policymakers in Washington. Yet the effect of U.S. anticommunist rhetoric has been to bolster the white minority regime's view that it alone stands as a bastion of western civilization against the onslaught of godless communism in Africa. This was evident in the way officials in Pretoria welcomed the advent of the Reagan administration.[13]

The South African government has a long history of justifying its policies with anticommunist rationales. Until recent years, they tended to lump the Soviet Union and the People's Republic of China together, even going so far as to argue that the Sino-Soviet split was a hoax and the two communist powers were secretly cooperating in an overall campaign of subversion.[14] Since the thaw in relations between Beijing and Washington, South African officials have focused most of their rhetorical attention on the Soviets.

South African spokesmen have been careful to link their survival with that of the entire "free world." During his fourteen years as Defense Minister, P.W. Botha stressed this connection. As Prime Minister he continues to use anticommunism to rationalize policies that have fueled conflict throughout the region. In a 1983 *New York Times* interview, Botha used the anticommunist theme to justify his government's support for insurgents in neighboring states: "if fellow Africans are threatened by the evils of Communism, we shall assist them when our assistance is requested."[15] There is mounting evidence, even from western diplomatic sources, that Pretoria is trying to destabilize neighboring regimes.[16] But the Prime Minister dismissed these charges, claiming they were "another stunt by Marxist forces, by Moscow and their satellites, to hide their efforts in the subcontinent because they want destabilization so as to enable themselves to get control of strategic points."[17] Botha used the same anticommunist motif to dismiss South Africa's main resistance movement, the African National Congress, as "a small clique of whites and blacks...controlled by the Communist Party with its headquarters in London and from there controlled by the Kremlin."[18]

A 1982 South African government report argued that in order to halt the "total onslaught" of communism and other "devilish ideologies" the already stringent security laws would need to be tightened.[19] Based on the assertion that organizations such as the ANC and the Pan Africanist Congress of Azania (PAC) are mere "proxy forces" for the Soviets,* the report reasoned that legal groups inside the country that promote aims similar to those of the outlawed groups are necessarily part of the total onslaught and therefore deserve similar kinds of government repression.

The South African legal code enshrines this guilt-by-coincidence style of reasoning as the law of the land. The Internal Security Act (1976), previously titled the Suppression of Communism Act, outlaws any doctrine that "aims at bringing about any political, industrial, social or economic change within the Republic by the promotion of disturbance or disorder, by unlawful acts or omissions" or which is deemed to incite "feelings of hostility between the European and non-European races of the Republic" aimed at effecting change through the promotion of disorder or unlawful acts.[20] In equally sweeping fashion, South African law deems a communist anyone judged to be advocating either the goals of communism or acts designed to bring about those goals.

So insistently have the ruling Afrikaners recited their communist threat theme that when the early Carter administration lobbied Pretoria for reforms, even solidly anticommunist U.S. officials became suspect. One conservative publication ventured: "to say that Professor Brzezinski is a Marxist is perhaps too drastic, but the degree of tolerance he displays towards Marxism is surprising for a man who should be strongly committed to the Western ideology."[21]

---

*A strange assertion given that PAC is staunchly anti-Soviet, a fact that even cursory examination of PAC literature would reveal.

The Cape Sea Route and Strategic Minerals

In the past decade, the communist threat theme has been brought to bear on the question of the strategic dependence of the United States on South Africa. With the 1973 oil embargo, the overthrow of Shah Reza Pahlavi in Iran, and a general buildup of Soviet and NATO naval forces in the Indian Ocean, U.S. planners have grown more attentive to the strategic assets of South Africa: its vast deposits of industrial minerals and its position astride the Cape sea route by which most of the petroleum from the Arab Gulf is shipped to the West. Conservative analysts make two basic arguments: the United States and its key allies are dependent on the Cape route and South Africa's strategic minerals, and this dependence necessitates a friendly policy toward the white minority regime.[22] The situation is usually portrayed in stark terms: "the Republic of South Africa is a potential bulwark standing in the way of ultimate Soviet hegemony over all of Southern Africa."[23]

The reasoning behind the Soviet-threat-to-the-sea-lanes argument assumes that Moscow intends to interdict the flow of oil to the West. Such an act would certainly disrupt the western economies, but with economic integration between East and West it would also have severe repercussions for Eastern Europe and the Soviet Union. The Soviets have shown an interest in competing with the West economically, but there is nothing to suggest the likelihood of such a major act of economic sabotage.

Even if the U.S.S.R. did plan to sever the West's oil lifeline, why would Soviet strategists choose to attack in such a distant region, when they could more efficiently bomb the oilfields or the Straits of Hormuz using planes based in the Soviet Union?

Any attempt by the Soviets to block the sea lanes would precipitate a major conflict with the West. This conflict would be fought primarily in Europe, with possible secondary theaters in the Mediterranean and along the Sino-Soviet border. There is no rationale, military or otherwise, for the Soviets to deploy off the coast of South Africa the submarines that would be required to stop shipments of western oil. In a major East–West conflict Warsaw Pact naval forces would be deployed in the North Atlantic, the North Sea, the Baltic, the Mediterranean, and the Sea of Japan, not off the coast of South Africa.

Moreover, the threat-to-the-sea-lanes theme assumes that a leftist regime in South Africa would cooperate with the Soviets in restricting western shipping around the Cape. Yet no empirical evidence supports this assumption. The leftist regimes in the region have sought to expand trade with the West, not restrict it. The leaders of Mozambique and Angola, like the ANC, are proud nationalists. Having suffered under white rule and foreign domination for centuries, they are not likely to turn their hard-won independence over to Moscow.[24] Neither Angola nor Mozambique has permitted Soviet naval bases on its shores. In sum, the possibility of an attack on the Cape route by the Soviets and/or leftist regimes in the region is extremely remote.

In contrast to the Cape route argument, the strategic minerals theme has a stronger factual base. American companies import substantial quantities of South African minerals. Four of these minerals are generally considered "essential to western industry and defense."[25] Table 4.1 lists the major uses of these minerals (chromium, manganese, platinum-group metals, and vanadium), the level of U.S. dependence on imports, and the major foreign sources of each mineral. It is clear from this data that the United States currently imports a significant portion of these minerals from South Africa. But examination of the world market and industrial applications of each mineral suggests that South Africa's exports are not essential.

Presently South Africa accounts for about one-third of world chrome ore production and roughly three-fourths of world reserves. But South Africa's deposits are predominantly low-grade; most of the world's high-grade ore is in Zimbabwe. Other producers— Turkey, Albania, the Philippines, New Caledonia, Madagascar, Yugoslavia, and Greece—have recently been expanding production and cutting into South Africa's traditional markets.[26] The dormant capacity in developed countries which could be revived for strategic and nationalist reasons, and the new capacity already available in developing countries, suggest that dependence on South Africa's chromium is not imperative.[27] In addition, U.S. consumption of chrome could be significantly curtailed without causing major disruptions. Some 40 percent of imported chromium is used in decorative stainless steel and could be replaced by other ferroalloys or aluminum.[28] A major use of chromium has been for decorative chrome in the auto industry where there is already a trend toward use of lighter weight substitutes such as plastic and aluminum. A 1976 study found that only 12 percent of imported chrome was used in strategically sensitive areas where there were no effective substitutes.[29] Also, the United States could lessen its dependence on South

Table 4.1: U.S. Import Dependence on Four Key Strategic Minerals

Mineral	Uses	U.S. Net Import Reliance[*] 1980	1981	1982	Import Sources (1978-81) (% of total U.S. imports)
chromium	Most important use is in manufacture of steel. Chromium alloys are used in the aerospace, defense, transportation, and power-generation industries.	91%	90%	88%	Chromite: South Africa (44%), U.S.S.R. (18), Philippines (17), other (21). Ferrochromium: South Africa (71), Yugoslavia (11), Zimbabwe (6), Brazil (3), other (9).
manganese	A desulfurizing and deoxidizing agent in steel production. Also used in manufacture of dry-cell batteries.	98	98	99	Ore: Gabon (32%), South Africa (24), Australia (18), Brazil (15), other (11). Ferromanganese: South Africa (42), France (25), other (33).
platinum group metals	Catalysts in petroleum refining, auto emission control systems, and production of nitrogenous fertilizers.	88	83	85	South Africa (56%), U.S.S.R. (16), Britain (11), other (17).
vanadium	Important alloy in iron/steel industry: jet engines, airframes, oil and gas pipelines.	35	34	14	South Africa (58%), Chile (10), Canada (8), other (24).

[*]Imports minus exports, plus adjustments for government and industry stock changes.

Sources: U.S. Department of the Interior, Bureau of Mines, *Mineral Commodity Summaries, 1983* (Washington, DC: Government Printing Office, 1983); U.S. Congress, Senate, *Imports of Minerals from South Africa by the United States and the OECD Countries* (Washington, DC: Government Printing Office, 1983).

African chrome through increased recycling of stainless steel scrap, which now supplies 15 to 20 percent of U.S. demand.[30]

Manganese, an essential ingredient in steel production, comprises only about 1 to 2 percent of steel production costs and therefore adequate supply, rather than price, is the key concern. In recent years, the world manganese market has been in surplus. In the event of a cutoff of South African manganese, nations such as Gabon, India, and Brazil would increase their exports. In the medium-term, Australia would be the country most likely to pick up slack in the market because its "mining operations and deposits are particularly suited to rapid expansion and large-scale production."[31] In the long-term, the world's seabeds, particularly the equatorial Pacific Ocean, hold a virtually endless supply of manganese in the form of rich metal-bearing nodules that also contain copper, cobalt, and nickel. Although it will take ten to fifteen years for this supply to be commercially viable, the United States and Japan are the countries which stand to benefit most from these resources.

South Africa has by far the largest known reserves of platinum group metals (PGM). But other countries such as Zimbabwe, with higher grade deposits than South Africa, and Canada possess deposits which have not yet been fully assessed. There is also the Stillwater Complex in Montana which "contains major resources of PGM" but has not yet produced significant amounts due to financial difficulties of its owner.[32] More importantly, the technology for recycling PGM from its catalytic uses shows great promise, and some 70 percent of U.S. PGM consumption is for catalytic purposes.[33] Currently about 10 percent of U.S. consumption comes from PGM recycled from catalysts and scrap metal but this percentage could be greatly expanded. A large proportion of world demand for platinum is for use in jewelry. In the event of an embargo this supply would be diverted into more essential uses. And, as the Bureau of Mines points out, there are substitute materials for many PGM functions.[34] These factors led a Rockefeller Foundation study of South Africa to conclude that with regard to platinum group metals, "the United States and the West could cope in the short and medium terms with a stoppage of South African exports."[35]

The United States has large deposits of vanadium and its import dependence is decreasing. American imports of vanadium in 1982 were only 29 percent of those in 1978.[36] A 1980 study reported "large reserves of vanadium in Canada and the United States as well as new methods of vanadium recovery from scrap metals will both serve to reduce the West's dependence on South African supplies."[37] In addition, vanadium can be replaced by other metals in nearly all of its alloying functions.[38]

The U.S. government has been increasing its stockpiles of strategic minerals in preparation for any emergency disruption of foreign supplies.[39] The building of stockpiles, in addition to the constant search for substitute materials, has resulted in a trend toward reduced industrial vulnerability to mineral supply interruptions.[40] Obviously, if antiapartheid constituencies in the West were mobilized to pressure their governments, this trend could be accelerated.

No matter how rapidly the industrial countries implement safeguards against mineral supply disruption, however, they will still remain dependent to some extent on South African minerals. It is important for policymakers to consider the political conditions that are most likely to interrupt South African mineral exports. The Rockefeller Foundation study found four possible scenarios for a disruption of these exports:

1. the United States, unilaterally or in concert with other nations, might voluntarily deny itself access to South Africa's mineral wealth by imposing economic sanctions, including a trade embargo, against South Africa;
2. the present South African government, in response to what it viewed as intolerable pressure from the United States and other nations, might retaliate by halting or reducing exports of some or all of its minerals;
3. internal upheaval in South Africa could hinder mining or transport operations, and for a time severely reduce or even halt entirely South Africa's mineral exports;
4. a new, unfriendly government in South Africa might manipulate, suspend, or discontinue the sale of some or all minerals to the United States and/or other Western countries.[41]

The U.S. government has been a staunch opponent of the first scenario—trade sanctions. A State Department official responsible for U.N. affairs told the author: "the only way the U.S. would agree to sanctions would be if South Africa invaded the United States." The antiapartheid movement may eventually mobilize enough pressure to force the government into an economic embargo, but for the near term, the first scenario is highly unlikely.

The second and fourth scenarios—a halt in mineral sales by a

South African government of either the Right or the Left—are highly unlikely due to the extreme dependence of the South African economy on its mineral exports. Some two-thirds of all South African export revenue is generated by sales of minerals and mineral products.[42] Most of these go to the West.

A majority government in South Africa, however radical, would be even less likely to cut mineral exports than would the current regime. A popular government would come to power with a mandate to raise the living standards of the masses. This could only be accomplished by increasing, not decreasing, mineral exports to the West.[43] In addition, the mineral export policies of other leftist regimes in the region cast doubt on the likelihood of the fourth scenario. Angola, Mozambique, and Zimbabwe have all sought increased trade with the United States, and leaders of the black liberation struggle in South Africa have indicated they would do the same.

Consequently, the third scenario—civil war—already in its early stages, seems the most likely scenario for altering U.S.–South Africa mineral relations. To play an effective role in preventing civil war, the United States will need credibility with the initiators of change in the black community, rather than one-sided alignment with defenders of the status quo. Traditional policy has failed to produce such balanced leverage.

In the conservative literature on U.S. mineral dependence, the authors focus on questions of physical supply. Nowhere in this literature is there a discussion of the central reason for U.S. mineral corporations operating in South Africa: high profits. Table 4.2 reveals that the rate of return on U.S. mining investments is much

Table 4.2: Rate of Return on Total Book Value, U.S. Firms' Direct Foreign Investment in Mining & Smelting

	Canada	Latin America & Caribbean	South Africa
1953-57	8.3%	10.4%	25.7%
1958-62	5.9	14.5	20.8
1963-67	9.9	19.9	43.3
1968-72	5.3	12.8	31.6

Source: Robert Pollin, "The Multinational Mineral Industry in Crisis," *Monthly Review*, April 1980, p. 28.

higher in South Africa than in other areas of the world. In South Africa, black miners work under conditions and pay scales that rank among the worst in the world. The coerced-labor conditions of apartheid help keep labor costs low and profits high.

It is damnably convenient for those profiting from the exploitation of South African workers to preach that communism is a greater danger than apartheid. This mainstay of the conservative position touches on the key flaw of the strategic literature defending normal relations with Pretoria. Nowhere does this literature acknowledge South Africa's most important commodity: black labor. The docks and repair facilities would never have been built, and no minerals would come out of the ground, were it not for black labor. It is the experienced, well-disciplined African workforce that undergirds the very existence of South Africa's strategic assets. Yet the strategic arguments ignore this central fact. The defenders of white minority rule literally dehumanize South Africa's importance to the United States.

The Pentagon and those corporations most dependent on military contracts form the political base for arguments emphasizing South Africa's strategic assets. Charged with global military responsibilities, the Pentagon plans the inclusion of South Africa on our side in a war against the Warsaw Pact. Corporations dependent on South African minerals are interested in "stability" and profits, not the human cost of that stability. Only when the costs of bolstering white minority rule become too high will military and corporate leaders end their support for the apartheid regime.

The Limits of Soviet Power

Another key component of the anticommunist theme deals with Soviet policy and influence in Africa. Stressing the hostile intentions of the Soviet Union's Africa policy, portrayed as part of a master plan for world domination, U.S. strategists allege that various African regimes and nationalist movements willingly or unwillingly play a supporting role in this global strategy.

Yet, even anticommunist scholars have noted that the U.S.S.R. does not appear to have a grand design or overall strategy for Africa.[44] Specialists in Soviet policy generally agree that the U.S.S.R. has four basic objectives in Africa: finding friendly port facilities for servicing Soviet commercial and naval vessels; expanding Soviet political and economic influence; denying influence to the United

States and its NATO allies; and denying influence to the Peoples Republic of China. Depending on the African country, these goals rank differently; there is "no evident hierarchy of priorities."[45] Often, objectives are in conflict with each other, inhibiting a coherent overall strategy.

Most experts have characterized Soviet policy in Africa as reactive and opportunistic, i.e., highly dependent on conditions in Africa. When conditions were favorable, as in the Angolan civil war, the Soviets made commitments. When conditions turned against them, however, the Soviets acquiesced to humiliating defeats. After giving Egypt more than half their military aid to Africa in the 1955-76 period, the Soviets were summarily thrown out. Several African states—the Congo, Guinea, Mali, Ghana, Sudan, Somalia—ejected the Soviets after receiving considerable amounts of aid. A 1980 study found that "no African government has been prevented from breaking its links with the Soviet bloc when it felt its interests required such action."[46]

Those who emphasize the communist threat point to two recent victories in Africa for the U.S.S.R. and its allies: Ethiopia and Angola. In the late 1970s, Soviet intervention in these countries reflected a new global assertiveness. Yet the conditions under which these interventions occurred suggest they were not a major departure from traditional Soviet policy.

A majority of African states, acting through the Organization of African Unity (OAU), approved the Soviet/Cuban interventions in Angola and Ethiopia. Somalia's irredentist aggression against Ethiopia, and the CIA/South African invasion of Angola made it politically feasible for the communist powers to intervene without much fear of African disapproval. Despite this ease of entry, it is questionable what the Soviets won in the long-term.

Although the U.S.S.R. has provided billions of dollars in military aid to Ethiopia, the regime of Mengistu Haile Mariam seems no closer to solidifying its rule now than it did when the Soviets first intervened in 1977-78. The ruling military junta—the Dergue—has not created a communist party, the country is wracked by economic difficulties, and the central government's army is fighting losing battles on numerous fronts against ethnic independence movements.[47] In addition, when the Soviets switched their allegiance from Somalia to Ethiopia they lost a major naval base at Berbera, Somalia. The multi-billion dollar complex built by the Soviets is now used by U.S. naval forces, hardly a victory for Soviet expansion.

In Angola, the MPLA regime is the closest ally of the U.S.S.R. in all of southern Africa. But despite massive Soviet aid, the MPLA leadership is divided on its policy toward the U.S.S.R. Luanda has not granted the Soviets military basing privileges. In only one area—fishing rights—have the Soviets gained materially from the Angolans. The more important areas of the Angolan economy, especially oil and diamonds, remain firmly linked to the western-dominated world market. The MPLA has assiduously courted western governments and corporations. Luanda instituted a very liberal investment code—easier on foreign profits than some capitalist governments in Africa—and they have been punctual in paying off their debts to western banks. David Rockefeller and other U.S. executives have testified to the flexible and pragmatic nature of the MPLA's economic and foreign policies.[48]

Indeed, Soviet involvement in Angola should have reverse implications for U.S. policy than are normally drawn by Pretoria's defenders. During the 1975-76 civil war, the single most decisive factor in turning international opinion, particularly African opinion, to the side of the MPLA was the invasion by several thousand South African troops. When Washington essentially aligned itself with Pretoria, it did as much to damage U.S. interests and secure a leftist victory as did the Cuban and Soviet military aid. The Cold War perspective is likely to produce similar results in South Africa.

Moscow's other ally in southern Africa, the FRELIMO regime in Mozambique, has been even more cautious than Angola in its foreign relations. As a guerrilla movement, FRELIMO was non-aligned. It had relations with China, the U.S.S.R. and many capitalist states. Once in power, FRELIMO moved carefully toward closer ties with the Soviets, but it has developed improved relations with most of the western powers as well. The bulk of Mozambique's military aid comes from the U.S.S.R. but the nature of this hardware is defensive—it does not pose a threat to South Africa. Like the MPLA, FRELIMO implemented a liberal investment code, sought to extend trade ties to the West, and denied military basing privileges to the Soviets. After some rough going during the early Reagan administration, U.S.-Mozambique relations began improving again in 1983.[49]

There is only one factor that could cause the MPLA and FRELIMO to increase their military dependence on the Soviet Union: aggression from Pretoria. In both countries, the original reason for inviting communist assistance, and the reason for its retention, has been Pretoria's policy of regional destabilization. The South African government has utilized a broad array of tactics: economic pressure, assassinations, sponsorship of anti-government forces such as UNITA and the Mozambique National Resistance (MNR), commando raids, air strikes, and full-scale invasions. As long as this aggression continues, the majority of African states will support outside military assistance to Mozambique and Angola, whatever the source of that aid.

The third leftist regime in the region, Robert Mugabe's ZANU government in Zimbabwe, has a cool relationship with Moscow. Zimbabwe's weapons, trade, investment, and aid come largely from the West. The Zimbabwean government's foreign policy of non-alignment enjoys broad popular support. It is difficult to imagine any possible developments that could cause Zimbabwe to become dependent on the Soviet Union.

The Soviet position in southern Africa is so weak that even the Reagan administration, albeit in secret, told a group of visiting South African generals that the communist threat in the region was overblown. *The Economist* gave the following synopsis of the American position:

> Russia had other fish to fry, the generals were told. In the words of Mr. Anatoly Gromyko, "in Africa, opportunities have changed." With its protege, Mr. Nkomo, toppled in Zimbabwe, and disenchanted with President Machel, Moscow was left with Angola, not a gratifying prospect even for the Kremlin. Eastern aid to the region was primarily military. Russia did not see why its valuable foreign exchange should end, like much economic aid to southern Africa, in a Johannesburg bank. Already saddled with Ethiopia, it could see no gain in further heavy involvement. The South Africans returned home rather deflated.[50]

Finally, there is the question of the relationship of the U.S.S.R. with the African National Congress of South Africa. The Cold War perspective stresses the military and diplomatic support Moscow gives to the ANC, and asserts that the ANC is dominated by the South African Communist Party (SACP).[51]

In reality, the ANC's roots in Christian pacifism are as strong as its roots in socialism.[52] This is one of the reasons for the ANC's cautious approach to the use of force. Although there is an official alliance between the ANC and the SACP, and some top leaders hold positions in both organizations, the SACP is not powerful enough to dominate the ANC. Ideologically, the ANC has stronger strains of African nationalism than Marxism. Like the other leftist movements in the region, the ANC is first and foremost a nationalist movement seeking independence and majority rule for its country. The ANC receives military assistance from socialist countries because the capitalist powers have refused to provide it. Africans reject the Cold War assertion that military aid from Moscow automatically brings with it political domination.[53] Indeed, developments in southern Africa since 1975 show "no evidence to support the premise that the liberation organizations are allied with the USSR against Western governments."[54]

The ANC did not import the socialist content of its program from Moscow or Havana. The organization's class analysis developed locally in response to the fact that apartheid and capitalism are two sides of the same coin.[55] To be committed to the eradication of apartheid requires a critical stance toward fundamental premises of the capitalist system. Black South Africans are well aware that local and foreign businessmen for centuries have been willing to make their fortunes from a system akin to slavery. This is why a large percentage of black South Africans are not afraid of socialism. The Johannesburg *Star* cited three surveys of black opinion to conclude that "the majority of urban blacks prefer to call themselves communists, marxists or socialists."[56]

In 1983, two new broad-based coalitions developed in opposition to the white government. The United Democratic Front, a pro-ANC formation, had by mid-1983 accumulated four hundred member organizations and over one million members.[57] The National Forum, a smaller group, is aligned with the ideology of the black consciousness movement. Both of these organizations, despite their differences, are opposed to capitalism. *The Christian Science Monitor* reported that, "one area of agreement [exists] between the two camps in black politics. That is a basic pro-socialist leaning and a view that oppression in South Africa is the product of a class struggle as well as one of racism."[58]

While Cold Warriors take for granted the incorporation of Africa into the western-dominated system of world trade and investment, many Africans, particularly those involved in the liberation movements of southern Africa, hold that it is precisely this tight integration into the capitalist world economy that has prevented balanced economic development and full political sovereignty. This is why the nationalist forces in southern Africa have refused to limit themselves to demands for formal political independence and have insisted on charting their own economic course as well.

Conclusion

The U.S. government has a long tradition of opposing independence movements that threaten the international status quo, even when the country in question has marginal economic or strategic assets, and even when the Soviets are in no way involved. Well before the Bolshevik revolution of 1917, Washington intervened against nationalist movements in Cuba, Puerto Rico, the Philippines, and even South Africa.[59] This tradition suggests that later U.S. interventions against the Russian, Chinese, and other socialist revolutions were not based solely on opposition to leftist doctrines.

The existence of a Bolshevik state since 1917, however, has provided a convenient rationale for U.S. leaders to oppose various independence movements around the world. When Calvin Coolidge sent the U.S. Marines back into Nicaragua in 1927, he claimed it was to save that country from "Bolshevism" allegedly seeping in from Mexico. In 1954, when Dwight D. Eisenhower authorized the overthrow of the democratically-elected Arbenz government in Guatemala, the action was justified on anticommunist grounds even though U.S. officials knew Arbenz was not a communist. The same anticommunist blinders caused U.S. leaders to intervenue against Patrice Lumumba's regime in the Congo. During America's long and costly invasion of Vietnam, policymakers justified their actions by claiming they were acting to contain communism.

With regard to Africa, U.S. policy in the post-war period has been dominated by a Cold War perspective that has led to numerous setbacks and embarrassments. The East–West paradigm systematically ignores African realities, creates the impression that only white nations deserve spheres of influence, and portrays Africans as nothing more than victims and dupes of outside forces. Helen Kitchen points out that, "the image of Africans as the passive victims of major foreign powers in the pattern of the nineteenth century is obsolete. It is the Africans themselves who are now responsible for the introduction of foreign powers...into African internal and regional conflicts."[60]

Moreover, this paradigm creates the illusion that competition between the United States and the Soviet Union is a zero-sum game, i.e., a loss by one side is automatically a gain for the other. The Third World regimes and nationalist movements are seen as so many pieces of political property that can be swapped back and forth between the major powers but can have no independent existence. Among the key transformations of the post-war period, however, has been the waning influence of both the Soviet Union and the United States in the Third World. Washington's political defeat in Iran is mirrored by Moscow's debacle in Egypt; Vietnam by Afghanistan. Both superpowers suffered the "loss" of China.

The non-aligned movement is a real and growing force in world politics, an expression of nationalism. The smaller nations have endured centuries of external domination and have little interest in choosing between one big power 'patron' or the other. They want the freedom to establish broad international relations, regardless of ideology. The East–West paradigm, forged in the bi-polar world of the 1950s, cannot accurately portray the multi-polar world of the 1980s.

The rhetoric of the communist threat theme does not accurately portray the reality in southern Africa. As in other cases of U.S. opposition to Third World nationalism, the explanation for this gap between rhetoric and reality must be found in the domestic political arena. If U.S. leaders were to tell the American people the truth— that most Third World revolutions are indigenous, popular movements spawned by poverty and repression—Americans would overwhelmingly reject a U.S. role in opposing these rebellions.

The anti-communist theme provides policymakers greater room for maneuver by quieting anti-interventionist voices in Congress and the general public.[61] The ultimate effect, however, has been a policy supporting anti-democratic regimes. These regimes protect American investments and cooperate with the Pentagon and CIA, but they also restrict their internal political processes and create conditions that breed revolution. Once a liberation struggle begins, international opinion often swings to the side of the popular rebellion, and the United States becomes isolated in its support for the regime. The preconditions of this process are well established in South Africa. The showdown may be many years off, but unless U.S. policy changes, Washington will be on the wrong side again.

Notes

1. Kevin Danaher, "The Political Economy of U.S. Policy Toward South Africa," Dissertation, University of California/Santa Cruz, 1982.
2. For background on the U.S. intervention in the Angolan civil war, see John Stockwell, *In Search of Enemies* (New York: W.W. Norton, 1978); Gerald Bender, "Kissinger in Angola: Anatomy of a Failure," in Rene Lemarchand, ed., *American Policy in Southern Africa* (Washington, DC: University Press of America, 1981); Ernest Harsch and Tony

Thomas, *Angola: The Hidden History of Washington's War* (New York: Pathfinder Press, 1976); Wilfred Burchett, *Southern Africa Stands Up* (New York: Urizen Books, 1978); Center for National Security Studies, *CIA's Secret War in Angola* (Washington, DC: CNSS, 1975); U.S. Congress, House, *United States-Angola Relations* (Washington, DC: GPO, 1978); and Mohamed A. El-Khawas, *Angola: The American-South African Connection* (Washington, DC: African Bibliographic Center, 1978).

3. Stockwell, *In Search...*, p. 43. Stockwell reports that CIA Director William Colby also saw the situation in Cold War terms.

4. Quoted from the 1976 Democratic Party platform plank on Africa, reprinted in Colin Legum, ed., *Africa Contemporary Record, 1976-77* (London: Rex Collings, 1977); p. C163.

5. For a detailed examination of this policy shift on South Africa, see Danaher, "The Political Economy...," pp. 331-349, 423-431.

6. For details on the struggle within the Carter administration over Africa policy, see David Ottaway, "Africa: U.S. Policy Eclipse," *Foreign Affairs* (special annual review: "America and the World—1979"); "U.S. Africa Policy: Hardening the Line," *International Bulletin*, 5 June 1978; "Cold War Cripples Africa Policy," *Washington Notes on Africa*, Summer 1978; Henry Jackson, "A Policy with No Plan," *Black Enterprise*, April 1979; Richard Deutsch, "Carter's Africa Policy Shift," *Africa Report*, May/June 1980; Bruce Oudes with Michael Clough, "The United States' Year in Africa: From Confidence to Caution," *Africa Contemporary Record* (New York and London: Africana Publishing Co., 1980). For background on the Carter administration's general shift to a more conservative foreign policy, see Bruce Cummings, "Chinatown: Foreign Poilcy and Elite Realignment," in Thomas Ferguson and Joel Rogers, eds., *The Hidden Election: Politics and Economics in the 1980 Presidential Campaign* (New York: Pantheon, 1981); Jerry W. Sanders, *Peddlers of Crisis: The Committee on the Present Danger and the Politics of Containment* (Boston: South End Press, 1983); Richard J. Barnet, *Real Security* (New York: Simon and Schuster, 1981); Alan Wolfe, *The Rise and Fall of the "Soviet Threat": Domestic Sources of the Cold War Consensus* (Washington, DC: Institute for Policy Studies, 1979).

7. "Reagan Aides Diagnose 'Regionalitis' in U.S. Africa Policy, *The New York Times*, 7 December 1980.

8. Quoted in "Reagan and Africa," *Africa*, no. 111, November 1980.

9. Quoted in Robert Lawrence, "Reagan's Africa Arsenal," *Southern Africa*, November/December 1980, p. 19.

10. *TransAfrica News Report* (special edition), August 1981, p. 3.

11. Ibid., p. 6.

12. Ibid.

13. "Botha Hails Reagan's TV Views on South Africa," *The New York Times*, 5 March 1981.

14. Hendrik J.A. Reitsma, "South Africa and the Red Dragon: A Study in Perception," *Africa Today*, vol. 23, no. 1, January/March 1976.

15. Joseph Lelyveld, "South Africa is Firm on Communism," *The New York Times*, 17 February 1983, p. A1.

16. See Chapter 1, note 77.

17. Lelyveld, "South Africa is Firm. . ."
18. Ibid.
19. "Afrikaners' Mood: Girding for the Soviet 'Onslaught'," *The New York Times*, 8 February 1982, p. A6.
20. John Dugard, *Human Rights and the South African Legal Order* (Princeton: Princeton University Press, 1978), p. 156.
21. *Current Affairs*, quoted in Heribert Adam and Hermann Giliomee, *Ethnic Power Mobilized: Can South Africa Change?* (New Haven and London: Yale University Press, 1979), p. 140.
22. See Robert J. Hanks, *The Cape Route: Imperiled Western Lifeline* (Cambridge, MA and Washington, DC: Institute for Foreign Policy Analysis, 1981); *Lifeline or Strategic Backwater: The Military Significance of the Cape Sea Route* (Sandton: Southern African Freedom Foundation, 1978); A.T. Culwick, "Southern Africa: A Strategic View," *Strategic Review*, vol. II, no. 3, Summer 1974; *South Africa: The Vital Link* (Washington, DC: Council on American Affairs, 1976); *The Resource War in 3-D: Dependency, Diplomacy, Defense* (Pittsburgh: World Affairs Council, 1980); Robert J. Hanks, "On Minerals, Metals, and U.S. Foreign Policy," *South Africa International*, vol. 11, no. 2, October 1980; "The Cape Route: Passageway to Survival," *Backgrounder* from the South African Embassy, Washington, DC, February 1980; "South Africa: Persian Gulf of Minerals," *Backgrounder* from the South African Embassy, Washington, DC, December 1980.
23. Robert J. Hanks, *Southern Africa and Western Security* (Cambridge, MA: Institute for Foreign Policy Analysis, 1983), p. v.
24. Robert M. Price, "U.S. Policy toward Southern Africa: Interests, Choices, and Constraints" in Gwendolen M. Carter and Patrick O'Meara, eds., *International Politics in Southern Africa* (Bloomington: Indiana University Press, 1982), pp. 56-57.
25. Foreign Policy Study Foundation, *South Africa: Time Running Out* (Berkeley: University of California Press, 1981), p. 310.
26. "South Africa: strategically downgraded," *Africa Confidential*, vol. 24, no. 10, 11 May 1983.
27. Ibid.
28. Barbara Rogers and Brian Bolton, *Sanctions Against South Africa: Exploding the Myths* (London: Manchester Free Press, 1981), p. 10.
29. Desaix Myers III, with Kenneth Propp, David Hauck, and David M. Liff, *U.S. Business in South Africa* (Bloomington and London: Indiana University Press, 1980), p. 238.
30. Foreign Policy Study Foundation, p. 314.
31. Ibid., p. 316.
32. Bureau of Mines, U.S. Department of the Interior, *Mineral Commodity Summaries, 1983* (Washington, DC: GPO, 1983), p. 117.
33. Foreign Policy Study Foundation, p. 317.
34. Bureau of Mines, p. 117.
35. Foreign Policy Study Foundation, p. 318.
36. Bureau of Mines, p. 168.
37. Desaix Myers III, et al., p. 240.
38. Rogers and Bolton, p. 10.
39. See *National Material and Mineral Program Plan and Report to Congress*, The White House, April 1982; and Bureau of Mines, U.S.

Department of the Interior, *Mineral Commodity Summaries* (individual years).

40. "South Africa: strategically downgraded."
41. Foreign Policy Study Foundation, p. 318.
42. Galen Spencer Hull, *Pawns on a Chessboard: The Resource War in Southern Africa* (Washington, DC: University Press of America, 1981), p. 194.
43. See Robert M. Price, "Can Africa Afford Not To Sell Minerals?" *The New York Times*, 18 August 1981. An extended presentation of the same argument is Price's essay in Carter and O'Meara, *International Politics in Southern Africa*.
44. See Chester Crocker's testimony to the Senate Subcommittee on Security and Terrorism, 22 March 1982; and David E. Albright, "Moscow's African Policy of the 1970s" in David E. Albright, ed., *Communism in Africa* (Bloomington and London: Indiana University Press, 1980).
45. Albright, p. 57.
46. Christopher Stevens, "The Soviet Role in Southern Africa" in John Seiler, ed., *Southern Africa Since the Portuguese Coup* (Boulder, CO: Westview Press, 1980), p. 54.
47. See Bereket Habte Selassie, *Conflict and Intervention in the Horn of Africa* (New York: Monthly Review Press, 1980); "The Horn: Sand against the wind?" *Africa Confidential*, vol. 23, no. 20, 6 October 1982; Alan Cowell, "For the New Ethiopia, Old Troubles Grind On," *The New York Times*, 26 June 1983, p. 12; Fred Halliday, *Soviet Policy in the Arc of Crisis* (Washington, DC: Institute for Policy Studies, 1981).
48. See "David Rockefeller Cites 'Advantage' To US of Normal Ties With Angola," *The Washington Post*, 3 March 1982; testimony of Melvin J. Hill, president of Gulf Oil Exploration and Production Co., in *United States Policy Toward Angola—Update*, Hearings Before the Subcommittee on Africa, House Committee on Foreign Affairs, 17 and 30 September 1980; Jay Ross, "Angola Interested in Better U.S. Ties," *The Washington Post*, 20 August 1981; and David J. Savastuk, "Angola: U.S. Business Involvement is Significant, Expanding," *Business America*, 9 August 1982.
49. "Mozambique: Diplomatic Turnaround," *The Nation*, 3-10 September 1983; "Long-Hostile Mozambique Now Supports U.S. Policy," *The Washington Post*, 5 February 1984, p. A1.
50. "Destabilizing Southern Africa," *The Economist*, 16 July 1983, p. 27.
51. See U.S. Congress, Senate, *Soviet, East German and Cuban Involvement in Fomenting Terrorism in Southern Africa*, Report of the Chairman of the Subcommittee on Security and Terrorism (Washington, DC: GPO, 1982).
52. See Mary Benson, *South Africa: Struggle for a Birthright* (New York: Minerva Press, 1969); Edward Roux, *Time Longer Than Rope: The Black Man's Struggle for Freedom in South Africa* (Madison: University of Wisconsin Press, 1964); Gail M. Gerhart, *Black Power in South Africa: The Evolution of an Ideology* (Berkeley: University of California Press, 1978); Peter Walshe, *The Rise of African Nationalism in South Africa: The African National Congress, 1912-1952* (Berkeley and Los Angeles: University of California Press, 1971).

53. As one ANC member put it: "The U.S. alliance with Russia in the Second World War didn't make it a colony of Moscow. Nor will some guns make us one." (Quoted in Carole A. Douglis and Stephen M. Davis, "Revolt on the Veldt," *Harper's*, December 1983, pp. 35-36.) Also see President Julius Nyerere, "Foreign Troops in Africa," *Africa Report*, July-August 1978. Prominent Afro-American groups such as TransAfrica and the Congressional Black Caucus have also criticized the notion that Soviet assistance to independence movements automatically translates into Soviet domination.

54. Ronald T. Libby, *Toward an Africanized U.S. Policy For Southern Africa: A Strategy for Increasing Political Leverage* (Berkeley: University of California Press, 1980), p. 80.

55. There is a large body of literature bearing out this point. See Chapter 1, note 3. Also see Marian Lacey, *Working for Boroko: The Origins of a Coercive Labour System in South Africa* (Johannesburg: Ravan, 1981); Shula Marks and Anthony Atmore, eds., *Economy and Society in Pre-Industrial South Africa* (London: Longman, 1980).

56. Cited in Ernest Harsch, "South Africa: Repression vs. mass radicalization," *Intercontinental Press*, 8 August 1983, p. 443.

57. *The Argus* (SA), 19 August 1983.

58. "South Africa's divided black activists work toward a clenched-fist unity," *The Christian Science Monitor*, 15 June 1983.

59. When the Afrikaner republics of the Transvaal and the Orange Free State fought a war of independence against Britain (the Boer War, 1899-1902), U.S. policymakers sided with the imperial power. Teddy Roosevelt commented on the propriety of great-power spheres of influence: "though I greatly admire the Boers, I feel it is in the interest of civilization that the English-speaking race should be dominant in South Africa, exactly as it is for the interests of civilization that the United States...should be dominant in the Western Hemisphere," quoted in Noer, *Briton, Boer, and Yankee*, p. 55.

    The Boers' lack of industrial experience and their use of protectionist policies convinced British and American leaders that Afrikaner independence would inhibit access to the mineral-rich interior. The laissez-faire 'freedom' of capital to penetrate any area of the globe required the denial of colonial peoples' freedom to construct full sovereignty. The United States joined Britain in establishing a foreign policy generally opposed to republicanism: an imperialist policy resisting efforts by smaller states to withdraw from the "free-trade" network dominated by Britain and the United States.

60. Helen Kitchen, "Eighteen African Guideposts," *Foreign Policy*, no. 37, Winter 1979-80, p. 73.

61. Barron and Immerwahr cite survey data showing that two-thirds of Americans polled disapprove of arms sales to South Africa, but when reference to a communist threat was added to the question, "opinion was evenly divided: 33 percent in favor, 32 percent opposed." Deborah Durfee Barron and John Immerwahr, "The Public Views South Africa: Pathways Through a Gathering Storm," *Public Opinion*, January/February 1979, p. 57.

Conclusion

> But the tragedy of South Africa is not simply in its own policy; it is the fact that the racist government of South Africa is virtually made possible by the economic policies of the United States and Great Britain, two countries which profess to be the moral bastions of our Western world.
>
> Rev. Martin Luther King, Jr.[1]

Reform is underway in South Africa, but it is designed to entrench minority rule. American investment is a major force, but it does more to bolster apartheid than undermine it. U.S. officials call for peaceful change, but they arm the perpetrators of violence. They claim that communism threatens South Africa, but the threat to the majority of Africans is apartheid.

As polarization and conflict in South Africa intensify, U.S. policy-makers cling to their dual goal of retaining South Africa as an economic partner and strategic ally while maintaining credibility on the question of apartheid. The duality in U.S. policy toward South Africa—verbally denouncing apartheid while materially sustaining it—began in the late 1950s. Prior to the political independence of black Africa and the enfranchisement of black America, occurring roughly at the same time, the main constituencies for U.S. policy toward South Africa were certain corporations and sections of some government agencies (e.g., the Pentagon, CIA, Commerce Department). As long as there were no antiapartheid constituencies with leverage on the government, politicians could safely ignore the issue of oppression in southern Africa. As Africans and Afro-Americans assumed greater roles in the world's political and economic institutions, however, U.S. leaders developed a policy "straddle" aimed at pleasing both the antiapartheid constituency, and those in the government and the corporate world who benefit from white minority rule.

The attempt by U.S. officials to reconcile economic/strategic interests with humanitarian concerns has grown more difficult because both sides gained strength and diverged over the years. While U.S. trade and investment in South Africa have steadily expanded, the international community has increased its pressure on Pretoria, and activists in America have grown more effective in agitating against white minority rule. This divergence is reflected in opinion poll data showing a wide gap between elite and working class attitudes on what to do about apartheid. A 1979 comparison of elite and mass opinion by the Council on Foreign Relations found:

> The greatest divergence between our elite respondents and the American people as a whole comes in the question of how best to deal with South Africa, where the elites appear less willing to adopt stern measures.
>
> If an American administration were to decide to adopt a policy of forceful pressures against South Africa, it seemingly would have to find its major public support among groups not represented, or poorly represented, in the elite population surveyed here, particularly blue-collar workers, unionists, and blacks.[2]

A study by the Carnegie Endowment for International Peace found that in response to a brief description of the South African system, 86 percent of Americans polled said it was "wrong" and only 2 percent said it was "right."[3] Another analysis of public opinion:

> ...found that by almost a two-to-one margin (46–26 percent), Americans favor the United States and other nations putting pressure on the South African government to give blacks more freedom and participation in government. Specifically, large segments of the public support cutting off arms sales to South Africa (favored 51–24 percent), getting U.S. companies in South Africa to put pressure on the South African government (46–28 percent), and preventing new U.S. business investments in South Africa (42–33 percent).[4]

Although there is considerable public support for tougher measures against apartheid, the U.S. government has consistently refused to go much beyond rhetorical condemnation. Of the three general policy options—friendly relations, symbolic pressure, material pressure—only the latter has never been tried.[5] The Nixon and Reagan administrations implemented friendly relations with the apartheid regime and conditions grew worse for the black majority. The Carter administration tried verbal and symbolic pressure but Pretoria shrugged off the criticism and cracked down even harder on its black opposition. No U.S. administration has ever tried a policy of real material pressure on the white minority. This is not due to a lack of leverage.

There are dozens of ways the United States could bring economic, political, and cultural pressure to bear on the apartheid regime.* As South Africa's top trading partner, and a leading member of numerous international organizations, the United States has more potential leverage on South Africa than does any other nation. What is lacking is the political will on the part of U.S. leaders.

The key factor inhibiting a tougher U.S. policy toward South Africa is that the same U.S. corporations that are deeply involved in the apartheid economy also wield extraordinary influence in Washington. The many authors who have documented the history of U.S. policy in southern Africa generally agree that "one policy area never became a matter of conflict for policy-makers, despite sporadic rhetorical gestures: overall economic policy toward the region."[6]

South Africa's leaders are fully aware of the political clout wielded by the large corporations. A secret South African study of the potential impact of economic sanctions argued that Pretoria's "stake in the multinationals is very large, not only for obvious economic reasons but because they exercise a restraining effect on policymakers abroad."[7]

The narrow domestic base of U.S. policy toward South Africa— only a few hundred corporations have direct investments there, and

---

*After eliminating "highly controversial" steps such as a total cutoff of trade and investment, or military aid to the liberation movements, Ferguson and Cotter list forty-one measures the United States could implement to pressure Pretoria for change. These include increasing official contacts with the liberation movements, encouraging American athletes and artists to observe the U.N. boycott, joining the U.N. Council on Namibia and the Committee Against Apartheid, tightening U.S. visa policy toward South African officials, offering asylum to refugees and military deserters, reducing nuclear cooperation, encouraging our NATO allies and Israel to reduce their collaboration, and erecting barriers to U.S. business ties. The full list is contained in Clyde Ferguson and William R. Cotter, "South Africa: What Is To Be Done?" *Foreign Affairs*, January 1978. The Rockefeller Foundation study of South Africa includes forty-five pages of detailed suggestions on how the United States could influence South Africa. See Foreign Policy Study Foundation, *South Africa: Time Running Out* (Berkeley and Los Angeles: University of California Press, 1981), pp. 410–454.

nine banks account for 65 percent of U.S. loans to South Africa[8]—has saddled us with a policy that is undemocratic at home as well as abroad. To reinforce white minority rule in South Africa, U.S. policy has required deception of the American people. If democracy must be based on an informed electorate, then the distortions used to justify U.S. inaction against apartheid can only be considered anti-democratic.

A more democratic policy requires a broader definition of U.S. interests in South Africa. Historically, the interests protected by U.S. policy have been private (class) interests, not the public (national) interest. Defining the "national" interest mainly in terms of protecting trade and investment severely limits U.S. policy alternatives and places us on the side of a repressive minority. The class-based definition of U.S. interests also limits policy to a short time horizon. Dominated by the logic of the profit motive, the official U.S. viewpoint emphasizes current and short-term stability of the regime. Instead, we should be preparing for the certain future of a majority-ruled South Africa.

Only an informed citizenry can counteract the political influence of big money. The problem confronting antiapartheid forces is that Americans, like others, are politically motivated by issues they sense affect them directly.[9] The antiapartheid movement must therefore educate Americans about the connections between white supremacy in South Africa and bread-and-butter issues here at home.

- Many of the corporations that are closing plants and laying off workers in the United States are making big profits and expanding their operations in South Africa.
- Banks that are 'redlining' poor neighborhoods in our cities, denying loans to low-income residents, are extending billions of dollars in loans to white minority interests in South Africa.
- The oil monopolies that are making record profits over-charging Americans for auto fuel and heating oil are violating international law and world opinion to provide the white minority regime with fuel and lubricants.
- Many U.S. corporations that invest in South Africa violate Equal Employment Opportunity guidelines in their American operations.[10]
- While tens of thousands of U.S. miners and steelworkers are unemployed, American companies are importing millions of

tons of government-subsidized South African coal and steel
every year.

   Making connections between apartheid and other political issues
is not just an intellectual exercise: it requires establishing organizational links with groups that do not focus on white supremacy. For
example, the antinuclear movement, with its broad support throughout the United States, could lend considerable strength to the antiapartheid movement. The very energy companies and national
security officials who locked our country into an over-dependence
on nuclear power and weapons also developed South Africa's
nuclear potential—despite Pretoria's refusal to sign the Non-Proliferation Treaty. Considerable evidence points to South Africa's possession of nuclear weapons. Pretoria's history of aggression against its
neighbors and its own black population makes it a high risk for
using a nuclear device in combat. These connections between the
problems confronting the antinuclear and antiapartheid movements
should lead to organizational ties between the two movements.
   The basic lesson of all political struggle is—unite friends, divide
enemies. Historically, U.S. elites have maintained a *de facto* alliance
with South African elites, to the detriment of the South African and
American people. They have been relatively successful in fighting
off attempts to break their cross-national class solidarity. The
general goal of the antiapartheid movement should be to build
solidarity between progressive forces in South Africa and those
outside, while interrupting cross-national elite collaboration.
   The core problem is much greater than official U.S. inaction
against apartheid. South Africa is only one of many anti-democratic
regimes whose principal capital, technology, and diplomatic support come from the United States. The Third World is rife with
right-wing dictatorships which, through their anticommunism and
support for private investment, gain the approval of Washington
and the tax dollars of American citizens. While this serves big
corporations and the national security state, it is producing a steady
deterioration in U.S. influence abroad, and requires ever greater
levels of disinformation at home. American policies that inhibit
democracy in countries such as South Africa require policy rationales that inhibit democracy in the United States.
   Transforming U.S. policy toward South Africa is only a partial
solution. What is needed is the democratization of decision making.
As long as our national interest is defined by, and in the interest of, a

wealthy minority, U.S. foreign policy will continue its undemocratic course at home and abroad.

Notes

1. Martin Luther King, Jr., *Where Do We Go From Here: Chaos or Community?* (New York: Harper and Row, 1967), p. 202.
2. William J. Foltz, *Elite Opinion on United States Policy Toward Africa* (New York: Council on Foreign Relations, 1979), p. 24.
3. *Africa News*, 25 May 1979, p. 10.
4. Deborah Durfee Barron and John Immerwahr, "The Public Views South Africa: Pathways Through a Gathering Storm," *Public Opinion*, January/February 1979, p. 54.
5. For a more detailed discussion of these three policy options see Kevin Danaher, "U.S. Policy Options Toward South Africa: A Bibliographic Essay," *A Current Bibliography on African Affairs*, vol. 13, no. 1, 1980-81.
6. John Joseph Seiler, "The Formulation of U.S. Policy Toward Southern Africa, 1957-1976: The Failure of Good Intentions," Dissertation, University of Connecticut, 1976, p. 393. Also see Thomas Karis, "United States Policy Toward South Africa," in Gwendolen M. Carter and Patrick O'Meara, eds., *Southern Africa: The Continuing Crisis* (Bloomington: Indiana University Press, 1979); Anthony Lake, "Caution and Concern: The Making of American Policy Toward South Africa, 1946-1971," Dissertation, Princeton University, 1974; René Lemarchand, ed., *American Policy in Southern Africa* (Washington, DC: University Press of America, 1981); Henry F. Jackson, *From the Congo to Soweto: U.S. Foreign Policy Toward Africa Since 1960* (New York: William Morrow and Company Inc., 1982). A former White House aide under Nixon summed it up this way: "Nor is there a wider readiness in the administration to confront the vast American corporate interests or the cozy CIA liaison with South Africa that have always quietly mocked the official public disapproval of the racist regimes." Roger Morris, *Uncertain Greatness: Henry Kissinger and American Foreign Policy* (New York: Harper and Row, 1977), p. 296.
7. Martin Bailey writing in *The New Statesman*, 8 July 1983, reprinted in *Facts and Reports*, vol. 13, no. P, 5 August 1983, p. 4.
8. See James Cason and Michael Fleshman, "Dollars for Apartheid," *Multinational Monitor*, November 1983, p. 19.
9. John E. Rielly, "The American Mood: A Foreign Policy of Self-Interest," *Foreign Policy*, no. 34, Spring 1979; and Robert W. Oldendick and Barbara A. Bardes, "A Cross-Time Comparison of Mass and Elite Foreign Policy Attitudes," paper presented at 1980 Annual Meeting of American Political Science Association, Table 5.
10. Corporate Data Exchange, *Pension Investments: A Social Audit* (New York: CDE, 1979).

Abbreviations/Glossary

Africans: With regard to SA, refers to indigenous people (Zulu, Xhosa, Tswana, Swazi, Ndebele, Sotho, Venda, Shangaan/Tsonga).

Afrikaners: Whites of Dutch/Huguenot descent who first arrived in SA in mid-17th century and whose language is Afrikaans.

AID: Agency for International Development, US Department of State.

ANC: African National Congress of South Africa. Oldest liberation movement in Africa, formed in 1912. Outlawed 8 April 1960 by Unlawful Organizations Act.

Apartheid: South Africa's system of white minority rule. Originated as system of labor control. Includes disfranchisement of all non-whites, and denationalization, bantustanization of Africans.

ARMSCOR: Armaments Development and Production Corporation. South African government-owned company producing and exporting weapons.

Azania: Name for South Africa used by PAC and Black Consciousness organizations. Not used by ANC.

AZAPO: Azanian People's Organization. Black Consciousness group still operating legally.

Bantu: Derogatory term used by some white South Africans to refer to Africans. Used correctly, refers to large linguistic group of Sub-Saharan Africa.

Bantustan: Barren, rural areas where Africans are forcibly resettled. Also called "homelands" or rural reserves.

BCM: Black Consciousness Movement. Broadly refers to organizations, most originating in the 1970s, espousing need for black pride and autonomy.

Blacks: Sometimes synonymous with Africans, but often refers to all non-whites (Coloureds, Indians, Africans).

Boers: Synonym for Afrikaners. In Afrikaans, "farmers."

BOSS: Bureau of State Security. Previous name of South Africa's civilian intelligence, currently National Intelligence Service.

CIA: Central Intelligence Agency

Coloureds: Persons of mixed white/black ancestry, assigned a social status between whites and Africans.

Contact Group: The five western nations (US, Britain, France, West Germany, Canada) negotiating with South Africa since 1977 for the independence of Namibia.

FLS: Front-Line States. Black-ruled states supporting liberation movements in the region: Angola, Botswana, Lesotho, Mozambique, Tanzania, Zambia, Zimbabwe.

Freedom Charter: Key document of the liberation struggle in SA. Adopted in 1955 by a broadly representative Congress of the People, a coalition of ANC and allied groups. Calls for egalitarian economy and non-racial political system.

FRELIMO: Front for the Liberation of Mozambique. Led the armed struggle against Portuguese colonialism, and has ruled since independence in 1975.

IMF: International Monetary Fund

ISCOR: Iron and Steel Corporation. Government-owned corporation producing most of SA's steel.

MNR: Mozambique National Resistance. South African-backed guerrilla movement opposed to FRELIMO.

MPLA: Popular Movement for the Liberation of Angola. Oldest of the country's nationalist movements. Ruling since independence in 1975.

NP: National Party. Largely Afrikaner party ruling South Africa since 1948.

OAU: Organization of African Unity. Since formation in 1963, the main continental association of independent African states.

PAC: Pan Africanist Congress of Azania. South African liberation movement formed in 1959 as a breakaway from ANC. Outlawed in 1960.

PFP: Progressive Federal Party. Liberal white opposition in South African parliament.

PLAN: People's Liberation Army of Namibia. Armed wing of SWAPO.

Rand: Main unit of South African currency. In recent years has fluctuated in rough equivalence to US dollar. Equal to $0.86 as of May 1984.

Robben Island: Maximum security prison holding many political prisoners off SA coast near Cape Town.

SA: South Africa

SADCC: Southern African Development Coordination Conference. Founded in 1979 to foster regional development and economic independence from SA. Includes Angola, Botswana, Lesotho, Malawi, Mozambique, Swaziland, Tanzania, Zambia, Zimbabwe.

SADF: South African Defence Force

SAG: South African government

SASOL: South African Coal, Oil and Gas Corporation. Government-owned company pioneering coal-to-oil conversion technology.

Soweto: South West Townships. On outskirts of Johannesburg, largest African 'city' with over one million residents.

SWAPO: South West African People's Organization. Founded in 1960 and recognized by UN as sole, legitimate representative of the Namibian people.

UN: United Nations

UNITA: National Union for the Total Independence of Angola. South African-backed rebels opposed to MPLA.

USG: United States government.

ZANU-PF: Zimbabwe African National Union (Patriotic Front). Ruling party in Zimbabwe since independence in 1980.

Country Profile

Geography

Area: 1,221,356 square kilometers.
471,566 square miles (not including Walvis Bay)
Roughly three times the size of California.

Land Use: 12% cultivable, 2% forested, 86% desert, waste, or urban.

People

Population: 30,938,000 (July 1983). African 72%, White 16%, Coloured 9%, Asian 3%.

Growth Rate: Africans 2.7%, Whites 1.7%, Coloureds 2.2%, Asians 2.4%.

Languages: English and Afrikaans (official), Zulu, Xhosa, Tswana, North and South Sotho, other.

Religions: Predominantly Christian; also traditional African, Hindu, Muslim, and Jewish.

Workforce: 12 million (approx.). Agriculture 30%, Industry and Commerce 29%, Services 34%, Mining 7%. By ethnicity: African 70%, White 18%, Coloured 10%, Asian 2%.

Literacy: Most Whites are literate; South African government estimates that roughly half of all Africans are literate.

Education: Primary and secondary school are free and compulsory for Whites but, until recently, have been neither free nor compulsory for Africans. In 1981 the government introduced compulsory education for 45,000 Africans, roughly 1.5% of African students. All education remains racially segregated.

Health: Infant mortality per 1,000: Whites—12, urban Africans—69, rural Africans—282. Malnutrition: while there are no recorded

cases of malnutrition among Whites, Professor Allie Moosa, head
of the Department of Pediatrics at University of Natal, estimates
that 96 Black children die of malnutrition every day. Doctors
available: Whites (nationwide)—1:400; rural Africans—1:40,000.
Doctors graduating from medical schools, 1968-77: White—97%,
Black—3%.

Economy

Currency: 1 Rand(R) = $0.86 (May 1984)

Gross National Product (GNP): R84.121 billion (1983)

Annual Growth Rate: -0.9% (1982), -1.0% (1983)

US Exports to SA: $2.13b (1983)

US Imports from SA: $2.03b (1983)

Major Trading Partners: United States, Great Britain, West Germany,
Japan, Switzerland, France, Italy, Israel.

Principal Exports: gold, diamonds, mineral products, iron and steel,
coal, fruits and vegetables.

Principal Imports: machinery, vehicles and transportation equipment,
chemical products, base metals, textiles, and plastics. (Official
statistics do not reveal imports of weapons and oil.)

Major Industries: mining, automobile industry, metal-working, machinery, textiles, iron and steel, chemicals, fertilizer, fishing.

Main Agricultural Crops: corn, wool, wheat, sugarcane, tobacco,
citrus fruits, dairy products.

Sources: Central Intelligence Agency, *The World Factbook—1982*
US Department of State, *Background Notes: South Africa*
Nedbank Group, *South Africa: An Appraisal*
Africa Fund, *South Africa Fact Sheet*
South African Embassy, Washington, DC

Chronology

1974

January

- Despite objections by his own Africa Bureau, Secretary of State Henry Kissinger permits US visit by SA Minister of Information, Cornelius Mulder. Meetings with VP Gerald Ford and senior Pentagon officials, including Vice Admiral Ray Peet, in charge of international security affairs and the Indian Ocean.

22 USG issues license for U.S. Nuclear Corp. of Oak Ridge, TN, to export 12.5 kilograms of highly enriched uranium to SA. Amended on 2 October 1974 to allow an additional 12.5 kilos.

April

6 Assistant Secretary of State for Africa, David Newsom, cites "problems in our aerospace industry" as a main reason for Nixon's relaxation of restrictions on aircraft exports to Portugal and SA.

25 Right-wing Caetano dictatorship in Portugal is overthrown by young, leftist military officers—the Armed Forces Movement—who favor decolonization in Guinea-Bissau, Angola and Mozambique. Many of the young officers were radicalized during tours of duty fighting liberation movements in Africa.

   With control of Angola and Mozambique going from rightist white settlers to leftist black nationalists, *this marks a key turning point in history of southern Africa.*

May

- Admiral Hugo Biermann, Chief of SADF, holds meetings in the Pentagon with Admiral Thomas Moorer, Chairman of the US Joint Chiefs of Staff, and J.W. Middendorf, Acting Secretary of the Navy.

22   Officials of SAG and USG sign nuclear cooperation accord that updates original agreement signed 8 July 1957 trading US financing, training and equipment for SA uranium.

August

8   Nixon resigns the Presidency.

September

27   UN Council on Namibia passes Decree No. 1 (endorsed by General Assembly 13 December) prohibiting foreign exploitation of Namibian resources.

30   UN General Assembly votes 98 to 23 (US), with 14 abstentions, to adopt resolution rejecting SAG's credentials as member.

October

2   Pentagon announces it is considering purchase (cost of up to $1b) of the French-South African "Cactus-Crotale," an all-weather, anti-aircraft missile.

30   UN Security Council resolution calling for expulsion of SA due to "continued implementation of apartheid," refusal to withdraw from Namibia, and "support to the illegal regime in Rhodesia," is vetoed by US, France and Britain.

December

16   Following 29 meetings held between 7 October and 28 November, in which 100 governments participated, UN General Assembly passes 5 resolutions against apartheid. The measures, *inter alia*, call for an arms embargo, urge release of political prisoners and elimination of repressive laws, and call on member states to increase aid to liberation movements. USG votes against two resolutions, abstains on two, and votes in favor of resolution calling for increased contributions to UN Trust Fund for South Africa and other organizations assisting victims of apartheid.

1975

January

11 Ford administration nominates William Bowdler to replace John Huro as US Ambassador to SA, and Nathaniel Davis to replace Donald Easum as Assistant Secretary of State for African Affairs. Kissinger is reportedly upset with Easum for leaning too far in favor of black Africa against the white minority regimes. Davis was US ambassador to Chile in early 1970s and is alleged to have participated in overthrow of Allende regime. Both appointments confirmed by Senate on 11 March.

15 Alvor Agreement signed in Portugal by MPLA, FNLA, UNITA and Portuguese government. It establishes structure for a transition government of all three groups and sets independence for 11 November 1975.

16 Rep. Charles C. Diggs (D-MI) is denied visa by SAG and declared *persona non grata*. Diggs, chairman of House Subcommittee on Africa, says that because he is black SAG fears his effect on SA black majority. SAG says it denied visa because Diggs was trying to interfere in SA internal affairs.

late Ford administration approves CIA request to channel $300,000 to FNLA in Angola.

29 Four American oil companies announce they are going to shut down operations in Namibia. Texaco, Continental, Getty, and Phillips have been under pressure from various church groups to cease prospecting for oil.

February

18 Standard Oil of California becomes the fifth oil company to end operations in Namibia because of pressure from US church groups.

27 Congressional Black Caucus asks President Ford to withdraw nomination of Nathaniel Davis to post of Assistant Secretary of State for Africa because of Davis' alleged involvement in overthrow of Allende in Chile.

March

• Encouraged by recent CIA shipments of weapons, FNLA launches attack on MPLA offices of Luanda and expels MPLA from northern sections of Angola. Later in the month 1,200 Zairean troops enter on FNLA's side. FNLA's leader Holden Roberto and Zaire's President Mobutu Sese Seko have collaborated with CIA for over a decade.

April

- Fourteen church-related organizations which own stock in IBM ask company to stop selling computers to SAG. Church groups contend computers help SAG implement apartheid, particularly the pass system.

14   *The Washington Post* reports that U.S. Nuclear Corp., of Oak Ridge, TN, has shipped 97 pounds of enriched uranium—about enough to make 7 atomic bombs—to SA over the past year. Although SAG has not signed the Nuclear Non-Proliferation Treaty, the US Nuclear Regulatory Commission approved the sale on the condition the fuel not be taken from its proposed destination, a research reactor at Pelindaba in the Transvaal. Deal is part of long-term nuclear cooperation between SAG and USG. (See ROGERS and CERVENKA)

June

3   In response to SA's continued presence in Namibia, UN member-states press for sanctions against SA but US, Britain and France block these efforts. SAG expresses pleasure over US action, as well as over appointment of Daniel Moynihan to post of US Ambassador to UN, replacing John A. Scali.

6   US, Britain, and France veto a Security Council resolution that would have placed a mandatory arms embargo on SA for its continued occupation of Namibia.

early   National Conference of Black Lawyers announces its support of campaign to expel SAG from United Nations

25   After 4 centuries of Portuguese colonial rule, Mozambique attains independence under rule of leftist FRELIMO and its leader Samora Machel.

July

17   Despite recommendation against it by three bureaus in the State Department (African Affairs, Policy Planning, Intelligence and Research), Kissinger authorizes CIA covert intervention in Angola. Project involves CIA recruitment of mercenaries in violation of US law, and over $30m in weapons aid to FNLA and UNITA.

August

- Senator Dick Clark (D-IA) travels to Angola and meets with leaders of MPLA, FNLA and UNITA. He returns more convinced that US should not intervene.

3-6   Advance units of SA armed forces enter southern Angola to train anti-MPLA elements and prepare for major invasion in late October.

31   Nathaniel Davis resigns as Assistant Secretary of State for African Affairs in opposition to US policy of covert military intervention in Angola.

October

20   Planeload of US arms, to be used in Angolan civil war, transferred directly to SA military personnel in secret rendezvous at Zaire's Ndjili airfield, Kinshasa.

23   Mixed invasion force, led by SA armored units, launches major invasion of Angola in attempt to prevent MPLA coming to power. The combined UNITA, FNLA, mercenaries, and SA forces battle to within 400 km. of Luandà before being stopped by combined MPLA/Cuban forces and eventually expelled (31 March 1976). SAG had been encouraged to invade by Kissinger but when attack bogged down, US support was not forthcoming.

November

6   In closed-door testimony to Senate Foreign Relations Committee, CIA Director William Colby admits that USG is covertly supplying arms, ammunition and vehicles to FNLA and UNITA in their fight against MPLA in Angola.

11   US Department of State announces that US will not participate in any way in UN's Decade for Action to Combat Racism and Racial Discrimination because resolution includes language which "determines that Zionism is a form of racism and racial discrimination."

11   Angolan independence—formation of the People's Republic of Angola under MPLA leadership with Dr. Agostinho Neto as first President. Most other governments will accept PRA but USG will remain one of very few refusing to recognize MPLA's legitimacy.

27   Nigeria recognizes People's Republic of Angola and begins sending aid.

December

- State Department pressures Gulf Oil Corporation to close down operations in Angola and to withhold quarterly payment of $125m to MPLA government.

19 Despite urgent pleas by Ford and Kissinger, US Senate votes 54 to 22 to prohibit further US covert aid to anti-MPLA forces in Angola. From January to November 1975 US policy was based on premise that MPLA could be squeezed out of government participation. When it became clear (November) that MPLA had a secure hold on Luanda, US policy shifted for a few weeks to favoring partition. On above date, with FNLA disintegrating, Senate refused Kissinger the money he needed for continued intervention. Only then did Kissinger come out in favor of a coalition government in Angola.

23 Kissinger makes his first public call for withdrawal of SA troops from Angola. Many see this as coming too late to be credible.

1976

January

- SA military begins formation of "32 Battalion," comprised largely of former FNLA troops commanded by white SA officers. The group is used for military operations in southern Angola. They target primarily civilian and economic targets and play a middleman role between SA military and UNITA. Reportedly, 32 Battalion is the brainchild of Colonel Carpenter, an American mercenary who fought in Zaire and Zimbabwe and is now an officer in the SA army.

22 OAU condemns SA invasion of Angola but does not condemn Cuban or Soviet involvement.

27 Despite last-minute appeal by President Ford, House of Representatives votes 323 to 99 to join Senate in banning US aid to FNLA and UNITA. Later (10 February), in an attempt to shift blame for US debacle in Angola, Ford will accuse Congress of having "lost its guts."

30 UN Security Council unanimously passes Resolution 385, condemning SA's illegal occupation of Namibia, military buildup

there, and use of Namibia for attacks against neighboring states. Also demands that SAG agree to UN-supervised elections in Namibia.

February

11 OAU recognizes MPLA government in Angola and admits it to full membership.

March

28 South African and mercenary troops are finally expelled from southern Angola back into Namibia.

31 UN Security Council condemns SA aggression against Angola, and demands that SAG pay Angola for the damage, estimated at $6.7m.

April

• Space Research Corporation of Vermont signs contract with SAG for arms deal worth estimated $50m.

14 SA Prime Minister, John Vorster—a former Nazi supporter— negotiates economic, scientific and industrial pact with Israel.

27 As part of key policy address in Lusaka, Zambia, Secretary of State Kissinger proclaims "a new era in American policy" toward southern Africa. His CIA intervention in Angola having failed, Kissinger switches to diplomacy in effort to prevent leftist guerrilla victory in Rhodesia. He criticizes white minority rule in attempt to rebuild American credibility with African states. His ten point plan, including more aid to black states in the region and proposals for negotiated solution in Rhodesia, foreshadows the more liberal approach of the Carter administration. Ronald Reagan, running against Ford in the Republican primaries, attacks the new policy for 'abandoning' traditional white allies in southern Africa.

May

20 State Department announces support for General Electric's request to sell two atomic power plants and 1.4m pounds of enriched uranium fuel to SA, but SA awards contract to French firm.

June

16 SA police open fire on Soweto schoolchildren protesting inferior quality of black education. Incident sparks months of rebellion in which hundreds are killed. The so-called Soweto rebellion is important for several reasons: militancy of black youth is raised to highest levels ever, many young Africans leave the country to

receive guerrilla training, and SAG's widespread repression brings world condemnation.

19   Emergency session of UN Security Council adopts by consensus a resolution condemning SAG for "its resort to massive violence" against student protestors.

23   US casts UN Security Council veto of Angola's application for membership.

23-24   Kissinger meets with Vorster in West Germany for secret talks dealing primarily with how to defuse the escalating guerrilla war in Rhodesia.

August

2   Kissinger delivers major American address on his new southern Africa policy to annual meeting of the Urban League.

3   Kissinger meets with Rev. Jesse Jackson to discuss US policy in Africa. Among topics discussed are why most black American ambassadors are assigned to African countries, why few blacks are employed by State Department, and recognition of Angola. Kissinger is trying to win black American support for his initiatives in southern Africa, and the meeting with Jackson is seen as an important step in this process.

5   SAG cancels visit of James Cone, a black American theologian, who was to address a seminar in SA on the role of black clergy in SA.

12   *The Christian Science Monitor* reports on official US displeasure over growing economic and military ties between Israel and SA.

27   USG protests to UN Secretary General Kurt Waldheim about Sean MacBride of Ireland, who heads UN Commission on Namibia. USG accuses MacBride of lobbying for greater pressure on SA to comply with UN Security Council Resolution 385 which sets 31 August as date for SA to disengage from Namibia.

31   Kissinger gives major Africa Speech to Rev. Leon Sullivan's Philadelphia-based Opportunities Industrialization Centers.

September

4-6   Kissinger meets with Vorster in Zurich to discuss situation in Rhodesia, Namibia and SA.

17   Demonstrations at several Soweto schools to provide Kissinger's visit to Pretoria for talks with Vorster. Six children are shot dead by police, 35 injured.

25 Congressional Black Caucus convenes Black Leadership Conference on Southern Africa. Meeting in Washington, 120 black leaders of labor, church, civil rights groups and government produce policy document criticizing US policy and outline an 11-point program that is still relevant in the 1980s. Document published in January/February 1977 issue of *The Black Scholar.*

October

19 US, Britain and France veto UN Security Council resolution calling for arms embargo on SA because of its role in Namibia. Previous triple vetoes were June 1975 (sanctions) and December 1974 (attempt to expel SA).

26 One and a half million Africans automatically lose their SA citizenship as Transkei bantustan is declared "independent." Fifteen US citizens attend ceremony. The unofficial US delegation is led by Andrew Hatcher, black former assistant press secretary to President Kennedy and currently a vice-president of New York public relations firm, Sydney S. Baron and Co. which has a $365,000/year contract from SAG. UN General Assembly votes 134 to 0, with 1 abstention (US) condemning SAG's bantustan policy and calling on all UN member states to refrain from any dealings with Transkei.

November

9 UN General Assembly passes by large majorities 11 resolutions condemning apartheid, criticizing Israel–SA relations, calling for end to military, economic and cultural collaboration with SA, and urging support for organizations aiding victims of apartheid. US votes No on 5, abstains on 4, and 2 are passed without a vote.

December

1 Black Consciousness leader Steve Biko meets Senator Dick Clark (D-IA) and gives him memo listing "a few minimum requirements" for US policy toward SA. These include dealing with "authentic black leadership," pressing for release of Nelson Mandela and other leaders, "cease showing any form of tolerance to Bantustan leaders" like Buthelezi, et al. "Whilst it is illegal for us to call for trade boycotts, arms embargo, withdrawal of investments, etc., America herself is quite free to decide what price South Africa must pay for maintaining obnoxious policies."

11 *The Nation* reports that total lending to SA by US banks and their overseas subsidiaries has surpassed $2b—nearly double what it was one year ago. This is in spite of the "unprecedented political turmoil."

30   In his first publicly-announced meeting with any foreign envoy, Secretary of State-designate Cyrus Vance confers with Ambassador R.F. Botha of SA.

1977

January

15   Andrew Young, Carter's appointee as US Ambassador to UN, calls for US training of black leaders who will take over when majority rule comes to SA. Young also suggests US subsidize an independent, antiapartheid newspaper in SA.

February

•   The five western members of the UN Security Council (US, UK, France, West Germany, Canada) begin discussions on Namibia which result in formation of the "Contact Group." This group takes over mediation between parties in Namibia dispute but fails to gain implementation of UN-supervised elections and independence. Critics charge the Contact Group is a device to take the issue away from UN and keep pressure off SAG.

11   Roelof "Pik" Botha, SA's Ambassador to the US, is named Foreign Minister. Move is seen as indicating SA's interest in strengthening relations with US at time when US policy toward southern Africa seems to be changing.

16   Carter announces that regarding applications to export computers to foreign police agencies, the State Department will recommend denial of the export license where it is believed the computer will be used in suppression of human rights.

28   Allard Löwenstein, Chief US delegate to the annual session of the UN Human Rights Commission in Geneva, endorses SWAPO call to isolate SA diplomatically.

March

•   US Ambassador to SA, William Bowdler, sends the State Department a confidential report on black attitudes toward US investment in SA. Report states that a growing number of young, urban blacks accept radical analysis: "This anti-capitalist reasoning contends that even if foreign firms offer minor reforms, it is only to create comfortable black middle class which will perpetuate exploitation of African masses." Report concludes that: "With radicalization of black attitudes, tendency to call for disinvestment grows stronger...role of American firms here will become increasingly controversial and rationale for continued presence will seem less and less persuasive to growing number of blacks."

● Carter signs Presidential Review Memorandum 4, outlining key elements of southern Africa policy. Memo gives great urgency to southern Africa's problems, favors peaceful change because armed struggle creates opportunities for Soviet influence, argues that vocal opposition to apartheid will help US standing in Third World, suggests cooperation with African and European states, and argues for "visible steps" to downgrade official US–SA relations.

1 Rev. Leon Sullivan, black civil rights activist and a director of General Motors, initiates the "Sullivan Principles," a voluntary corporate code of conduct for US companies in SA. Code calls for desegregation of dining/restroom facilities, equal pay for equal work, and more training for blacks. Critics question potential impact because less than one percent of SA blacks work for US firms. By 1984, less than half of US firms in SA have signed on, and Sullivan denounces poor performance of US firms.

5 Carter meets with Chief Gatsha Buthelezi. They agree on two basic positions: "peaceful change" for black South Africans, and continued US investment in SA.

17 Addressing the UN General Assembly, Carter calls for majority rule in SA.

22 Rep. Cardiss Collins (D-IL) announces that USG licensed some $300,000 worth of guns and other equipment for export to SA in 1976 despite UN arms embargo. Among material classified as non-military and thus allowable for export to SA were shotguns, billie clubs, and tear gas guns. Collins says: "I am convinced that no one at the Commerce Department really has a sound grasp on exactly what is going on regarding the licensing of these so-called non-military weapons to South Africa."

April

15 Referring to SA's "major role...in the peaceful resolution of Rhodesia and Namibia" President Carter asserts that "to a major degree the South African government is a stabilizing influence in the southern part of the continent."

15 Carter announces that Vice President Mondale will henceforth be coordinating Africa policy. Some critics argue that Mondale had been doing this since March, but this announcement was intended

to put Andrew Young in his place after he characterized the SA regime as illegitimate.

May

- SA freighter, Tugelaland, sails from New York en route to Cape Town but stops at Caribbean island of Antigua to pick up 155mm cannons and shells produced by Space Research Corp. of Vermont and illegally sold to SAG.

17   In a television question-and-answer session with Los Angeles residents, President Carter says: "We've gone to Vorster now and given him a request—a little bit stronger than a request—saying that if you don't do something about Namibia, then we're going to take strong action against you in the United Nations." Vorster didn't, and Carter didn't.

19-20   Following 2 days of meetings in Vienna with SA Prime Minister Vorster, VP Walter Mondale says continuing racial discrimination and denial of political rights will lead to a "worsening of relations" with US and escalation of violence in southern Africa. Press gives much attention to Mondale's call for "one-man-one-vote" in SA. Vorster rejects US position.

21   During visit to SA, Andrew Young urges SA businessmen to learn from experience of US South and achieve peaceful change "through the marketplace."

June

3   Carter appoints Richard M. Moose to replace William E. Schaufele, Jr. as Assistant Secretary of State for African Affairs. After serving three and one half years Moose will go to work for the prominent New York investment firm, Lehman Brothers, Kuhn Loeb.

16   Despite western votes to the contrary, SA is formally ousted from the policy-making board of the International Atomic Energy Agency, the last UN executive body where it was still represented. Reason for expulsion—SA's exploitation of Namibian uranium.

18   Police and demonstrators clash during Solidarity with Soweto march in New York City.

20   Addressing group of 300 businessmen in Rye, NY, SA Foreign Minister, Pik Botha, criticizes Carter administration pressure for black political rights, saying "we are not going to negotiate our own suicide."

July

- Carter orders all government departments to provide details of their links with SA.

1 Incorporation of TransAfrica, black American lobby group for Africa and the Caribbean. Stemming from a September 1976 Black Leadership Conference on Southern Africa, sponsored by the Congressional Black Caucus, TransAfrica's progressive policies are shaped by its director, Randall Robinson, a lawyer and former aide to Congressman Charles Diggs (D-MI).

1 Addressing annual convention of NAACP in St. Louis, Secretary of State, Cyrus Vance, focuses on US relations with Africa. Key points: a "reactive American policy that seeks only to oppose Soviet or Cuban involvement in Africa would be both dangerous and futile," US policy "should recognize and encourage African nationalism," racial justice in southern Africa must be promoted peacefully, and US leverage in southern Africa is limited.

13 Report presented to House International Relations Subcommittee on Africa says US, UK, France and Italy have provided arms to SA despite 1963 UN arms embargo, to the point that SA's arms stockpile is worth over $3b, far exceeding all previous estimates.

20 US Justice Department accuses representatives of SA sugar interests of making cash contributions and providing free air fare to staff and members of House Agriculture Committee between 1970 and 1974 in attempt to increase US purchases of SA sugar. Justice contends South African Sugar Association contributed to campaign of Rep. W.R. Poage (D-TX) on two occasions and provided executive jet transport for him on two trips to SA. Also implicated is South Africa Foundation and its director, John Chettle. Foundation sponsored trip to SA by Rep. John Flynt (D-GA) and his wife. Flynt is chairman of House Committee on Standards of Official Conduct, currently probing Korean influence-buying in Congress.

24 *The Sunday Times* of Johannesburg reports that agents of SA Bureau of State Security (BOSS) have been trained in US and West Germany, and that BOSS agents work undercover in many nations, including US, UK, France, etc. Quoting Deputy Director of BOSS, Alexander van Wyk, *The Times* says US and SA security services regularly trade information. US State Department refuses to comment on report.

August

6 Speaking in San Francisco, Tanzanian President Julius Nyerere criticizes US policy as "prompted more by super-power competition than by a genuine concern for equality and justice in Southern

Africa." He lays considerable blame on western corporations: "All these investors were profiting from apartheid, and have an interest in sustaining it." (full text published in *The Black Scholar*, October 1977).

8   Soviet news agency TASS warns that a Soviet Cosmos satellite has sighted a nuclear weapons testing facility in the Kalahari Desert, SA. Western press ignores the report until two weeks later when France makes similar claim. Carter warns Vorster against conducting a nuclear test. Vorster tells Carter SA does not intend to develop nuclear weapons. Later Vorster denies making any promises. Although State Department denies prior knowledge of test facility, records of US "Big Bird" satellite's flight patterns show that the area of the test facility was well-photographed during July and August.

12   *Newsweek* reports that "...some US intelligence analysts concluded that the bomb the South Africans had planned to set off actually had been made in Israel." Magazine quotes a "high-ranking Washington official" as saying "I know some intelligence people who are convinced with near certainty that it was an Israeli nuclear device."

19   South Carolina Governor James B. Edwards (later chosen by President Reagan to head Energy Department) defends remarks he made during recent trip to SA trying to encourage investment in SC. Despite public criticism, Edwards refuses to apologize for his remark that: "The black influence in American politics prevented the white South African government from getting its fair share of sympathy and understanding."

20   On instructions from Secretary of State Vance, US Ambassador in Pretoria asks SA Department of Foreign Affairs for assurance that: 1) SA does not have, or intend to develop, nuclear explosives for any purpose, 2) the Kalahari facility sighted by satellites was not a test site, and 3) there will be no nuclear explosive testing in SA. Next day SAG gives these assurances.

22-26   More than sixty governments and many non-governmental organizations are represented at UN-sponsored World Conference for Action Against Apartheid in Lagos, Nigeria. Many leaders call for greater material support to guerrilla movements in southern Africa but US Ambassador to UN Andrew Young argues for nonviolent tactics. UN Secretary General Kurt Waldheim says: "There can be no peace in South Africa so long as three-quarters of its people are excluded from the mainstream of its national life."

September

12   After being beaten severely, Black Consciousness leader Steve Biko becomes the 45th known black activist to die in police

custody—the 21st in 18 months. Before arrest Biko told US reporter there had been "lots of good talk from the Carter administration without any demonstrable shift in US policy."

23 Eleven US Congressmen ask Donald Sole, SA Ambassador to US, to allow Red Cross to take part in autopsy of Steve Biko (SA black leader killed 12 September while in police custody). Sole refuses.

28 Three Congressmen, Thomas J. Downey (D-NY), Andrew Maguire (D-NJ), and Edward J. Markey (D-MA), send letter to other members asking them to join in forming Ad Hoc Monitoring Group on South Africa. Letter notes that in past 18 months 21 political prisoners have died in hands of SA police, and the situation calls for US group to monitor treatment of political prisoners. By January 1978 the group has 30 members. Group will be spied on by SAG agents. (See DOWNEY)

October

- Tufts University sells 11,000 shares of Citicorp stock because its subsidiary, Citibank, made loans to SAG following the Soweto riots.

- Amherst College board of trustees adopts SA-related policy for its investment portfolio: supports adoption of Sullivan Principles, supports shareholder resolutions prohibiting bank loans to SAG, and considers selective divestment of stock in firms that fail to meet goals of Sullivan code.

- University of Massachusetts' board of regents votes to sell all SA-related stock. School divests some $631,000 from 21 companies—roughly half the total portfolio.

- Smith College sells 42,014 shares of stock—worth $687,728—in Firestone Tire & Rubber because company was not sufficiently responsive to school's inquiries regarding Firestone's operations in SA.

3 Nine conservative Congressmen introduce resolution calling for Andrew Young's impeachment due to his alleged support for "Marxist," "Communist," and "terrorist" leaders in Africa. Measure dies in committee.

13 In a letter to Carter, Vorster gives assurances that SA "neither has nuclear explosives nor intends to develop them for any purpose, peaceful or otherwise." Vorster later denies this, saying "I am not aware of any promise that I gave to President Carter."

19 SAG initiates widespread repression of the Black Consciousness Movement: 40 prominent black leaders arrested, 7 white opposition leaders banned, the 2 leading African newspapers closed with

some journalists and editors arrested, 18 African organizations and the Christian Institute outlawed. Crackdown touches off scattered anti-government violence and clashes with police.

19   State Department complains that SA's crackdown on black organizations and journalists is "a very serious step backwards" from policies the Carter administration is trying to promote in SA.

21   Responding to government crackdown against black opposition in SA, Congressional Black Caucus sends memo to President Carter listing "immediate action items." They include: recall US ambassador, downgrade US mission to SA, eliminate US commercial, defense and agricultural attachés, deny tax credits to US firms investing there, stop Export–Import Bank credits, end nuclear cooperation, support Security Council action at UN, end all US–SA exchange programs, and strongly affirm US support for one-person-one-vote in SA. White House will respond on 27 December.

21   Ambassador William Bowdler temporarily recalled to the US as part of Carter administration's reaction to recent government repression in SA.

31   US House of Representatives passes symbolic resolution condemning SAG's recent repression and calling on Carter to take action against SA. Measure later dies in the Senate.

31   US, Britain and France veto 3 UN Security Council resolutions calling for ban on foreign investment in SA, end to nuclear cooperation, and cessation of arms sales. Security Council unanimously adopts Resolution 417, condemning SAG in general terms for "massive violence and repression against the black people" but containing no punitive measures.

November

● One of SA's top financial experts, Dr. Robert Smit, and his wife are shot to death in their home by unknown assailants. At one time SA's representative to the International Monetary Fund, Smit had helped secretly transfer large funds from SA to be used in SAG's foreign propaganda and influence-buying schemes. Smit discovered $33m of government funds diverted to a Swiss bank account. He found it belonged to Dr. Nicholas Diederichs, the State President of SAG. Smit supported secret projects but opposed SAG officials pilfering. It is suspected this was the reason for his murder. (See WINTER)

1   US temporarily withdraws a commercial attaché and naval attaché from SA to protest SAG crackdown on opposition forces and murder of Biko.

4   UN Security Council unanimously approves Resolution 418 implementing mandatory arms embargo against SA. Resolution proclaims "that all states shall cease forthwith any provision to South Africa of arms and related materials of all types." However, the western powers and Israel will not strictly enforce this measure.

10   US National Council of Churches calls on member churches to make efforts toward withdrawal of all funds from financial institutions doing business with SA.

23   Polaroid ends distributorship with Frank and Hirsch Pty., its distributor in SA, after learning that it has been selling Polaroid products to SAG in violation of a 1971 understanding not to do so.

23   More than 130 US companies operating in SA launch a Chamber of Commerce. This coincides with Carter administration review of commercial relations. US Commercial Attaché returns from Washington and attends inauguration of the Chamber's offices saying he had spoken to Administration officials just before he left and "received no indication that the Administration is opposed to American business in South Africa."

30   In special election called by Vorster, National Party scores biggest parliamentary majority ever—135 seats to the opposition's 30.

December

2   SA police cleared by courts in death of Steve Biko. White House is "shocked."

5   SAG declares second black homeland, Bophuthatswana, independent. Another 2,500,000 black South Africans lose their citizenship.

14   State Department announces approval for the sale of 6 Cessna planes worth $500,000 to SA. Cessna is planning to sell an additional 44 planes worth $3m to SA.

14   UN General Assembly approves by large majorities 14 resolutions condemning apartheid and calling for various actions to put pressure on SAG for change. US votes No on 5, and abstains on 4.

16   UN General Assembly votes 113 to 0, with 10 abstentions, to impose an oil embargo on SA. US and NATO allies are among those abstaining.

27   National Security Advisory Zbigniew Brzezinski responds to 12 policy recommendations sent from Congressional Black Caucus 21 October 1977 to the White House. Brzezinski stresses that "our influence and leverage within South Africa are limited." He

explains why the Administration opposes CBC proposals. Admits that cooperation agreement between Pentagon and SAG regarding the "operation of Eastern Test Range Tracking Station 13 near Pretoria...is presently under review."

1978

January

- Henry Ford II visits SA for first time in ten years and says his company will not withdraw its investments.

13   Commerce Department's Office of Export Administration levies a $25,000 fine against the SA subsidiary of Gardner-Denver Co. of Dallas, TX for selling mining and drilling equipment to Rhodesia from 1972 to 1976.

19   Executive Board of NAACP issues policy statement calling for total withdrawal of US firms from SA. In July 1978 NAACP national convention ratifies policy.

25   As part of report titled *U.S. Corporate Interests in Africa*, Senate Africa Subcommittee chairman Dick Clark (D-IA) endorses a shift in policy "to actively discourage American foreign investment" in SA. Report finds "the net effect of American investment has been to strengthen the economic and military self-sufficiency of South Africa's apartheid regime."

29   Carter rejects recommendation for higher tariffs on the import of chrome alloys from SA.

31   Employee of de Kieffer and Associates, a Washington, DC law firm registered as agent for SAG, poses as Congressional aide to gain access and tape-record closed hearings on human rights abuses in SA. This could be violation of US espionage laws. The perpetrator, Eva Neterowicz, had resigned from job with Rep. Dan Rostenkowski's office in October 1977 to take job with de Kieffer. Neterowicz is not prosecuted.

February

- University of Wisconsin board of regents votes to sell all SA-related investments. School divests $10.2m of stocks and bonds from 24 companies.

- Ohio University board of trustees votes to sell all school's common stock in SA-related firms. Affected is $38,000 worth of common stock—1.3% of school's $3m endowment fund—in 4 companies: Mobil, International Telephone and Telegraph, TRW, and Monsanto.

- Earlham College board of trustees announces investment policy regarding SA-related companies: calls on companies to adopt Sullivan Principles and accept African workers' right to organize and bargain collectively.

- Duke University president Terry Sanford announces that school will not sponsor shareholder resolutions urging companies to withdraw from SA but will vote proxies in favor of such resolutions when they are introduced by others. Sanford justifies this compromise position by saying that taking an activist role would be too costly for the university.

6   Michigan state legislature adopts Resolution 462 urging Congress and the President "to impose immediate sanctions against the South African government in response to that country's disregard for human rights and dignity.

16   Commerce Department issues new regulations (EAR 175) restricting export of US–origin commodities and technical data to SA military and police. Two years later, State Department officials tell Congress: "We do not believe that these controls have severely and permanently hampered our overall export levels to that country." Reagan administration will drop the restrictions.

24   AFL–CIO Executive Council calls on US corporations to divest themselves of SA affiliates and sever all ties with SA corporations. Also demands an end to USG operations that promote the flow of capital to SA.

March

- Sixty US corporate executives tour Rhodesia, SA and Tanzania. Despite President Nyerere's strong criticism of US corporate assistance to the white minority regimes, the businessmen generally agree on continued investment and loans.

- Olin Corp. of Connecticut is charged with falsifying export applications for the shipment of 3,200 firearms and 20m rounds of ammunition to SA. Fined $510,000 for its illegal actions, Olin becomes the first US corporation to be sentenced for breaking the arms embargo.

- United Auto Workers' President, Douglas Fraser, urges banks lending to SA to pledge publicly not to make any more loans, and calls on Carter administration to actively discourage further US investment in SA.

12   Citicorp announces it will no longer make loans to SAG but will make private-sector loans which "create jobs and which benefit all South Africans." Despite its stated opposition to apartheid, Citicorp led all US banks in lending to SA during 1972-78: Citicorp was involved in 27 loans totaling $1.6b.

20   Representatives from US and Swedish Embassies in SA try to attend a trial of political dissidents (the Bethal trial) who allege they have been tortured while in police custody. Justice Curlewis bars the foreigners from attending the trial.

21   In pursuance of the Lagos Declaration, the UN General Assembly proclaims the year beginning on this date "International Anti-Apartheid Year." The detailed program calls on governments to implement total sanctions against SA.

22   General Aircraft Manufacturers Association announces USG approval of sale to SA of 70 to 80 light aircraft worth over $3.5m.

26   London *Observer* reports secret $18m fund for destabilizing Angola by subsidizing UNITA guerillas. SA, Iran, Saudi Arabia, Morocco and France are implicated.

April

14   Colby College board of trustees adopts guidelines for investments in firms doing business with SA: endorse Sullivan Principles, seek information regarding the firms' racial practices, sell stock in firms that "do not demonstrate adequate initiative" in eliminating racist practices.

17   Following the largest antiapartheid demonstrations in US sports history, International Tennis Federation expels SA from Davis Cup competition in Nashville.

21   Gabriel Hauge, Chairman of Manufacturers Hanover bank, admits that SA's racial policies pose credit risk and his bank will review its lending policies. During 1972-78 "Manny Hanny" is second largest international lender to SA with $1.2b total.

late Harvard University announces policy on SA-related investments: avoid banks that lend to SAG, ask US firms in SA to follow progressive labor practices "even where such action impinges on profitability," ask firms to adopt Sullivan Principles, support shareholder resolutions requesting withdrawal from SA when it is clear company's presence supports apartheid.

May

● Antioch University board of trustees instructs its portfolio manager to sell all school's investments in firms with SA ties.

● John Stockwell, former head of CIA's Angola Task Force during 1975-76 war, publishes *In Search of Enemies,* highly critical of US role in Angola and documenting US collaboration with SA's 1975 invasion.

1 House Banking Committee votes 28 to 16 to prohibit Export–Import Bank lending to US firms exporting to SA. On 2 June 1978 full House votes 219 to 116 in favor of watered-down version based on the Sullivan Principles. Bill is signed into law by Carter on 10 November 1978. It effectively ends ExIm lending to SA-related transactions.

4 SA invasion force penetrates 150 miles into southern Angola to attack SWAPO refugee camp at Kassinga. Of 3,000 Namibians in the camp—mostly women and children—867 are killed, 464 wounded, and over 200 taken prisoner.

4 Carter tells a press conference: "we have no intention to intercede in any war in Angola." Yet on the same day CIA Director Admiral Stansfield Turner and a Brzezinski aide meet with Senator Dick Clark in what Clark interprets as an effort to change the 1976 Congressional prohibition against US military involvement in Angola.

10 State Department begins inquiry into charges that Jan H. Van Rooyen, SA Embassy Economic Minister, meddled in US internal affairs by criticizing Senator Dick Clark (D-IA) who is running for reelection this year. Clark is chair of Foreign Relations Subcommittee on Africa which has been critical of apartheid. Clark will lose reelection bid amid rumors that SAG channeled money to his Republican opponent, Roger Jepsen.

19 Exposure of secret "contingency plan" by General Motors' SA subsidiary to mobilize white employees in collaboration with SAG in case of black rebellion. Detailed security plan reveals that GM leadership is on the side of the white minority regime.

23 In a closed-door White House meeting with Senators, Carter objects to congressional restraints that prevent him from aiding the UNITA forces of Jonas Savimbi. Senator Moynihan, who attended the session, says: "for about a month now, officials... have been telling us they want to provide aid to Savimbi."

24 *The Washington Post* reports that Carter plan is to transfer arms via third parties to UNITA and Eritrean guerrillas in Ethiopia to

tie down Cuban forces and prevent them from assisting Rhodesian guerrillas.

June

- Columbia University board of trustees adopts new investment guidelines under which the university will: withdraw money from banks lending to SAG, divest itself of securities in firms that "respond in a manner manifesting indifference... to the prevailing repressive policies in South Africa," inform portfolio companies of Columbia's concern over conditions in SA.

8   President Julius Nyerere of Tanzania criticizes the "hysterical voices" in the Carter administration who seek to inject Cold War politics into African struggles. He denounces western plans for a pan-African military force as "the height of arrogance." Nyerere warns Carter that US–African relations will suffer if he listens to Brzezinski.

11   Angolan President Agostinho Neto sends private message to Carter stating his government's desire for better relations with US, including a negotiated settlement in Namibia, and demilitarization of Angola–Zaire border. Neto notes that they will not accept US preconditions on purely domestic Angolan affairs (e.g., Cuban troops, relations with UNITA, and commitment to socialism).

12   In a *U.S. News and World Report* interview Andrew Young says that "even the best of our experts tend to think of Africa through a European mind-set."

25-29 Carter's top nuclear negotiator, Gerard Smith, holds talks in Pretoria with SA Foreign Minister Roelof (Pik) Botha and head of the SA Atomic Energy Board, Dr. Abraham J. Roux. In response to US request to sign Nuclear Non-Proliferation Treaty (NPT), SA officials list their demands: resumption of US deliveries of highly enriched uranium for SA's research reactor, deliveries of low-enriched uranium for 2 commercial reactors under construction, approval of US export permits for technology destined for SA's enrichment facility, and diplomatic assistance in regaining SA's seat on the Board of Governors of the International Atomic Energy Agency.

28   SAG-sponsored seminar for American business executives opens in Houston. Former President Gerald Ford is major speaker. He receives $10,000 for his services.

July

14   South African Council of Churches condemns foreign investment in the country, claiming investment and loans from abroad have supported "the prevailing patterns of power and privilege."

20   SAG implements the Protection of Business Act which prohibits foreign firms from disseminating information about their activities without consent from Minister of Economic affairs.

27   UN Security Council adopts 2 resolutions on Namibia. Resolution 431 establishes the UN Transitional Assistance Group (UNTAG) which would comprise 7,500 troops and 1,200 civilians from various countries to monitor ceasefire and elections. Resolution 432 declares that Walvis Bay must be reintegrated into Namibia and SAG should not do anything to the port city "prejudicial to the independence of Namibia or the viability of its economy."

August

10   Assistant Secretary of State for African Affairs, Richard Moose, testifies on Capitol Hill against 3 pieces of legislation aimed at curtailing US investment in SA. Bills sponsored by Bingham (D-NY), Solarz (D-NY), and Diggs (D-MI), are attacked by other Carter officials and fail to become law. Carter wants to avoid precedent of cutting economic ties with non-communist ally. Also, negotiations on Rhodesia are at critical stage and Carter wants to retain cooperation of SAG.

14   German magazine *Der Spiegel* carries interview with SA Foreign Minister Roelof Botha in which he is asked if Washington encouraged SA to invade Angola in 1975. Botha replies: "I could tell you much about it. 'Encourage' would be the understatement of the year."

22   Former Texas Governor and presidential candidate John Connally arrives in SA for week visit. During trip Connally claims SA's racial system "is not all that rare in the world," and promises US support.

23   *The Wall Street Journal* reports on Justice Department investigation of lobbyists for SA sugar growers who gave gifts, free trips to SA, and offers of jobs to several Congressmen. The secret largesse was bestowed upon Rep. W.R. Poage (D-TX), Rep. William Wampler (R-VA) who was ranking Republican member of Agriculture Committee which provided sugar quotas allowing South African Sugar Association to export sugar to US, and Rep. John Flynt (D-GA) who was chairman of the House Ethics Committee.

September

20   Under pressure from revelations in 'Infogate' scandal, SA Prime Minister Vorster resigns and, after one-week succession struggle, is replaced by Defence Minister P.W. Botha.

29   UN Security Council approves Resolution 435 which will become the definitive framework for an internationally acceptable settle-

ment in Namibia. Measure calls for UN-supervised ceasefire, elections, and framing of constitution. If accepted by all parties, plan would take one year to implement. SAG resists plan because it calls for removal of SA troops, and SAG military intelligence has reported SWAPO would win large majority of vote.

October

- Vassar College adopts policy of "highly selective divestment" from companies involved in SA. Aspects of the policy include: urging firms to adopt Sullivan Principles, engaging in shareholder activism to press companies on elimination of racist practices, selling holdings in banks that lend to SAG. Under the latter provision, the school sells $4.2m in bonds from Irving Trust, Bank of America, Manufacturers Hanover Trust, First National Bank of Chicago, and the federal government's Export–Import Bank.

- Carleton College's board of trustees adopts policy of selective divestment of stock from firms exhibiting certain behavior in SA: lending to SAG, selling goods to SA police/military, failing to adopt Sullivan Principles, or having main operations in SA.

10 Carter signs into law a total trade ban against the government of Idi Amin in Uganda. These sanctions devastate the Ugandan economy and within 6 months Amin is toppled.

12 US Congress renews year-old ban on aid to Angola and Mozambique.

16 On visit to SA, Secretary of State Vance delivers message from Carter to SAG leaders. Note reportedly promises official visit to Washington by Prime Minister P.W. Botha, and less US criticism of SA if SAG will accept UN plan for independence of Namibia. Vance also asks UN to extend deadline for action against SA.

November

- Howard University adopts policy of not holding stock of any company doing "substantial business" in SA. Howard sells off some $2m of SA-related stock without incurring a financial loss.

- Following a policy adopted in April 1978, University of Washington board of trustees votes to sell the school's holdings—worth $150,000—in Dresser Industries due to refusal of firm to adopt Sullivan Principles.

- Ohio State University sells 10,000 shares of stock—worth $250,000—in International Flavors and Fragrances because company failed to respond to inquiry about activities in SA.

7 Senator Dick Clark (D-IA), Chairman of Senate Africa Subcommittee and strongest antiapartheid voice in Congress, is defeated

in reelection bid by right-wing Republican Roger Jepsen. *The New York Times* (22 March 1979) will report that Eschel Rhoodie, former SA Minister of Information, says SAG was a major financial backer of Jepsen's campaign. The US federal prosecutor investigating the charges, James Reynolds, will be removed from the case by Reagan in 1982 and replaced by a Jepsen crony, Evan Hultman. No charges ever filed against Jepsen.

17   SA Reserve Army member Richard Beck arrives in Chicago to pick up $25,000 worth of guns and is arrested by US Customs agents, thus being the first South African to be charged with violating the arms embargo. Beck is eventually convicted in a jury trial but is acquitted by the presiding judge who overturns the jury's verdict—the only time the judge had done such a thing in 18 years on the bench.

20-27   In its yearly debate on apartheid, the 33rd session of the UN General Assembly adopts 15 resolutions calling for solidarity with political prisoners in SA, urging international community to increase pressure on SAG, condemning Israel for close ties to SA, requesting member states and Security Council to impose oil embargo, calling for halt to all nuclear cooperation with SA, urging reduction in economic ties, *et al.* All pass by large majorities. USG isolated in opposition, votes No 7 times and abstains 4 times.

30   Carter meets with SA Foreign Minister Pik Botha to urge SA cooperation on Namibia issue. Speaking in San Francisco, Andrew Young opposes economic sanctions against SA because Namibia has been promised independence and majority rule.

December

- Cornell University board of trustees adopts new guidelines for selective divestment of SA-related holdings: solicit information from companies regarding their SA operations, make no investments in firms whose main operations are in SA, hold no equities in banks lending to SAG, consider selling stock in firms that refuse to abide by code of fair employment practices.

- Bucknell University's board of trustees forms subcommittee for reviewing investments in SA-related stock. New policy prohibits investing in firms that refuse to sign Sullivan Principles.

- A US court fines United Airlines $50,000 for having trained Rhodesian pilots in 1972 and 1973 in violation of sanctions.

8   Michigan State University board of trustees begins program to sell off stock in companies active in SA. The divestment will involve $8.5m worth of stock—roughly 45% of the school's $18m portfolio.

21   George McGovern (D-SD), new chair of Senate Africa Subcommittee, returns from Africa trip and calls for US disengagement from Rhodesia and recognition of MPLA regime in Angola.

1979

January

- Colgate University's board of trustees accepts recommendation of faculty/student advisory committee to establish guidelines for investments in SA-related companies: stop investing in firms whose main operations are in SA, stop investing in banks lending to SAG, support shareholders resolutions aimed at ending corporate support for apartheid, and sell stock of firms that are "intractable and insensitive to moral considerations."

13   After State Department had initially denied him entry visa, SA boxer Kallie Knoetze knocks out Bill Sharkey in 4th round of scheduled 10-round fight in Miami Beach. Knoetze's US entry was opposed by civil rights groups because as a SA policeman in 1977 Knoetze shot a 15-year-old black boy in the legs. Fight was originally scheduled for New York but organizers moved it to Miami to avoid antiapartheid protests.

March

- University of Michigan board of regents votes to sell school's 14,613 shares in Black & Decker Manufacturing because company "was unwilling to comply with university requests for information regarding labor practices and the Sullivan Principles."

- University of Illinois board of trustees revised policy on SA-related investments. New policy calls for: supporting shareholder petitions for withdrawal from SA by firms refusing to abide by Sullivan Principles, and divesting from firms that refuse "to abandon unethical practices."

- Hampshire College board of trustees instructs its money managers to dispose of all holdings in SA-related companies and avoid all such holdings in the future.

- As part of corporate effort to relax USG restrictions on certain exports to SA, the American Chamber of Commerce in SA warns

US Secretary of Commerce that its 250 member companies in SA are losing business due to the export restrictions. In 1981 the Chamber will claim that US firms are losing $500m in business per year. Later that year, the Reagan administration will begin loosening commercial restrictions.

4   Under new Islamic leadership of Ayatollah Khomeini, Iran, formerly supplying 90% of SA's oil, breaks diplomatic relations with SA. In response to cutoff of Iranian oil, SAG announces complete clampdown on information regarding oil supplies.

6   Thirty-fifth session of UN Human Rights Commission adopts by large majorities 4 resolutions criticizing white minority rule and calling on member states to pressure SAG. US votes No on 3 and abstains on 1.

14   SA planes bomb SWAPO refugee camp in southern Angola. Angolan government later claims that between March 1976 and June 1979 SA forces have inflicted 1,383 deaths and more than 1,800 wounded in Angola.

21   BBC broadcasts interview with Eschel Rhoodie, former SA Minister of Information, in which he says SAG paid American "opinion formers and decision takers" to propagate pro-SA views. Documents obtained by BBC reveal SAG gave money to US politicians and labor union officials, and assisted John McGoff in his unsuccessful attempt to buy *The Washington Star.*

22   Under pressure from antiapartheid activists, Columbia University announces it has divested $2.7m from 3 banks because of their loans to SAG. Amount is less than activists wanted, representing about 1% of university's total investments, of which 35% is in companies doing business with SA.

28   By a vote of 12 to 0, with 3 abstentions (US, UK, France), UN Security Council adopts resolution condemning SA for military attacks on Angola and calling on member states to assist Angola.

April

● Brandeis University board of trustees announces it will selectively sell stock in companies that refuse to sign Sullivan Principles, make loans to SAG, or sell goods to SA police/military. As part of program, school will sell $50,000 fixed income investment in Crocker National Bank, and a $350,000 Ford Motor Co. bond.

● Ohio State University adopts policy of selling holdings in SA-related firms that fail to demonstrate progress in implementing the Sullivan Principles.

2   SAG announces that in 1974 it transferred $11.5m to a Swiss bank account to assist conservative US publisher John McGoff in effort to purchase *The Washington Star.*

4   SAG agents secretly remove film from camera on board American embassy plane in SA. Hundreds of negatives indicate that there had been systematic US surveillance of strategic regions of SA, including the secret Pelindaba uranium-enrichment facility. SAG accuses US of spying and expels 3 diplomats. In retaliation Carter expels 2 SA military attachés from Washington.

7   Johannesburg press reports that SAG, using American publisher John McGoff as conduit, offered financial support to New York daily, *The Tribune,* as part of efforts to gain influence in American media. The offer was rejected by *The Tribune*'s owners.

17 Voters in Berkeley, CA, approve referendum calling for public monies to be "removed from banks and other financial institutions doing business in or with South Africa." Roughly $4.5m is involved.

22 While transporting a plane to SA for Globe Aero Ltd. of Lakeland, FL, pilot Douglas Patrick is arrested for entering Angolan air space. Luanda releases the pilot 3 weeks later.

25 Department of Energy announces it has State Department clearance to buy SA's SASOL 1 data bank from any corporation that can arrange a deal.

late Black religious leaders from 38 states and 52 cities attend International Freedom Mobilization Against Apartheid conference in New York. The church leaders reject the Sullivan Principles, call for immediate US corporate disengagement from SA, and declare their "unequivocal support of the national liberation struggle waged by the South African people under the leadership of the African National Congress."

late Boston University trustees announce investment policy that will: selectively sell stock in firms with SA subsidiaries that fail to actively promote equal opportunity; refrain from contact with banks that lend to SAG; sell all SA-related non-voting stocks because they "confer no investor powers on the university." Total divestment: $6.6m.

28 Johannesburg *Sunday Times* reports that USG gave SAG intelligence photos taken from US ambassador's plane while flying over Angola, Tanzania, and Zambia. Disclosure comes after SAG expelled 3 US diplomats for taking aerial photos of SA installations. USG denies allegations.

May

- Yale University sells $1.7m worth of stock in J.P. Morgan & Co. because of firm's loans to SAG.

- Trustees of Knox College set guidelines for SA-related investments: no purchase of stock in firms not signing Sullivan Principles or similar code; divesting from firms that refuse to adopt non-racist practices.

- Responding to growing pressure from students, University of Delaware board of trustees establishes policy of monitoring SA-related activities of companies whose stock is owned by UD. Sullivan Principles are used as standard for correct corporate conduct.

12 Carnegie Endowment for International Peace releases results of poll saying 86% of Americans interviewed oppose apartheid and "believe the U.S. should work actively for reform in that country."

20 *The Baltimore Sun* reports that Tufts University (MA) will divest from companies involved in SA. Of a total endowment of $31m Tufts has $6.4m in SA-related stock.

21 *The Los Angeles Times* reports University of California and Stanford University will back shareholder resolution calling on General Motors to stop selling vehicles to SA police/military. Resolution fails but it is the first time these institutions vote their stock against corporate management on any issue. The move follows two years of student antiapartheid protests involving hundreds of arrests for civil disobedience.

24 UN General Assembly votes 96 to 19 (US), with 9 abstentions, to reject SA's credentials.

31 UN General Assembly votes 118 to 0, with 16 abstentions (US), to adopt resolution condemning SA for its continued occupation of Namibia, supporting the liberation struggle of the Namibian people led by SWAPO, and urging the Security Council to put greater pressure on SA to leave Namibia.

June

- State University of New York sets investment policy that will: consider companies' adherence to the Sullivan Principles when making investments; seek information on employment practices of firms not signing Sullivan code; and divest from companies not providing "satisfactory responses" to SUNY inquiries.

11   PAC leader David Sibeko assassinated in Dar es Salaam, Tanzania. Sibeko had been one of the most dynamic and effective SA blacks doing antiapartheid work in the US.

22   SA Minister of Cooperation and Development, Piet Koornhof, tours US declaring "apartheid is dying" but bantustans, pass laws, and other apartheid policies continue.

July

20   After initially denying him a visa, SAG bows to Carter administration pressure and allows the Rev. Jesse Jackson to tour SA. During stay Jackson says several things that would put a black South African behind bars: calling for withdrawal of foreign investments, referring to apartheid as "legalized genocide," and calling the government a "terroristic dictatorship." Jackson loses credibility with young, militant blacks by meeting with Chief Gatsha Buthelezi.

31   *The Washington Star* reports that a federal judge in San Francisco has fined *Sacramento Union* co-publisher John McGoff and his lawyer $10,000 for refusing to answer questions about the money used to buy the newspaper. It is alleged they used SAG money.

August

•   During US visit, Gatsha Buthelezi calls for continued US investment in SA.

14   Rockefeller Foundation announces it is funding a large-scale study of US involvement in SA. Group is headed by Franklin Thomas, President of the Ford Foundation, and in 1981 will issue its 517 page report—*South Africa: Time Running Out.*

15   Amid controversy following secret meeting with PLO representative in New York, Andrew Young is forced to resign as UN ambassador, thus silencing the Carter administration's strongest antiapartheid voice. Incident adds to growing tension between American Jews and blacks. Young is replaced by his deputy Donald McHenry. In late February 1984 it will be revealed that the Reagan administration held nine months of secret talks with the PLO, yet no officials are punished.

16   *The Washington Post* reports that Riggs Bank, Washington's largest commercial bank, with some $5.4m in loans to SA, will not change its lending policies despite pressure from human rights groups.

30   Fluor, the US construction corporation involved in the SASOL synthetic fuel project in SA, announces an agreement covering future use of SASOL technology in the US.

September

10 Angolan President Agostinho Neto dies of pancreatic cancer in a Moscow hospital. Planning Minister Jose Eduardo dos Santos succeeds him as President.

12 SAG declares Venda bantustan "independent." Another half million blacks lose their SA citizenship.

22 US Vela satellite detects intense double flash of light (characteristic of nuclear blast) in the Indian Ocean near SA. USG does not release the information until 25 October when ABC TV News reports event. While many experts claim SA tested bomb, Carter administration covers up, claiming Vela made mistake, despite fact Vela has never previously erred.

October

3 American Chamber of Commerce in SA announces it will build a private commercial high school in Soweto to train blacks in administrative and commercial skills. Funded by some 70 US companies, the PACE Commercial High School charges $1,400/year tuition and will eventually enroll 600 students. The American Chamber of Commerce says the school "will provide a source of commercially well-trained blacks...and enhance the image of business, both here and overseas."

3 *Africa Confidential* reports that Eaton Corporation of Cleveland, OH is planning a joint venture with SA parastatal, the Economic Development Corporation, to build a gear and axle plant producing components for heavy trucks used by SADF.

20 Black American boxer John Tate fights Gerrie Coetzee in Pretoria despite antiapartheid protests. Tate wins.

November

• Delegation of the House Armed Services Committee is given red carpet treatment while on its biennial tour of SA. They visit Simonstown Naval Base and other facilities. Chairman Melvin Price (D-IL) is quoted as saying that SA is important to US strategic interests

• Black employees at Department of Energy's Argonne nuclear laboratory near Chicago protest presence of two white South Africans enrolled in a six-week course on nuclear technology. Despite the protests to Washington, the South Africans are allowed to complete the training.

2 By a vote of 12 to 0, with 3 abstentions (US, UK, France), UN Security Council adopts resolution condemning SA's aggression

against Angola, warning SA to respect Angola's territorial integrity, and calling on member states to assist Angola.

22   General Tire and Rubber Co. of South Africa, 26% owned by General Tire of Akron, Ohio, fires 625 black workers demanding recognition of their trade union. Action follows Ford Motor Co.'s decision a day earlier to fire 700 black workers who struck to protest strained relations with white workers.

December

12   UN General Assembly adopts by large majorities 17 resolutions condemning apartheid and calling for various measures to isolate SAG. US votes No on 8, abstains on 3, and supports only those resolutions which are symbolic rather than substantive.

12   UN General Assembly adopts by large majorities 7 resolutions aimed at ending SA's illegal occupation of Namibia. Two are adopted by consensus and US abstains on the other 5.

31   *The Washington Post* reports that the White House Office of Science Policy, investigating 22 September incident off coast of SA, has initially concluded it was nuclear test. Under political pressure, the group will later issue report saying Vela satellite was mistaken—flash recorded by satellite was caused by meteorite, not nuclear blast. Independent experts claims this is highly unlikely but coverup is successful, in that no further investigation into the incident is conducted.

1980

January

• Group of 12 Congressmen, led by James Wright (D-TX) make an unpublicized trip to SA and visit the SASOL coal-to-oil conversion plants, among other sites.

• Assistant Secretary of State for African Affairs, Richard Moose, meets with SADF Chief Magnus Malan.

9   Ford Motor Co. of SA reinstates more than 500 black workers who had been on strike since November.

16 NAACP Board of Directors adopts measure calling upon US corporations to withdraw their investments from SA, and reaffirms its previous call for economic sanctions.

17 Pentagon sources tell *The Baltimore Sun* that 2 SA patrol boats harrassed and nearly collided with a US cruiser rounding the Cape toward the Indian Ocean.

February

21 CBS News reports Israel exploded nuclear device in ocean near SA on 22 September 1979 with SA cooperation. CBS says SAG first offered Israel chance to test atomic bomb in SA in 1966. *The Washington Post* (22 February) reports: "the CIA has told key Congressional committees that if there was a test near South Africa last September 22, Israel was its leading candidate as the source."

March

• Israeli Defense Minister, Ezer Weizman, pays secret 3-day visit to SA for discussion of security matters.

2 Over 1,000 Afro-American leaders, representing over 300 organizations, meet in Richmond, VA for the National Black Agenda Conference. They adopt resolution calling on US "to sever all economic, diplomatic, political and cultural relations with South Africa." "These measures should include a ban on new investment by U.S. companies, a program of tax penalties designed to require withdrawal of current investments, a ban on new bank loans to South African borrowers, and termination of all exportation to and importation from South Africa."

4 Following nationwide voting, Rhodesian Registrar of Elections announces that ZANU-PF has won a landslide victory, taking 57 seats in the 100-seat parliament. Robert Mugabe becomes Zimbabwe's first black Prime Minister.

13 Angolan Mission to the UN in New York is bombed by the anti-Cuban terrorist group Omega 7.

31 Nebraska state legislature adopts antiapartheid measure calling on the Nebraska Investment Council to remove from its list of approved investments corporations and banks that invest in SA.

April

1 Meeting in Lusaka, Zambia, 9 southern African states (Angola, Botswana, Lesotho, Malawi, Mozambique, Swaziland, Tanzania, Zambia, Zimbabwe) form the Southern African Development Coordination Conference (SADCC) to promote regional development and lessen economic dependence on SA.

1   Prestigious Washington law firm of Smathers, Symington and Herlong is hired by SAG to lobby and disseminate political propaganda. *Rand Daily Mail* calls contract a "spectacular public relations coup" because Smathers and Symington are prominent Democrats with "top contacts in and out of the US Government." Smathers was Senator from Florida (1950-68), and Symington served in House (1969-76). The firm replaces Donald de Kieffer, whose contract as lobbyist was terminated in 1979, and who would later be appointed by President Reagan to office of US Special Trade Representative.

11   UN Security Council unanimously adopts resolution condemning SA for recent military raids on Zambia.

22   While delivering a plane to SA for Globe Aero Ltd. of Lakeland, FL, pilot Thomas Willett makes an emergency landing in Angola and is arrested. Six months later he is released.

May

14   Speaking at congressional hearing, US Assistant Secretary of State for Human Rights, Patricia Derian, says that Prime Minister Botha has made no significant improvements in situation of SA blacks and "time is running out for the prospects of peaceful change."

18   *Sunday Post* (Johannesburg) reports that last year SA became leading exporter of coal (ahead of Poland and Australia) to the US. SA data cites 1,130,900 tons sold to US companies.

25   At their national convention, Coalition of Black Trade Unionists adopts measure calling on "the American trade union movement to withdrawn their bank accounts, including pension funds, from banks that make loans to South Africa and also from banks that loan money to companies that invest in South Africa."

June

•   SA subsidiary of Goodyear Tire and Rubber Co. fires over 1,300 black workers striking for higher pay. Goodyear then selectively rehires most of them.

7   Under code name 'Operation Smokeshell', SA air and ground forces launch major invasion of southern Angola. Some 4,000 troops with much heavy artillery and air support penetrate 100 miles. Angola claims 416 civilian and 32 military casualties. SA claims 200 SWAPO casualties and over 100 tons of military equipment captured.

12   In SA at invitation of SAG, Joseph Churba, an advisor to Reagan and President of the Center for International Security, says he will advise Reagan, if elected, to end US compliance with arms

embargo, aid SA security efforts, and establish US naval presence at Simonstown.

13   UN Security Council unanimously adopts resolution that condemns SAG for widespread repression of recent student protests, calls for release of Nelson Mandela and other political prisoners, and demands SA stop military attacks on neighboring countries.

16   Space Research Corporation founder Gerald Bull and former company president Rogers Gregory receive 6-month prison terms for violating arms embargo against SA by exporting 155mm artillery cannons and shells. In October, a British television program charges that the cannons were used for testing a tactical nuclear weapon, said to be detected by the US Vela satellite in September 1979.

27   Despite abstentions by US, France and Britain, UN Security Council adopts resolution calling for full implementation of the arms embargo, denouncing SA's attacks on Angola, and requesting member states to aid Angola.

30   Writing in *The Washington Post*, former Ambassador Andrew Young criticizes ongoing repression in SA and calls for greater pressure by western governments.

July

- Antiapartheid groups at University of California/Los Angeles (UCLA) elect or influence enough members of the board controlling student funds to transfer $25m out of banks lending to SA.

3-11   Chairman of House Africa Subcommittee, Rep. Stephen Solarz (D-NY), accompanied by William Gray (D-PA) and Benjamin Rosenthal (D-NY), makes an 8-day tour of SA. Their published findings, *South Africa: Change and Confrontation*, report that there is "a universal feeling among black leaders that Prime Minister Botha has failed to live up to his early promises about initiating extensive reforms."

22   Vice President Walter Mondale leads a 72-member trade delegation to Nigeria and is criticized by major Nigerian newspapers for letting US policy toward SA slide into irrelevance.

August

- Formation in Washington, DC of the US–Southwest Africa/Namibia Trade and Cultural Council run by Marion Smoak and Carl Shipley. Council's basic goal is to promote the Democratic Turnhalle Alliance (DTA), the political party in Namibia most closely aligned with SAG. Smoak was White House Chief of Protocol under Nixon and will serve on Reagan's transition team at the State Department's Africa Bureau.

2-9   National Bar Association of America (some 8,000 mostly black lawyers) at its annual conference in Dallas, calls for comprehensive sanctions against SA. NBAA also endorses campaign for Nelson Mandela's release from prison. NBAA report is submitted to House Africa Subcommittee.

September

5   *The Wall Street Journal* reports that Rev. Leon Sullivan is criticizing US firms for insufficient aid to SA blacks and says he may call for disinvestment if conditions do not improve.

22   Citibank involvement in a $250m consortium credit to SA for black schools and housing is reported. The move does not stop criticism of the bank by religious and other groups, who withdrew $6.5m in March to protest Citibank's SA ties.

26   SASOL, SAG's synthetic fuel corporation, announces contract to act as consultant and co-licenser for synthetic fuel project in North Dakota. SASOL's annual report states that "of the first $100m allocated by US Department of Energy for design work on synfuel projects, $60m will go to projects with which SASOL is involved either as consultant or potential licenser."

30   While delivering a plane to SA from Globe Aero Ltd. of Lakeland, FL, pilot Dick Lauer accidently lands in Botswana and is picked up by Botswana authorities before SA military can rescue him.

October

•   Presidential candidate Ronald Reagan forms a 23-person Strategic Minerals Task Force, mostly business executives and mining company officials, to advise on how best to wage the "resource war" against the Soviet Union.

25   US boxer Mike Weaver defeats South African Gerrie Coetzee in World Boxing Association heavyweight championship at Sun City, Bophuthatswana.

November

4   Ronald Reagan is elected President with 51% of vote. Republicans also win majority in Senate for first time in 26 years.

December

•   Eastern Rugby Union of America accepts $25,000 donation from Johannesburg businessman Louis Luyt. Same month they invite SA's "national" rugby team (Springboks) to tour US.

3   Contingent of black American businessmen, accompanied by public relations specialists, leaves New York for an 8-day tour of Bophuthatswana, one of SA's dependent bantustans.

8   Columnist Jack Anderson reports that Israel, Taiwan and SA will soon begin joint production of cruise missiles. "U.S. intelligence agencies have known for years that the three nations were working together on nuclear weapons development," but the addition of this sophisticated delivery capability means that "South Africa would annihilate targets anywhere in the southern part of the continent."

16 UN General Assembly adopts by large majorities 18 resolutions condemning apartheid, calling for international isolation of SAG, requesting greater assistance to liberation movements, and condemning Israel for close relations with SA. US votes No on 10, abstains on 5, and votes Yes on 3 non-substantive resolutions (calling for release of political prisoners, and urging support for UN Special Committee on Apartheid and UN Trust Fund for South Africa).

16 According to US intelligence source quoted by the Johannesburg *Star* (18 February 1981) SAG tests another nuclear explosion in the southern Indian Ocean.

16 President Carter signs Public Law 96-533 (International Security and Development Cooperation Act of 1980). Section 118 modifies the Clark Amendment: assistance may not be furnished to Angolan insurgents unless (1) the President determines that such aid is in the national interest, (2) the President provides details of the aid and its recipients, (3) Congress passes a joint resolution approving the above.

26 Columnist Jack Anderson reveals that former CIA recruiter, David Bufkin, signed a sworn statement that the CIA violated the Neutrality Act by recruiting US mercenaries to fight against the MPLA in Angola's civil war, despite USG assurances that CIA was not involved.

1981

January

6   Two weeks before Ronald Reagan's inauguration his ex-campaign manager, John Sears, registers with the Justice Department as a paid foreign agent of SAG. His fee is $500,000 per year.

30   Within weeks of Ronald Reagan's inauguration, SA commandos launch their first cross-border raid into Mozambique to attack ANC houses in Maputo suburb, Matola. Twelve ANC members, a Portuguese technician and 1 South African killed. Pretoria follows attack with menacing troop movements along Mozambican border and violations of Mozambican air space.

February

4   While delivering an airplane to SA from Globe Aero Ltd. of Lakeland, FL, pilot Geoffrey Tyler makes unscheduled landing in southern Angola. Angolan authorities suspect Tyler of delivering weapons and propaganda material to UNITA and charge him with espionage.

March

2   UN General Assembly votes 112-22 (US) to reject SA's credentials.

3   In television interview with Walter Cronkite, President Reagan asserts SA is reforming and US should be "helpful." He adds: "Can we abandon a country that has stood beside us in every war we've ever fought, a country that is essential to the free world, that has minerals?" Reagan apparently does not know that Nationalist Party sided with Nazis in World War II.

4   Mozambique expels four US embassy officials on espionage charges. Mozambique alleges they are part of a spy ring that for many years has supplied information to Pretoria and the former white regime in Rhodesia. State Department denies charges. In retaliation, on 20 March the Reagan administration announces cutoff of over $5m worth of wheat, rice and corn destined for Mozambique.

6   UN General Assembly adopts by large majorities 10 resolutions opposing SA's illegal occupation of Namibia and calling for support of antiapartheid forces. US abstains on every vote.

9-15   Five high-ranking SA military intelligence officers pose as diplomats to gain entry to US and meet with officials at Pentagon,

National Security Council, and Congress. This breaks long-standing US policy of no visits by SA military. State Department says it didn't know their real identities and asks them to leave. Reagan administration claims no top officials met with the South Africans but it is later learned that UN Ambassador Jeane Kirkpatrick did meet with them.

17   South African jets strike nearly 200 miles into Angola to bomb Namibian refugee camps. State Department expresses "concern" but refuses to condemn the attack.

17   *The New York Times* reports that group of 132 Americans, including Rev. Jesse Jackson, Mayor Richard Hatcher of Gary, IN, Mayor Kenneth Gibson of Newark, NJ, and Rev. Joseph Lowery of the Southern Christian Leadership Conference, sent a letter to Reagan urging him to support UN policies aimed at ending SA control of Namibia.

19   Reagan administration formally submits to Congress proposal to repeal Clark Amendment. Rationale is that it restricts President's ability to make foreign policy.

20   Nigerian President Shehu Shagari warns Reagan administration against tilting toward SA and giving arms to UNITA: "If the United States is willing to support rebels in a sovereign African nation, it would be extremely serious. . . it would be very unwise."

25   Delegation of African diplomats meets with UN Secretary General Kurt Waldheim to tell him of their concern over the rightward shift in US policy toward SA.

26   *The Guardian* (Br.) reports on opposition in SA to Reagan's plan to repeal the Clark Amendment. Dr. Nthato Motlana: "If the Americans want to get the Cubans out of Angola, the way to do it is to get the South Africans out of Namibia." *The Sowetan* wanted to know why the West regarded people like Savimbi heroes, and people like Robert Mugabe 'terrorists'. Dr. Mike Hough, Director of the Institute of Strategic Studies at Pretoria University, asserted that Washington was more interested in making moves against the Soviets than in aiding democracy in Angola.

26   Congressional Black Caucus calls for the dismissal of UN Ambassador Jeane Kirkpatrick due to her secret meeting with SA military officials. Congressman William Gray (D-PA) says the Reagan policy toward SA is "a slap in the face to 26 million black Americans."

27   Johannesburg *Star* reports that 36 Democratic Congressmen have sponsored a resolution urging Reagan not to invite P.W. Botha to

the US until his government renounces apartheid. This follows rumors that Reagan is planning to give Botha an official invitation.

27   *The Wall Street Journal* reports that "several major U.S. compan- ies, mostly oil producers" are urging Reagan not to destabilize the Angolan government. They argue that the ruling MPLA is a "knowledgeable, understanding and reliable business partner." The fact that there have been only "four minor attacks on oil- company operations in five years of guerrilla warfare" is largely due to presence of Cuban troops.

29   *The Baltimore Sun*'s UN correspondent reports that "There is no doubt in the minds of observers here that the advent of the Reagan administration is behind the renewed disinclination of the South Africans to permit the implementation of the Western- devised UN plan for a peaceful transfer in Namibia. . . ."

31   Reagan officials announce they are seeking modification of UN plan for independence in Namibia (Res. 435). They favor constitu- tional agreements prior to elections in order to restrict the power of what is likely to be a SWAPO government. SAG officials welcome the proposal, acknowledging that they have sought these constitutional provisions for months.

April

4   *The Washington Post* reports that Reagan administration wants SA readmitted to the International Labor Organization following its 17-year exclusion from that body due to apartheid.

15   Reagan's Assistant Secretary of State for Africa, Chester Crocker, meets in Johannesburg with top SAG officials as part of 10-nation tour of Africa. Crocker is not officially confirmed by Senate until 9 June.

16   Frontline States meet in Luanda on eve of Crocker visit and condemn US policy toward Namibia, and Reagan's attempts to repeal the Clark Amendment. They reiterate full support for SWAPO.

27   State Department announces SA Foreign Minister Pik Botha has been invited to US for talks with Reagan officials, thus drawing immediate and irate criticism from African diplomats at UN.

29   House Africa Subcommittee unanimously rejects Reagan's attempt to repeal the Clark Amendment which prohibits US covert opera- tions in Angola. Full Foreign Affairs Committee later (12 May) sustains the Subcommittee's action by a vote of 19 to 5.

30   US, France and Britain block 5 UN Security Council resolutions aimed at pressuring SA to allow independence in Namibia.

May

8 *The Washington Post* reports that J.A. Parker, who headed Reagan's transition team at the Equal Employment Opportunity Commission, and who is President of the Lincoln Institute, a conservative think tank dealing mainly with black issues, has registered as a lobbyist for the Venda bantustan. Parker will be paid $3,000/month "to establish a presence" in Washington for this 'country' that is recognized by only one government: Pretoria.

13 At Houston airport US Customs agents seize $1.2m in weapons bound for SA. The guns are a different caliber from SA's and Customs agent Charles Conroy says "the UNITA forces in Angola were the obvious place for the final destination of the arms." Two British arms dealers arrested in the raid say they were hired by the South African Armaments Corp. Ltd. (ARMSCOR) to buy the arms from Colt Industries of Connecticut. False documents were used to conceal the purchaser and destination.

13 Senate Foreign Relations Committee votes 10-2 to repeal Clark Amendment, but prohibits aid to Angolan rebels unless the President (1) explains to the chairman of the committee and its House counterpart why the assistance is needed, and (2) certifies that "substantial progress" has been made toward "an internationally acceptable settlement" in Namibia, and that the assistance will not impede that progress. This comes one day after House Foreign Affairs Committee voted 19-5 to retain Clark Amendment.

14 Congressman William Gray (D-PA) introduces bill (H.R. 3597) aimed at prohibiting new US investment in SA.

14-15 Reagan, Haig, and other top officials meet with SA's Foreign Minister Pik Botha to discuss closer relations between the two nations. Botha's visit is the first by any African official with Reagan in the White House. In return for a more open friendship with the US, Reagan wants Pretoria to agree to eventual independence for Namibia. Some 500 antiapartheid activists demonstrate in front of the White House. Botha later sends secret letter to Reagan/Haig supposedly recapping the agreed basis for cooperation but US officials find the Botha version of the talks so politically unacceptable they choose not to respond.

16 Senior State Department official announces "constructive engagement" policy toward SA. Although failing to give details, the official says the new policy "represents above all the reality that there is a limit on the US capacity to use negative pressure to achieve positive results in South Africa."

17 *The Sunday Tribune* (SA) reports that General Vernon Walters, former deputy chief of CIA and top ambassador-at-large for Reagan administration, is to start "exploratory talks on the forma-

tion of a South Atlantic Treaty Organization that would include the armed forces of South Africa and South American dictatorships." Later reports suggest this attempt to form a SATO foundered because Brazil valued its ties to Angola and other African states more than a potential alliance with SA.

21 Rockefeller Foundation study, *South Africa: Time Running Out*, calls for arms and investment embargoes against SA until blacks get "effective share" of power.

30 Jack Anderson reports that the US embargo on computer sales to SA police and military, imposed in 1978 by Carter, has not been enforced. Article lists numerous cases in which firms such as Control Data, IBM, and Digital Equipment Corp. supplied high-tech items to police, military, and labor-control system.

31 Afro-American lobby group, TransAfrica, releases leaked State Department documents detailing meetings between USG and SAG officials. The memos reveal a shared interest in objectives: limiting Soviet influence in southern Africa and bringing SA into western alliance. However, important differences on Namibia: USG needs internationally accepted settlement but SAG knows free elections will bring SWAPO to power.

June

1 *The New York Times* reports on contents of leaked State Department documents outlining Reagan strategy for southern Africa: "They have decided on a strategy of tying final agreement on independence for South-West Africa to a withdrawal of Cuban forces from Angola and a commitment by the Marxist leaders in Angola to share power with Western-backed guerrillas, and they say they believe that key black-ruled African states will have no choice but to go along."

4 Compromise agreement reached between 3,500 striking black workers and SA subsidiaries of Ford, GM and Firestone.

9 Following 85 days of delay by Sen. Jesse Helms (R-NC), Senate votes 84-7 to confirm Chester Crocker as Assistant Secretary of State for African Affairs.

10-11 US Deputy Secretary of State William Clark meets in SA with Prime Minister P.W. Botha, Foreign Minister Pik Botha, and Defense Minister Magnus Malan. As follow-up to Pik Botha's talks in Washington last month, the discussions focus on Namibia and what concessions Pretoria will need to make in order for Washington to move into closer alliance.

11-12 Oliver Tambo, president of the African National Congress of South Africa, meets in New York with executives of top US corporations and foundations. Represented at the meetings are Ford, General Motors, General Electric, Citibank, Bank of America, Manufacturers Hanover Trust, Carnegie Foundation, and the African American Institute.

17 Testifying before the House Subcommittee on Africa, former UN Ambassador Donald McHenry says that efforts to arrange elections in Namibia have failed because Pretoria is convinced that free elections would result in a SWAPO victory, and therefore SAG has adopted a strategy of endless delay. "What is likely is that they will gulp up all of the carrots and ask for more."

27 The 50-member Organization of African Unity (OAU) unanimously adopts resolution condemning the Reagan administration for its "collusion with the South African racists." The resolution accuses Washington of attempting to circumvent UN efforts for a fair settlement in Namibia. Reagan administration responds with harsh attack on OAU declaration, saying it was based on "serious distortions" of US policy.

30 Reagan administration issues new guidelines which allow the sale of medical equipment and supplies to the SA military on a case by case basis, even if they are intended for military use. The new regulations also permit sale of metal detectors used in combating sabotage.

July

• US Customs agents conclude 5-month investigation into conspiracies to ship military hardware to SA. Three men are found guilty but given light probation sentences. They are Jack Holiday, who runs a California aviation sales company, Gideon Schiff, who holds Canadian and Israeli citizenship, and Omar Aly Khan, described as an engineer holding British and Indian citizenship.

1 *The Christian Science Monitor* reports that Portugal is urging the Reagan administration not to support UNITA's war against the Angolan government.

14 US State Department announces it will issue visas to SA rugby team, the Springboks, to tour the US. The 30-member team includes several members of the SA armed forces, thus raising questions regarding possible violation of UN arms embargo.

24 SAG announces it has denied request from visiting US congressional delegation to meet Nelson Mandela. Mandela's daughter, Zinzi, is quoted as saying that if they wanted to speak to the ANC "it would have been easier for them to have contacted an ANC representative right at their doorstep in Washington."

29   One of America's most sophisticated aircraft, the EC 135 Advanced Range Instrumentation Aircraft, arrives in SA for 3-day visit. Although manned by military personnel, the plane is under contract to NASA and therefore is classified as a 'civilian' aircraft, not in violation of the UN arms embargo. Purpose of visit is to track US satellite launch.

August

- Officials from US and Swaziland sign agreement to open CIA listening post in Mbabane, capital of Swaziland. Station will open in late 1981 under control of Foreign Broadcast Information Service which, although listed as organ of Commerce Department, is functionally part of the CIA. Normal operations will include monitoring electronic and print media but critics speculate that microwave eavesdropping on regional telephone/telegraph communication is other possible function.

- Two SA military officers begin training at US Coast Guard station on Governor's Island, NY.

- Group of SA nuclear experts visits Goodyear's Portsmouth Gaseous Diffusion Plant in Piketon, OH, where uranium isotopes are purified.

7   TransAfrica charges that US officials knew SAG was creating assassination squads to kill ANC leaders exiled in neighboring states. (Joe Gqabi was gunned down in Salisbury the previous week.) Randall Robinson, Director of TransAfrica, says his information comes from classified Defense Department documents. State Department declines comment.

13   France's Ambassador to SA calls on the diplomatic community to protest Pretoria's brutal treatment of squatters near Capetown. USG refuses to go along with protest.

14   Brooklyn offices of the South African Military Refugee Aid Fund (SAMRAF) are ransacked and hundreds of files and other records are stolen. Clifton Westraad, a South African exile and war resister who had been seeking assistance from SAMRAF, later shows up in SA, exchanging the stolen goods for safe reentry.

15   8 Days magazine reports that retired Chase Manhattan Bank Chairman David Rockefeller has written to Reagan, and met with White House officials urging a more friendly US policy toward Angola. Rockefeller reportedly praised Angola's "liberal investment code and sound economic management policies," saying Angola's economy seemed poised for a takeoff. Rockefeller and other corporate leaders advised the White House against supporting Jonas Savimbi.

23 SADF launches "Operation Protea" invasion of southern Angola. Roughly 10,000 troops, headed by 32 tanks and 82 armored vehicles converge on Angolan army base at Xangongo. Farther north, Cahama and Chibemba are bombed by SA Air Force. SA Defense Minister Magnus Malan denies invasion is taking place. From this point on, SA troops will permanently occupy large sections of southern Angola.

26 Angolan army halts SA advance at Cahama. Angola appeals to UN for assistance. France, UK, and West Germany condemn SA invasion. US State Department says attack must be seen in light of Cuban troops in Angola and SWAPO attacks in Namibia, refuses to condemn invasion.

26 Columnist Jack Anderson reveals top-secret CIA planning document aimed at increasing US capabilities for destabilizing regimes such as Libya, Cuba, and Angola. "CIA chief William J. Casey is eager to stir up mischief for such unfriendly regimes...and he isn't too particular whom the CIA finds to do the dirty work." Anderson quotes the document as saying that increased support to antigovernment forces is a "critical need...especially in Angola."

27 Jack Anderson discusses CIA plans to revert to interventionist ways, but because the agency's own capabilities have been weakened "the CIA is using foreign forces, some of them of dubious reliability, to carry out its clandestine activity." "CIA strategists are actively planning undercover operations in cooperation with such countries as Egypt, Israel, Turkey, Pakistan, Guatemala, South Africa, South Korea and the People's Republic of China."

28 Rep. Howard Wolpe (D-MI), chairman of the House Africa Subcommittee, holds press conference following 8-member congressional tour of Africa. Findings: SA was obviously a "police state" with anyone opposing the system facing tremendous risk; it was evident that SAG had made a sharp turn to the right; Reagan policy had effectively strengthened right-wing whites; all blacks they talked to in SA and elsewhere were skeptical of Reagan policy and supported the Clark Amendment; there was growing alarm in African states over SA's military aggression.

29 Chester Crocker gives major address on southern Africa to the American Legion. Mostly standard rhetoric, but some tidbits: "South Africa is an integral and important element of the global economic system" and "the Reagan Administration has no intention of destabilizing South Africa in order to curry favor elsewhere." The Reagan administration "seeks to build a more constructive relationship with South Africa." Main goal is to strengthen the "proponents of reform and nonviolent change." Claims that "UNITA represents a significant and legitimate factor in Angolan politics."

31   US breaks with its major European allies to veto UN Security Council resolution condemning SA for recent invasion of Angola. Congressional Black Caucus calls the veto "a dastardly act" that marks "an all-time low in the morality of the Reagan administration's foreign policy." Rep. Walter Fauntroy (D-DC) warns that this veto will encourage SA to continue its "reckless military action" in the region.

31   High-level delegation from OAU warns Reagan administration that African nations are running out of patience for SA to grant Namibian independence.

September

- Some 100 representatives of 24 corporations and 40 religious agencies meet in New York to discuss the role of US investment in SA. The conference does little to bridge gap between church activists, who say investment in SA supports apartheid, and corporations, who say their activities benefit blacks.

3   A new SA force invades Angola from Namibia, driving east toward Mavinga. Observers speculate that the new invasion is designed to resupply scattered UNITA bands. Angolan government puts total number of South African troops in Angola at 15,000.

3-14 UN General Assembly holds special session on Namibia, votes 117-0 (US abstaining) to condemn SA for illegal occupation of Namibia, also criticizes US for 31 August veto in Security Council.

4   UN General Assembly votes 117 to 22(US) to reject SA's credentials and expel SA representatives. Previous expulsion was November 1974.

11 France's Socialist government authorizes SWAPO and ANC to open offices in Paris. Prime Minister Francois Mitterand says that France's "commitment of friendship with the United States does not include supporting all the world's dictatorships."

13 US Voice of America radio begins broadcasting from a 50,000 watt AM station in Selebi-Pikwe, Botswana. This brings millions of people in SA's most populous industrial area (Pretoria-Johannesburg) within reach of VOA propaganda. Signal also covers Harare and Bulawayo, Zimbabwe's two major cities.

15 *The Christian Science Monitor* reports on recent meeting of National Council of Churches which criticized Reagan administration for supporting apartheid by tilting toward SA.

16 *Africa Confidential* reports that Globe Aero Ltd. of Lakeland, FL "is supplying a substantial number of planes to South Africa for

possible counter-insurgency purposes." Globe Aero purchases planes, modifies them according to clients' specifications, and then flies them to foreign destinations. "...Globe pilots enjoy close cooperation with South African military personnel..." On several occasions Globe pilots have created international incidents (see 22 April 1979, 22 April 1980, 30 September 1980, and 4 February 1981).

21   Chester Crocker and SA's chief negotiator on Namibia, Brand Fourie, meet secretly in Zurich to discuss US proposals for settlement in Namibia.

23   Writing in *The Washington Post*, Bishop Desmond Tutu, General Secretary of the South African Council of Churches, says western corporations in SA are making minor improvements for a small number of workers without challenging apartheid: "They are making apartheid more comfortable rather than dismantling it."

29   After heated debate, the World Medical Association, meeting in Lisbon, votes to readmit SA to membership following 5 years exclusion from the group. US supports readmission. Black African delegates walk out after vote.

29   At American University in Washington two security guards are injured and sociology professor Gary Howe is arrested as 300 students protest presence on campus of SA Embassy official Leo H. Evans.

30   US Senate votes 66-29 in favor of repealing the Clark Amendment. Sen. Nancy Kassebaum (R-KS), chair of Senate Subcommittee on Africa and author of the repeal proposal, argues that less than half the current Senate were members when the Clark amendment was passed in 1975 and "it's time to wipe the legislative slate clean."

30   In compliance with standing US policy, State Department denies visas for two Bophuthatswana officials. Because US does not recognize the bantustans as independent countries, it does not accept passports issued by the 'homeland' governments.

October

●   US Commerce Department grants license to export Sperry Univac 1100 series computer to Atlas Aircraft Corp., a subsidiary of South African Armaments Development and Manufacturing Corp. (ARMSCOR) in which SAG owns controlling interest.

1   *Windhoek Advertiser* (Namibia) reports US officials offered SAG secret bilateral security agreement if SAG would accept UN elections in Namibia.

4   Washington, DC police defuse bomb addressed to home of Sybrand Visagie, SA's top representative to IMF. No one claims responsibility for bomb.

early   SAG warns foreign correspondents in SA, especially Americans, that they must be more careful in their reporting. Last week, SAG gave Cynthia Stevens, Associated Press correspondent, two weeks to leave country without specifying reason. SAG also initiated legal proceedings against Nat Gibson, UPI bureau chief, for alleged disclosure of defense-related information. Charges later dropped.

9-11   Meeting at Riverside Church in New York, the Conference in Solidarity with the Liberation Struggles of the Peoples of Southern Africa brings together politicians, church leaders, trade unionists, antiapartheid activists and representatives of ANC and SWAPO to hear testimony and plan strategy for supporting the liberation movements.

13   *The Sowetan* reports that 25 members of the US Congress have written a letter to the SA Minister of Justice expressing 'concern' over the detention and banning of black journalists.

17   State Department denies that recent granting of visas to top SA police officials is change in US policy. Reagan officials claim that standing policy only prohibits visits of active military officials, not police or retired military personnel. Retired SA Army major general Neil Webster, leading a 13-member delegation to US, claims visit is a "breakthrough" that could not have occurred prior to Reagan administration.

19   *Rand Daily Mail* reports that the Associated Actors and Artists of America (the umbrella organization representing all major actors' unions) decides that its members should boycott SA. The association, which includes the Screen Actors Guild, has over 240,000 members through its affiliates.

22   *The Christian Science Monitor* reports that "the latest US 'carrot' being dangled before South Africa appears to be enriched uranium fuel pellets." Four Reagan nuclear specialists are holding talks with SA officials to work out details on how US can supply Pretoria with enriched uranium for its 1,800-megawatt Koeburg plant due to begin operating in 1983.

28   District of Columbia officials cancel rugby match between Durban (SA) Collegians and local Potomac Rugby Union players following outcry by area residents and politicians.

November

- AFL-CIO Executive Council establishes a special fund to assist black trade unions in SA. They contribute $25,000 and encourage affiliated unions to contribute to the fund. The fund will finance training for SA unionists, and support other US labor programs aimed at fostering AFL-CIO-style trade unionism in SA. As part of its effort to stimulate US trade union support for SA workers trying to organize US corporate subsidiaries, the AFL-CIO has asked SA unions for a list of American companies they have targeted for unionization efforts.

early   West German government and US Lutheran officials protest the torture of 4 Lutheran ministers by bantustan police in SA. A Lutheran parishioner and leader of the Black Peoples Convention was killed while in detention.

7   US International Communication Agency cancels government-sponsored tour of Africa by US scholar, John Seiler, due to his article criticizing Reagan policies in southern Africa.

December

- Israeli Defense Minister Ariel Sharon makes unpublicized 10-day trip to SA and war zone in Namibia. Sharon denounces UN arms embargo and asserts SA needs more weapons.

early   UNITA leader, Jonas Savimbi, meets in Washington with top US officials, including Chester Crocker and Alexander Haig. This marks Savimbi's third trip to Washington since Reagan took power. Official US policy regards UNITA as a "legitimate political force" in Angola, and informed sources believe Reagan is supplying indirect aid to Savimbi.

4   *Rand Daily Mail* reports that an American naval attaché, Commander Royce L. Caplinger, has been posted to the US embassy in Pretoria as a further step in Reagan administration's plan to improve relations. Caplinger to take post 26 January 1982.

4   Ciskei bantustan receives "independence" from SAG. More than 2 million black South Africans automatically lose their citizenship. In keeping with traditional policy, US refuses to recognize Ciskei as a nation.

10   Chester Crocker testifies to Congress that: "While the basic structure of apartheid remains intact, there was some improvement in practice on some human rights fronts through non-enforcement of some existing racial laws."

11   W. Haven North and Ted D. Morse, officials of the US Agency for International Development's Africa bureau, complete a 2-week

tour of SA during which they questioned SA officials, educators and black political groups on their attitudes toward possible US aid to black schools in SA.

17   UN General Assembly adopts by large majorities 16 resolutions condemning apartheid, calling for greater international pressure on SAG, and seeking more support for victims of apartheid. US isolated in opposition, votes Yes on 2, No on 12, and abstains on 2.

1982

January

3   *The New York Times* reports that in SA Reagan's 'constructive engagement' policy "is generally viewed with suspicion or hostility by politically sophisticated blacks."

15   Launching year of intense but unsuccessful diplomacy on Namibia, Chester Crocker meets Angolan Foreign Minister Paulo Jorge in Paris. This follows Crocker meetings in London with SA's Director General of Foreign Affairs Brand Fourie.

20   US Navy Ensign Stephen Baba of Maryland is sentenced to 8 years imprisonment by military tribunal for passing electronic-warfare secrets to SA Embassy in Washington, DC.

25   Joel Lisker and Bert Milling, staffers of Jeremiah Denton's (R-AL) Senate Subcommittee on Security and Terrorism, are in SA to check on links between ANC/SWAPO and Soviets in preparation for upcoming hearings on same subject.

February

•   AFL-CIO's African American Labor Center (AALC) launches a SA program to provide leadership training to black trade unions. Original grant of $875,000 is intended to help "close the wide gap" between black and white workers in SA.

5   Trade union leader, Dr. Neil Aggett, is found dead in his cell at security police headquarters in Johannesburg. He becomes 46th South African—the first white—to die in political detention since 1963. Death sparks largest sympathy demonstrations since 1977 death in detention of Steve Biko.

9   US State Department releases annual human rights report containing criticism of SAG for bad prison conditions, torture, large number of crimes carrying harsh sentences, etc.

9   Two House subcommittees (Africa, International Economic Policy and Trade) hear testimony regarding USG controls on exports to SA. Evidence presented that Reagan has weakened restrictions, US has provided important technology (e.g., computers).

10   PACE commercial high school, funded by some 70 US companies in SA, officially opens in Soweto. School will ultimately enroll 600 students at $1,400/year tuition for training in commercial, administrative and secretarial skills. American Chamber of Commerce in SA says the PACE school "will provide a source of commercially well-trained blacks...and enhance the image of business, both here and overseas."

22-23   Top SA military officials, including Lt. Gen. P.W. van der Westhuizen, chief of staff for intelligence of SADF, meet with State Department officials, including Deputy Secretary Walter Stoessel.

25   UN Commission on Human Rights passes 4 resolutions condemning apartheid and calling for action against SAG. US officials stress "abhorrence of apartheid" but fail to support any of the measures.

26   Reagan administration implements new export guidelines lifting ban on sales of certain nonmilitary items to SA police and military. These will include computers, helicopters, and airplanes. Since the 1963 UN arms embargo, 5 US presidents imposed trade restrictions on SA police/military but Reagan reverses this 20-year trend.

26   Donald deKieffer, for 9 years a paid agent of SAG and now general counsel in White House Trade Representative's office, leaves for SA to discuss US trade policy with US businessmen and SAG officials.

28   OAU adopts resolution condemning US, Britain, and Israel for "collaboration in economic, military and nuclear fields with the racist regime of South Africa."

28   National League of Cities conference in Washington unanimously passes resolution calling for divestment of public employee pension funds from companies doing business in SA and Namibia.

28   SAG names Dr. Brand G. Fourie as new ambassador to US. Fourie holds an MA from New York University and has worked over 40 years on foreign affairs for SAG.

March

2   Nearing the end of a 10-nation tour of Africa, David Rockefeller, retired chairman of Chase Manhattan Bank, says he does not think African Marxism is a threat to the US or to American business in Africa.

11   State Department says they have eased longstanding restrictions on admitting SA military officers into US in hopes of facilitating Namibia negotiations.

18-19   Antiapartheid activists, UN officials, and African diplomats meet in New York as part of special UN sessions calling for "Solidarity with Peoples Struggling Against Racism and Racial Discrimination."

21   Former CIA Director Stansfield Turner visits Prime Minister Botha in Cape Town and takes special tour of war zone in northern Namibia.

22   Senate Subcommittee on Security and Terrorism begins several days of hearings regarding connections between Soviet Union and liberation movements in southern Africa. Chester Crocker states his belief that the Soviets do not have a grand design for southern Africa.

24   Senators Edward Kennedy (D-MA), Paul Tsongas (D-MA), Rudy Boschwitz (R-MN), and Larry Pressler (R-SD) introduce Senate Concurrent Resolution 77 calling for, in part, denial of export licenses "for items controlled for national security purposes and any helicopters or airplanes destined for South African military and police entities." This and similar non-binding resolution in House, H.Con.Res. 304, are in response to Reagan's 26 February 1982 relaxation of export controls regarding SA police/military. Both resolutions die in committee.

26   US Commerce Department issues license for Control Data Corp. to export a Cyber 170/750 computer to SA's government-run Council for Scientific and Industrial Research (CSIR). Critics argue the computer has nuclear and cryptographic applications.

29   Senate confirms Herman Nickel as new US Ambassador to SA. A former editor of *Fortune* magazine, Nickel wrote article for *Fortune* praising US investment in SA which was reprinted by Ernest Lefever's Ethics and Public Policy Center. Nickel also wrote piece for Lefever attacking boycott of Nestlé infant formula and it was later learned that Ethics and Public Policy Center received $25,000 from Nestlé.

30   House Africa Subcommittee chair, Howard Wolpe (D-MI), introduces staff report highly critical of USG efforts to enforce arms

embargo against SA. Report recommends strengthening US enforcement efforts, and supports call for Congressional investigation of CIA role in shipping arms to SA.

April

9   US votes in favor of UN Security Council resolution asking SAG to commute death sentences of 3 ANC members convicted of treason for an attack on a rural police station. SAG eventually commutes death penalty to life imprisonment.

13   *The Washington Post* reports that 2 US firms, Edlow International of Washington, DC, and SWUCO, Inc. of Rockville, MD, played a key role in SA acquiring nearly 100 tons of enriched uranium despite USG opposition.

20   Dr. Edward Teller, "father of the H-bomb," is in SA to address Pretoria University's Institute of Strategic Studies on the subject "The Influence of Technology on 20th Century Warfare."

26   US Department of Commerce approves sale of 2,500 shock batons to SA. The batons, designed for "crowd control," each carry shock of 3500 volts. Sale is violation of Section 502(b) of the Foreign Assistance Act which prohibits exports to police/military in nations with consistent human rights violations. Batons are shipped in August, and sale is only discovered in September. Commerce Department officials say license approval was "an honest mistake," a "simple, unfortunate screw-up."

30   According to a report published by The Africa Fund in NY, Harry Oppenheimer's SA-based Anglo-American conglomerate is rapidly expanding its investments in North America.

May

5   Col. Mike Hoare, leader of SA mercenaries who failed in 25 November 1981 coup attempt in Seychelles, says the CIA had been informed beforehand of coup plot.

13   In a letter to Sen. Charles Percy (R-IL), Commerce Secretary Malcolm Baldrige details the Reagan administration's shift to a more "flexible" policy with regard to the export of US nuclear technology to SA. The new policy applies to "dual use commodities," i.e., technology that can be used for nuclear power generation but also has military applications. The letter states that USG has approved 5 export licenses for nuclear technology to SA since May 1980. Items shipped include vibration test equipment used to test warheads and ballistic re-entry vehicles, and computers and multichannel analyzers that can synthesize data from hundreds of cables at nuclear test blast sites. The letter was in response to Sen. Percy's inquiry into a pending US sale of 95 grams of helium-3, which can be used to make tritium for a thermonuclear device.

13 House Foreign Affairs Committee votes to reimpose export restrictions on nonmilitary goods to SA police/military.

14 Six-man investigative team of SA Catholic Bishops' Conference issues report detailing allegations of widespread atrocities against civilians by SA troops in Namibia. Report lists numerous charges of rape, looting, torture and murder.

17 Theo-Ben Gurirab, SWAPO UN representative, after attending meetings in Tanzania is denied re-entry visa by US State Department in violation of UN rules. Informed speculation is that Gurirab is on special White House list of undesirable organizations and individuals to be prevented from attending UN Special Session on Disarmament which opens 7 June.

17 New daily newspaper, *The Washington Times*, starts in the nation's capital. Funded by Rev. Sun Myung Moon's Unification Church, with one-third of staff 'Moonies', many editorial positions are held by people with long tradition of support for white minority rule (e.g., James Whelan, Smith Hempstone, John McGoff, Carlyle Reed, and William Rusher).

17 IMF issues confidential report criticizing apartheid as a serious impediment to SA economic growth.

June

10 Two House Subcommittees (Africa, International Economic Policy and Trade) approve two resolutions restricting US business involvement with SA. H.R. 3597, by Gray (D-PA), would prohibit new investment, establish mechanism to monitor compliance, and establish civil and criminal penalties. H.R. 3008, by Solarz (D-NY), would make mandatory fair employment codes, prohibit import of Krugerrands, and ban loans to SAG. Passed same day is H.R. 6393, by Bingham (D-NY), seeking to reimpose 1981 export controls on US goods to SA military/police. None will become law.

17 Mayor of Philadelphia signs into law the strongest divestment bill passed by any major American city to date. It requires some $70m of the city's pension funds to be withdrawn over a 2-year period from US corporations doing business in SA.

July

4 In SA for meetings with officials, Sen. Sam Hayakawa (R-CA) praises Reagan policy toward SA. A member of the Senate Africa Subcommittee and confidante of Reagan, Hayakawa says that friendly ties between the two governments will be better than criticism.

mid Some 13,000 auto workers strike Ford, GM, and Volkswagen plants in Port Elizabeth and Uitenhage over wage dispute.

17 Jack Anderson reports that State Department is blocking entry to US of SA veteran antiapartheid activist Victor Goldberg, a founder of the SA Congress of Democrats. Because State has declared that expired organization a communist front, Goldberg can join his wife and son living in Louisiana only if he renounces principles of the Congress of Democrats. Ironically, SAG has issued visa to Goldberg.

August

● Three top SA military officers, Lt. Gen. van der Westhuizen (head of SA's military intelligence), Maj. Gen. Lloyd (commander of SA forces in Namibia), and Gen. Geldenhuys (Chief of the Army), meet with Reagan officials in Washington.

3 Columbia University announces it will give honorary doctorate to Bishop Desmond Tutu, Secretary General of SA Council of Churches and outspoken opponent of apartheid. This is only third time such award given to non-New Yorker.

5 AFL-CIO Executive Council gives annual George Meany Human Rights award to Dr. Neil Aggett, SA trade unionist killed in police detention earlier this year, and Chief Gatsha Buthelezi, head of KwaZulu bantustan.

10-20 Ford Motor Company closes all 4 of its plants in SA for 10 days due to labor dispute with black workers. Though Ford is generally considered one of the more enlightened employers, black workers struck over wages and the precise form wage bargaining should take. Company offered only $1.90/hr. as minimum wage.

11 Three black American jurists, including a federal judge, are detained and questioned for 2 hours by security police in Ciskei. The 5-member tour of back American jurists, invited to SA by a local black lawyers' association, also reports being tailed by plain-clothes police in Cape Town and being questioned at a roadblock on their way to a pass-law court. US District Court Judge Thelton Henderson of San Francisco says that the experience, while distressing, helped him to understand what it is like to be black in SA.

14 *The Economist* reports: "For the umpteenth time South Africa has launched a major military operation into southern Angola just when the Namibia negotiations have reached a sensitive stage. It raises again the old question: does the South African government really want a settlement in Namibia..."

25   World Alliance of Reformed Churches expels the 2 all-white Dutch Reformed churches in SA (roughly half of SA's Afrikaners are members) due to the "heresy" of apartheid.

26   South African Patent Office awards patent for a new type of telescopic gun sight to American Daniel R. Shepherd.

26   Following a meeting with black American leaders and a representative of the ANC, Kentucky governor John Brown cancels plans to promote business ties between SA and his state. Move is considered major blow for SAG officials who had worked for more than a year on establishing formal trade ties with this state government.

30   Henry Kissinger meets in Pretoria with P.W. Botha, Foreign Minister Pik Botha, and Defence Minister Magnus Malan. Kissinger supports Reagan's "constructive engagement" policy. Though not on official mission, Kissinger admits he will report to USG leaders.

September

4   Following summit meeting in Lusaka, Zambia, Frontline States' leaders issue statement categorically rejecting US attempt to link Namibian independence with Cuban withdrawal from Angola.

6   Speaking at a conference in SA Henry Kissinger warns that current SAG reform efforts "will not provide the ultimate solution to the problem of power sharing." Suggests more rapid change.

6-17   AFL-CIO delegation visits SA for discussions with labor, management and government. Group includes Vice Presidents Sol Chaikin and Frederick O'Neal, International Affairs Director Irving Brown, and Director of African American Labor Center Patrick O'Farrell. Some of SA's more militant black unions refuse to meet with the Americans.

11   *Rand Daily Mail* (SA) reports on 1978 US State Department cable explaining secret plans by US companies to help SA circumvent international trade sanctions. The cable, from the US Embassy in Pretoria, says US firms "have already made plans to camouflage their operations through subterfuges arranged with affiliates in other countries."

16   Bishop Desmond Tutu, general secretary of SA Council of Churches, ends 19-day visit to US during which he met with church and government leaders. Tutu is critical of apartheid and Reagan administration's "constructive engagement" policy. Upon returning to SA his passport is revoked.

26   *The Washington Post* reports that ARMSCOR (SAG's armaments corporation) has launched international marketing drive for new

mobile artillery system developed with aid of data obtained from US corporation, Space Research of Vermont. The "G6" 155mm cannon is reportedly capable of firing a tactical nuclear warhead. Other sources, e.g., former CIA officer John Stockwell, say the CIA helped SAG develop this long-range weapon.

27   CIA Director William Casey meets in SA with top government and military leaders to discuss security situation in region. Some press reports claim Casey proposed a US-backed *cordon sanitaire* to secure SA's borders. Visit is part of several-nation tour with Casey meeting intelligence chiefs in Nigeria, Zaire, Zambia, and Mozambique.

30   Senate Foreign Relations Committee holds closed meeting on proposed export of helium-3, a dual-use nuclear item, to SA.

October

1   UN General Assembly adopts Cuban-sponsored resolution calling for clemency for 3 ANC members facing death penalty in SA. Vote is 136 to 1 with 1 (US) abstention.

11   US Embassy in Johannesburg says US diplomats are making first official visits to the 'homelands' Washington has never recognized as independent nations. They say visits are aimed at gathering information and do not represent change in policy of nonrecognition.

14   Western diplomats in Pretoria report that negotiations on Namibia are deadlocked and there is no longer any chance for an early settlement. State Department officials continue to express optimism.

20   UN General Assembly passes resolution calling on IMF to refrain from granting any credits to SA. Vote is 121 to 3 (US) with 23 abstentions.

21   Speaking at University of Witwatersrand, Robert S. McNamara, former Secretary of Defense and president of World Bank, predicts that white rule in SA will be overthrown in racial explosion within 20 years, and advises US to make clear it will not aid whites when showdown comes.

25   As part of 7-nation tour of Africa, Senators Mark Hatfield (R-OR), Paul Laxalt (R-NV), and Thomas Eagleton (D-MO), meet in Pretoria with Prime Minister P.W. Botha, Foreign Minister Pik Botha, and Defence Minister Magnus Malan. They also meet with KwaZulu leader Gatsha Buthelezi.

28   US and SA officials sign consular convention that codifies protections and immunities granted to consular staffs of the two nations.

Next week the 2 countries will bring number of attachés in each other's capitals to full strength.

November

1   As part of 4-day official visit to SA, US Information Agency Director, Charles Wick, meets with SA cabinet ministers to explore ways to increase cultural and information exchanges. Later, in testimony to Congress, Wick will say: "Some of them have marvelous minds, those black people over there."

3   *The Washington Post* reports on 2 US intelligence documents: one, an extensive CIA analysis of the ANC, says ANC is gaining strength and may intensify guerrilla struggle; the other is brief report that SAG is considering suppression of news regarding successful guerrilla attacks in order to guard white morale.

3   Despite unprecedented opposition, the IMF grants $1.1b loan to SA. Thirty-five members of Congress opposed the loan, and some members of IMF executive board argued that SA did not technically qualify, but US representative Richard Erb argued strongly in favor. Amount of loan is roughly equal to cost of SA's war in Namibia and Angola over past 2 years.

8   *Daily News* (SA) reports that a gasoline storage depot on the northern Natal coast owned by Mobil Oil Co. was heavily damaged by bombs and ensuing fire.

8   *The Star* (SA) reports that, according to US Department of Commerce data, US investment in SA has increased 13.3% since start of Reagan's "constructive engagement" policy.

10   Vice President George Bush leaves on 7-nation tour of Africa during which he is severely criticized for friendly US relations with SAG. Critics even include moderate African leaders such as Kenya's Daniel Arap Moi.

13   Following meetings in Lagos between Vice President George Bush and Nigerian Vice President Alex Ekwueme, joint communique details wide rift between the 2 governments regarding SA and Namibia. Nigeria favors mandatory sanctions against SA but US insists on linking SA pullout from Namibia with Cuban expulsion from Angola.

13-18   Two top SA police officials, Maj. Gen. Lothar Neethling (Chief of Police Forensics) and Maj. Gen. H.V. Verster (Head of Counter-Terrorism Unit), attend annual convention of International Association of Chiefs of Police in Atlanta. They also visit Washington.

23   ABC TV News producer, Christopher Isham, reports that 12,000 feet of film and 80 reels of sound tape, part of a documentary on

black trade unions in SA, were maliciously erased while in the custody of South African Airways. Lab experts agree the film was sabotaged. ABC crew reshoots footage and eventually airs documentary, including some damaged sections.

27 Thirty-one member states of the OAU issue communique claiming that the Reagan administration's "increased economic, military and nuclear collaboration" with SA have "emboldened it to carry out even more brutal repression against opponents of apartheid."

29 *Africa News* publishes interview with Winnie Mandela, wife of imprisoned ANC leader Nelson Mandela, in which she says: "The West and those countries that have trade links with South Africa are those who are protracting our struggle. They are prolonging our suffering. Although they know that they are doing so, they also know that we will take over this country..."

December

2 Two House subcommittees (Africa, International Economic Policy and Trade) hear testimony regarding USG controls on exports to SA. Administration officials claim restrictions are still in effect but evidence shows Reagan has removed many export restrictions.

8 Chester Crocker holds third meeting in 4 months with Soviet Deputy Foreign Minister Leonid Ilichev regarding southern African affairs.

9 UN General Assembly passes 10 resolutions condemning apartheid, and calling on member states (especially Israel and NATO countries) to stop collaborating with SAG. Each measure passes by large majority. US votes No on 9, and 1 passes without vote.

13 UN General Assembly unanimously adopts (US not participating) resolution condemning SA for 9 December raid into Lesotho and calling on Security Council to prevent future SA aggression against neighbors.

15 UN Security Council unanimously approves resolution 527 condemning SA for its "premeditated, aggressive" raid against Lesotho on 9 December that killed 42 people.

16 Powerful bombs explode in suburban New York offices of IBM Corp. and South African Railways, causing extensive damage but no casualties due to phone warning by the "United Freedom Front." In a communique the group denounces SA raid on Lesotho, US support for $1.2b IMF loan to SA, and corporate support for apartheid. Little is known of UFF.

16 Bartholomew Hlapane and his wife are assassinated in their Soweto home. On 25 March 1982 Hlapane, a former ANC

member, had testified against the ANC to the US Senate's Sub-committee on Security and Terrorism.

20   Diplomatic sources confirm that Daniel J.J. Opperman, SA's top intelligence agent in Washington, returned to SA in mid-October under unusual circumstances. *Rand Daily Mail* reports that Opperman had been involved in "harassment" of US antiapartheid groups. Two Washington antiapartheid groups, TransAfrica and the Southern Africa Support Project, had reported office break-ins during the previous year. State Department refuses to comment on why Opperman was forced to leave.

31   Michigan Governor William Milliken signs into law bill requiring state's colleges to divest holdings in companies doing business in SA.

1983

January

10   Speaking to some 250 delegates and observers at the 13th annual African-American Institute conference in Harare, Zimbabwean Prime Minister Robert Mugabe sharply criticizes the Reagan administration for its warm relations with SA and Reagan's insistence that a settlement in Namibia be coupled with a Cuban troop withdrawal in Angola. Also present is Rep. Howard Wolpe (D-MI) who comments on the "loss of American credibility" with African leaders since Reagan began "going easy on racist South Africa."

11   Massachusetts legislature overrides Gov. Edward King's 31 December 1982 veto of bill requiring divestment of $100m of state pension funds invested in SA.

18   *The Star* (SA) reports that Reagan administration has blocked move by Lt. Gen. Charles Sebe, chief of Ciskei security police, to visit US to buy helicopter. But State Department did allow Bophuthatswana cabinet ministers to visit US on SA passports early last year.

25   Reagan administration publishes new export regulations lifting ban on sales to SA of all but the most sensitive non-military items. This is third relaxation of export restrictions in less than a year.

27 *The New York Times* announces that Chrysler Corp. plans to sell its 25% stake in Sigma Motor Corp., the third largest auto and truck maker in SA. At an estimated value of $50m, this is one of the largest US business withdrawals from SA.

February

3 In the US for talks, KwaZulu Chief Gatsha Buthelezi says that SAG plan for Coloured and Asian representation in parliament amounts to slamming the door in the face of Africans, and that US should not support the proposed reforms.

8 Atlanta City Council passes measure proclaiming formal welcome to SA draft evaders. Other cities with similar policies include Santa Monica, Baltimore and Washington, DC.

8 During an 8-nation tour of Africa, UN Secretary General Javier Perez de Cuellar rejects US efforts to link the withdrawal of Cuban soldiers from Angola with the independence of Namibia.

10 Following a 2-year battle with US immigration authorities, SA draft evader Dominic Holzhaus wins grant of political asylum in US. He is first to do so under Reagan administration.

15 In testimony before House Africa Subcommittee, Chester Crocker admits it was USG, not SAG, that "raised a new proposition" by linking demand for Cuban troop withdrawal from Angola with Namibian independence. The linkage issue "was our effort. I am not denying that." Crocker claims chance for settlement is "reasonably good" but he is roundly criticized by Subcommittee members.

15 In a *Washington Post* editorial Senate Africa Subcommittee Chair, Nancy Kassebaum (R-KS), criticizes Reagan policy toward SA. On recent trip to SA she learned that blacks see constructive engagement "as a *carte blanche* for Pretoria." Quiet diplomacy has not achieved enough and "a stronger and more public stance" is now necessary.

16 Executive Committee of the Council of Churches in Namibia, representing 81% of Namibian Christians, sends letter to members of the western Contact Group stating that "the Cuban presence in the sovereign state of Angola is not a threat to the Namibian people." Letter criticizes USG for linking Namibian independence to Cuban troop withdrawal.

19 Stuart K. Spencer, one of Reagan's top campaign strategists, registers with the Justice Department as a paid foreign agent of SAG. Spencer helped manage Reagan's campaign for California governor in 1966, was a key strategist in the 1980 presidential

victory, and still consults with Reagan on the 1984 campaign. Sources close to Reagan downplay any conflict of interest, saying SAG is just another client.

March

2   *Cape Times* (SA) reports that Reagan administration last week blocked moves by third world members of International Atomic Energy Agency (IAEA) to oust SA.

3   Over 150 activists and legislators attend Capitol Hill briefing on US-SA nuclear relations. Sponsored by Washington Office on Africa, antiapartheid and antinuclear groups, session focuses on legislation, HR 1020 by Rep. Charles Rangel (D-NY), that would ban all nuclear exports to SA and end training for South Africans at US facilities.

3   *Cape Times* (SA) reports that US State Department has agreed to deliver to SA a quilt for Winnie Mandela autographed by 45 members of congress and incorporating official colors of USA and ANC. Gesture was initiated by Sen. Paul Tsongas (D-MA) after he heard of police raid on Mandela's home in which police confiscated bedspread with ANC colors.

12   Meeting in New Delhi, India, Seventh Conference of Heads of State of Non-Aligned Countries condemns Reagan administration's constructive engagement policy toward SA, charging that it encouraged Pretoria "in its intensified repression of the South African people, its escalating aggression against its neighbours, and its determined intransigence over Namibian independence."

16   SA police search Johannesburg home and office of *Washington Post* correspondent Allister Sparks ostensibly looking for evidence that Sparks illegally quoted banned activist Winnie Mandela. (In November 1983 Sparks will be charged with 2 crimes: quoting Mandela in a Dutch publication, and reporting in the London *Observer* on a TransAfrica allegation that SA security police have a special assassination unit for killing opponents in neighboring countries. If convicted, Sparks could be fined several thousand dollars and jailed for several years. The charges eventually will be dropped.) Bernard Simon, writer for AP-Dow Jones service, is arrested for allegedly removing documents from Sparks' office. Police also threaten *Newsweek's* SA bureau chief, Holger Jensen.

17   State Department spokesman John Hughes, reacting to yesterday's SA police raid on Allister Sparks, "strongly condemns" SAG efforts to restrict or intimidate press. Referring to recent State Department human rights report, Hughes notes that "there has been a progressive deterioration of press freedom in South Africa over the last decade."

17   Chester Crocker meets at State Department with Lt. Gen. Johann
      Coetzee, SA's chief of security police. State says talks are part of
      Namibia negotiations but fails to explain what SA's internal secur-
      ity chief has to do with Namibia. It is Coetzee's force that is
      responsible for the ongoing harassment of the South African
      Council of Churches for their vocal opposition to apartheid.

23   Mr. Henning Pieterse, a vice-consul for information at SA consu-
      late in New York, is given police escort from Orange County
      Community College in Middletown, NY as students shout epithets
      and refuse to let him address a political science class.

April

● Group of Harvard undergraduates establish the Endowment for
   Divestiture as a new technique for pressuring universities to divest
   from companies operating in SA. Graduating seniors who often
   donate funds to Harvard's endowment can now give to this
   divestiture fund: the money will only be turned over to the
   university when Harvard divests from all SA holdings.

1   Winding up a 4-day visit to Washington, Zambian President Ken-
     neth Kaunda criticizes US for failure to pressure SAG for change.
     He compares tough US reaction to repression in Poland with mild
     US criticism of SAG. Kaunda says he supports Cuban presence in
     Angola as necessary for protection against South African raids.

4   Commander Barreiros, until recently chief of staff of FNLA, says
     CIA is still assisting FNLA against MPLA government in Angola.
     Barreiros left FNLA because of disillusionment with leadership,
     and surrendered to Angolan authorities.

6   State Department criticizes SA police shooting of Saul Mkhize, a
     black accountant who was leading villagers of Driefontein in
     resistance to SAG efforts to forcibly remove them from lands they
     had occupied for many generations. Although unarmed, Mkhize
     was shot in the chest at close range.

12   US Ambassador to SA, Herman Nickel, hands over $25,000 from
     his discretionary fund to SA charitable organizations for drought-
     relief activities.

13   In 11th round of US-Angola talks on Namibia, top Angolan
     official, Lt. Col. Manuel Alexandre Rodrigues, meets in Washing-
     ton with Secretary of State George Shultz. No progress reported.

21   As part of growing opposition to US policy in southern Africa,
     coalition of 24 religious, political and labor groups assail Reagan's
     constructive engagement policy. Coalition includes NAACP, Uni-
     ted Auto Workers, Lutheran World Ministries, Congressional Black

Caucus, National Urban League, National Bar Association, American Federation of State, County and Municipal Employees, Americans for Democratic Action, and United Church of Christ. They issue a report, *Namibia: The Crisis in US Policy Toward Southern Africa*, highly critical of Reagan's insistence on linkage between Namibia settlement and removal of Cuban troops from Angola.

22   *The Star* (SA) reports on top-secret US intelligence document leaked to TransAfrica, showing Reagan administration had advance knowledge of SA military buildup for invasion of Angola last August but chose to do nothing about it.

24   Black SA journalist Joe Thloloe, who in 1982 became the first foreign recipient of the Louis Lyons award given annually by Harvard's Nieman Foundation for "conscience and integrity in journalism," is sentenced to 2½ years in jail for possessing a banned book. Thloloe spent 10 months in jail before the trial. He was also held for 8 months in the late 1970s without ever being charged with a crime. Thloloe's jailing follows a series of recent actions against journalists.

25   French Foreign Minister Claude Cheysson criticizes US linkage of Namibian independence with Cuban troop withdrawal from Angola. He says "it is not appropriate that the Namibian people should serve as hostages" to be used in attaining other foreign policy goals.

25   Nedbank, the largest SA-owned banking group, opens branch in New York, becoming the first SA bank to have a full branch in US.

May

3   In passing State Department budget authorization bill, the House Foreign Affairs Committee accepts amendment that would prohibit importation of Krugerrands, ban commercial bank loans to SAG unless money was for social welfare, and require US firms in SA to abide by the Sullivan Principles. Amendments will not become law.

6   Rep. Robert Mrazek (D-NY) introduces House Concurrent Resolution 122 "expressing the sense of the Congress that the Republic of South Africa should cease its 'black spot' policy of removing black South Africans from their ancestral land and relocating them." Resolution calls for US condemnation of SA's homeland policy and continued non-recognition of bantustan governments.

10   In *Washington Post* editorial Rev. Leon Sullivan, board member of General Motors and author of Sullivan code of corporate conduct in SA, complains that over half US companies in SA have not

accepted his equal employment principles and of those who do participate in program one-third are receiving failing grades for non-compliance. He reasons that since these companies "have been the main beneficiaries of cheap labor and profits from this evil and unjust system and among its main supporters," they should either help change that system or be forced to withdraw.

19   Confidential staff report of the IMF criticizes the deleterious effects on economic growth of SA's apartheid policies. Report never mentions the word 'apartheid'.

26   In New York address to the foreign ministers of key black African states, Secretary of State George Shultz asserts that the main obstacle preventing SA from granting independence to Namibia is the presence of Cuban troops in Angola.

27   House Foreign Affairs Committee approves subcommittee recommendation to restore controls on exports to SA police/military that were instituted in 1978 under Carter but lifted by Reagan.

June

5   City College of New York awards honorary law doctorate to Nelson Mandela. Degree is accepted for Mandela by Rev. Maxime Rafransoa, general secretary of the All African Council of Churches, because US State Department denied request from City College president to facilitate delivery of degree to Mandela or have Winnie and Zinzi Mandela come to NY.

6-12   Nineteenth summit of heads of state of the Organization of African Unity "strongly condemns the Reagan Administration for its self-proclaimed alliance with the racist Pretoria regime, the violation of the arms embargo and policy of 'constructive engagement'. . . ."

23   Speaking before the National Conference of Editorial Writers in San Francisco, Under Secretary of State for Political Affairs, Lawrence Eagleburger, gives the most detailed defense of administration policy in southern Africa in 2 years. Critical of apartheid, the speech is seen as a response to growing criticism of Reagan administration's friendly relations with Pretoria.

25   In *Washington Post* interview, Bishop Desmond Tutu, General Secretary of SA Council of Churches, calls Reagan policy toward SA an "unmitigated disaster." Church leader says: "We find it galling that the leader of the so-called free world should be hobnobbing so closely with our oppressors."

27   *Business Week* reports the Reagan administration "has quietly laid plans to bolster trade relations with South Africa, but it is keeping

the decision under wraps to avoid criticism from civil rights groups."

30   *Sunday Tribune* (SA) reports that the South African Council of Churches at a recent national conference adopted divestment measures instructing member churches to withdraw financial and other support from companies and other institutions that are engaged in defending apartheid.

July

8   Writing in the *New Statesman* (Br.), Martin Bailey reports on a secret 1979 cable from US Embassy in SA to then-Secretary of State Vance summarizing a secret SA study on economic sanctions. The cable cites the report to the effect that "multinationals, including US subsidiaries, are determined to undercut any sanctions action and have already made plans to camouflage their operations through subterfuges arranged with affiliates in other countries." The cable also notes that Pretoria's "stake in the multinationals is very large, not only for obvious economic reasons but because they exercise a restraining effect on policymakers abroad."

11-13 Meeting in Vienna, UN-sponsored International Conference on the Alliance Between South Africa and Israel, attended by dozens of governments and non-governmental organizations, presents documentation and criticism of growing military and economic ties between the 2 states.

26   In Senate confirmation hearing, Thomas Ellis, a Reagan appointee to Board for International Broadcasting which oversees Radio Free Europe and Radio Liberty, admits that he owns extensive holdings in SA, belongs to all-white country club, and is a former director of the Pioneer Fund which financed research into theories that blacks are genetically inferior to whites. He recently spent 12 days in SA at expense of SAG. When asked about apartheid he refuses to criticize SAG, saying it is doing the best it can in a bad situation.

28   *The Sowetan* (SA) reports on an address by Dr. John Dommisse to the World Federation of Mental Health, meeting in Washington, DC. Dommisse, an expatriate SA psychiatrist, calls for international censure of SA's medical bodies because of their silence on the adverse effects of apartheid on the health of blacks.

29   *The Star* (SA) reports that more than 200 US participants in the World Council of Churches' sixth general assembly meeting in Canada signed a statement to President Reagan opposing US policy toward SA. Referring to US policy as "destructive engagement," the statement criticized the economic support to SA pro-

vided by US corporations and the International Monetary Fund, and the "US policy which supplies arms to South Africa through Israel—thereby evading the UN arms embargo against South Africa."

30 Columnist Jack Anderson reports on confidential cable from US consulate in Johannesburg stating that US investment in SA "is probably in excess of $14.6b," not the $2.6b figure "we have always glibly bandied about." Cable notes that US investors own 57% of mining shares on Johannesburg stock exchange, and US bank loans to SA total more than $4b. Cable concludes: "All of this suggests that the potential for U.S. disinvestment could be more important to the South African economy than we had previously assumed."

August

• *Africa Now* reports that Reagan officials admit refusing to vote for African Development Fund loan to Angola for political reasons. MPLA regime is on list of alleged human rights violators whose requests for credit are to be blocked. SA is not on list.

1 In what will become some of the heaviest fighting of the 8-year Angolan civil war, UNITA troops, actively assisted by SA planes and troops, begin major offensive in Angola.

3 House of Representatives passes International Financial Stability and Recovery Act (referred to as IMF authorization bill) which includes amendment introduced by Julian Dixon (D-CA). The amendment directs US representative to IMF to "actively oppose" any IMF loans to "any country which practices apartheid."

4 Lesotho notifies USG that due to economic and military pressure from SA it will be forced to expel some 3,000 black SA refugees residing there. In addition to a military assault in December 1982 that killed 42 people in Lesotho's capital, Maseru, SAG has closed its border with Lesotho, thus keeping Lesotho migrant workers from traveling to their jobs in SA (a major source of income for Lesotho).

10 World Council of Churches concludes annual assembly representing 300 denominations with roughly 500 million Christian members. Assembly denounces apartheid, saying that racism destroys the "human dignity both of the racist and the victim"; calls on churches to support liberation movements and others opposing apartheid; calls SWAPO the "legitimate representative of the Namibian people" and calls for independence of Namibia.

10 Two Soweto men, Jacob Machigo and Peter Moloi, are imprisoned for 3 years and 1 year for possession of cassette with pro-ANC song by Harry Belafonte and Miriam Makeba.

14   Attended by 124 nations, the UN World Conference to Combat
      Racism calls for heavier sanctions against SA and condemns Israel
      for growing collaboration with SA in military and economic
      fields. Proposed measures to put more international pressure on
      SA pass by vote of 104-0 with 10 abstentions. The US and Israel
      boycott the 2-week conference because of UN resolution equating
      Zionism with racism.

16   Operating under a federal program to investigate illegal shipments
      of military equipment to unfriendly nations, US Customs officials
      seize 6 aircraft in Northeast Pennsylvania that were bound for
      Namibia. The single-engine Mooney 201s were confiscated after
      officials found discrepancies in the shipper's export declarations.
      The investigation was referred to US District Attorney in Scran-
      ton.

18   Zimbabwe's Prime Minister Robert Mugabe condemns US policy
      toward SA saying Reagan's constructive engagement policy has
      encouraged SA aggression against its neighbors and has made SA
      "more intransigent" regarding a settlement in Namibia. Mugabe is
      scheduled for an official visit to Washington in September.

18   Investigators from US Justice Department's Criminal Division
      visit ANC's UN Mission office in New York and demand access to
      ANC files. ANC refuses but Justice Department warns ANC and
      SWAPO that it intends to inspect their files, correspondence and
      financial records. This represents a new level of harassment by the
      Reagan administration.

27   Speaking to several hundred thousand demonstrators in Washing-
      ton, DC, to commemorate the 20th anniversary of Martin Luther
      King, Jr.'s historic march on Washington, Rev. Allan Boesak, SA
      Coloured minister and President of the World Alliance of
      Reformed Churches (70 million members worldwide), denounces
      US policy toward SA and calls for increased activism against
      apartheid. Other speakers at march, including Rev. Jesse Jackson
      and NAACP Director Benjamin Hooks, denounce apartheid and
      US support for SAG.

September

6   City Council of Washington, DC, passes Bill 5-18 requiring DC
      government to divest some $60m in city employee pension funds
      from banks and corporations doing business in SA. (All DC
      legislation must be approved by Congress, and in March 1984
      they allow Bill 5-18 to become law.)

6   US immigration judge dismisses deportation proceedings against
      SA poet and antiapartheid activist Dennis Brutus, thus granting
      asylum in US. Decision ends 2½-year effort by Reagan administra-
      tion to deport Brutus.

8   As part of growing ties between Israel and bantustan governments, Ciskei officials announce purchase of "about six" Ameri-
can-built aircraft from Israel and agreement that Israeli Air Force
instructors will train Ciskei pilots.

13   Following talks at the White House between Reagan and Prime
Minister Mugabe of Zimbabwe, Reagan aide explains that principal disagreement between them is over Mugabe's "urgent request"
that US drop demand that Cuban troops withdraw from Angola
before settlement in Namibia.

14   In a House Africa Subcommittee hearing on political change in
SA, Prof. Thomas Karis details the growing strength of the ANC,
and Prof. Stanley Greenberg explains how recent SAG reforms are
designed to divide the African population and perpetuate minority rule.

14   Singer Harry Belafonte and tennis star Arthur Ashe officially
launch new phase in the cultural boycott of SA. Their recently-
formed organization, Artists and Athletes Against Apartheid
(AAAA), includes among its members Muhammed Ali, the OJays,
and the National Football League Players Association. They hope
to convince US performers not to visit SA. According to Randall
Robinson, head of TransAfrica and one of the chief organizers of
AAAA, the group hopes to reach a membership of 10,000.

14   US Securities and Exchange Commission announces settlement of
3-year probe into questionable financial relations between SAG
and conservative US publisher John McGoff. SEC had charged
that McGoff, newspaper magnate and friend of Gerald Ford, had
illegally failed to disclose $11.3m received from SAG to purchase
US newspapers, including *The Washington Star*. McGoff and his
holding company, Global Communications Corp., were not
judged guilty or innocent but were let off by promising not to
break SEC rules in the future.

23   Six Democratic presidential candidates endorse pending legislation aimed at limiting trade and investment ties to SA. Letter
endorsing amendments to the Export Administration Act, introduced by Rep. Stephen Solarz (D-NY), criticizes Reagan's constructive engagement policy saying it "has produced neither substantial democratization within South Africa nor a settlement in
Namibia."

27   *The New York Times* reports that the State Department has
approved request from 7 US companies to provide some $50m
worth of technical services to SA's Koeberg nuclear power plants
near Cape Town.

October

1   US AID announces $3m grant over 4-year period for black SA businessmen.

2   SA press reports Reagan administration has opened a special trade promotion office in Johannesburg with the goal of increasing US–SA trade by $1b per year. Under the Commercial Foreign Service of US Commerce Department, the new office goes against traditional USG disclaimer that "we neither encourage nor discourage" trade with SA but is consistent with earlier moves by Reagan to ease trade restrictions.

3   Detroit Deputy Police Chief Richard Dungy complains that 3-man SA police delegation to convention of International Association of Chiefs of Police is on a "shopping expedition" for law enforcement hardware.

3   *Africa News* reports announcement by Colorado Coalition Against Apartheid (comprised of religious, peace and community organizations) that SAG has decided not to open consulate office in Denver as planned. Reagan administration had approved the diplomatic expansion but CCAA collected over 3,000 signatures on petition opposing the move.

5   *The Guardian* (Br.) reports that SAG has again revoked the passport of Bishop Desmond Tutu, General Secretary of the South African Council of Churches, this time preventing him from attending an African-American Institute seminar in the US.

6   *Rand Daily Mail* reports US bank loans to SA rose sharply in 1982 to nearly $3.7b but mostly consisted of short-term credits because of bankers' concern over political situation. Major lenders include Citibank, Chase Manhattan, Morgan Guaranty, Bank of America, and Manufacturers Hanover.

6-9   SA's Vice President, Alwyn Schlebusch, meets in Washington with George Bush, Chester Crocker, Senate Majority Leader Howard Baker (R-TN), Senate Minority Leader Robert Byrd (D-WV), and Speaker of the House Tip O'Neill (D-MA). The meetings with O'Neill and Byrd were arranged by the law firm, Smathers, Symington and Herlong, paid agents of SAG.

7-9   Three hundred college students from around US meet in NY to plan antiapartheid strategy. They agree to hold 2 weeks of coordinated action 21 March–4 April 1984. The meeting is probably the most significant of its kind in past 5 years.

10   *Newsweek* reports that CIA "training, arms, and financial assistance are given to the [UNITA] military forces in Angola."

11   SA Embassy in Washington holds day-long conference for some 150 US corporate executives aimed at convincing them: 1) SA is changing for the better, and 2) US firms should resist divestment movement and continue investing in SA. Site of conference, Madison Hotel, is picketed by dozens of antiapartheid demonstrators.

mid   Over 100 US business executives meet secretly in Cape Town to discuss common problems. Meetings are addressed by P.W. Botha, Magnus Malan, Gatsha Buthelezi, and US Ambassador Herman Nickel.

17   SA commandos plant bombs on the roof of an apartment building in Maputo, Mozambique, injuring 5 people and damaging some ANC offices. Building is in a sensitive suburban area that also contains President Samora Machel's residence, military headquarters, and residences of many foreign diplomats.

25   Publication of *Seventh Report On the Signatory Companies to the Sullivan Principles*. Findings: roughly half of US firms in SA won't sign on, dwindling number of signatories willing to report on activities, one-third of those reporting receive lowest rating, and data suggesting that pay scales and training for blacks are not improving rapidly. Results cause Rev. Sullivan to criticize US firms for not doing enough.

27   House of Representatives approves Export Administration Act which includes 4 antiapartheid amendments that would limit US investment and trade with SA. Senate version of act will not include any antiapartheid provisions. Final compromise version will drop House amendments.

28   UN Security Council votes 14-0, with US abstaining, to condemn SA's "obstruction" of a Namibia Settlement, and rejects as "extraneous and irrelevant" the Cuban troop withdrawal issue.

November

●   Meeting in Nairobi, Kenya, the International Planned Parenthood Federation suspends membership of South African Family Planning Association because of apartheid.

●   City government of Santa Cruz, CA, decides to remove city funds from banks and corporations doing business with SA.

9   In a closed meeting at Exxon headquarters in NY, representatives of over 100 US corporations which have signed the Sullivan Principles discuss political problems associated with their holdings in SA. Many feel the Principles have been played out and deeper changes are needed. This year was the first in which a large

number of signatory companies (29 of 145) dropped out of the program.

17   Congress approves $1.5m for aid to human rights groups in SA to be administered by AID during 1984/85.

28   Meeting in New Delhi, India, the Commonwealth nations officially criticize US policy in southern Africa, calling on the Reagan administration to drop its demand for linkage between a Cuban troop withdrawal from Angola and independence for Namibia. The Commonwealth leaders, including Contact Group members Britain and Canada, blame US "misconceptions" regarding southern Africa on Reagan's "total preoccupation" with East–West competition.

December

● Yale University's senior class overwhelmingly approves a plan to keep their class fund from investments in SA. For next 25 years money donated by class of 1984 will be invested only in companies and banks not involved in SA.

● SA students enrolled in educational programs funded by USG are invited to meet with Chester Crocker and US Ambassador to SA Herman Nickel. The students vote to boycott the meeting, saying they do not want their scholarships politicized.

1   UN General Assembly strongly condemns SA for blocking independence of Namibia and urges the Security Council to adopt comprehensive mandatory sanctions against SA. US opposes measure.

5   For the second time in a week, UN General Assembly votes overwhelmingly in favor of mandatory sanctions against SA. US, NATO allies and Israel oppose the measures aimed at diplomatic, economic and cultural isolation of SA.

5   Bipartisan group of 13 senators and 90 representatives forms new congressional caucus that will "watch out for [human rights] activists around the world who are physically threatened" because of their work. The new group, Congressional Friends of Human Rights Monitors, was initiated by Rep. Tony Hall (D-OH) in cooperation with Americas Watch, Helsinki Watch and the Lawyers Committee for International Human Rights. One of the first cases is that of Father Smangaliso Mkhatshwa, general secretary of the Southern African Catholic Bishops' Conference and co-patron of the United Democratic Front, who was arrested in SA 30 October 1983 for political activities.

6   As Chester Crocker meets in Rome with SA Foreign Minister, R.F. Botha, SA military begins new offensive into southern Angola.

The 2,000-man force encounters stiff resistance from SWAPO, Angolan and Cuban forces. Invasion lasts over a month. SAG announces heavier casualties (21 dead, 1 captured) than in any previous invasion of Angola. Reagan administration fails to criticize invasion.

7 French government criticizes Contact Group on Namibia, citing the "unacceptable manuevering" by USG aimed at linking independence of Namibia with removal of Cuban troops from Angola.

19 As punishment for Zimbabwe's votes in UN against US on Grenada invasion and Soviet downing of Korean airliner, USG cuts Zimbabwe's AID funds almost in half, from $75m to $40m. The cuts come at a time when Zimbabwe is suffering from southern Africa's worst drought in a century. Prime Minister Mugabe denounces the action, saying "we would rather be without a single cent from any source if securing aid meant selling or compromising our sovereignty."

1984

January

6 UN Security Council censures SA for its recent offensive into southern Angola. Vote is 13-0 with 2 abstentions (US and Britain).

6 Report published by the American Friends Service Committee shows that the Reagan administration has allowed more commercial military sales to SA ($28m) than in previous 30 years combined.

12-23 South Africa Foundation sponsors all-expense paid trip to SA for 7 conservative members of Congress: Sen. Steve Symms (R-ID), Rep. Danny Burton (R-IN), Rep. Sam Hall (D-TX), Rep. Ken Kramer (R-CO), Rep. Manuel Lujan (R-NM), Rep. Eldon Rudd (R-AZ), and Rep. Robert Young (D-MO).

17 Speaking at debate among Democratic presidential candidates, Walter Mondale says he supports effort to ban Krugerrand sales in the US, prevent further US investment in SA, and extend embargo on military sales to SA. Sen. Gary Hart (D-CO) says he supports "all-out economic sanctions" unless SA agrees to implement fair labor practices.

21   US pop group Chicago arrives in SA to perform 6 concerts at Sun City, Bophuthatswana.

22   London *Observer* reports that US and SA officials held "secret meetings" in Zaire to discuss plans for supplying arms to UNITA. Report is based on leaked Zairean memo which also says Israeli military advisors are now in Zaire's Shaba province bordering Angola. Earlier report in London *Times* gave evidence that Israel was shipping arms to UNITA.

27   Democratic presidential candidate Jesse Jackson condemns Reagan policy of linking Namibian independence with Cuban troop withdrawal from Angola. He contrasts US opposition to martial law in Poland with friendly ties to SA, and says it is time US put Africa on a par with Europe in its foreign policy.

February

● The Manpower and Management Foundation (a SA business organization) and Israel United Appeal (SA's equivalent of United Jewish Appeal) pay former Secretary of State Alexander Haig more than $30,000 to make an 8-day tour of SA and Namibia, meeting with top government and corporate officials.

7   Bipartisan group of congressional representatives introduce bill HR 430 calling on SAG to release Nelson Mandela from prison and Winnie Mandela from banning orders. Rep. George Crockett, Jr., (D-MI) member of Congressional Black Caucus, leads the effort.

10   State Department issues annual human rights report with evidence that SAG is guilty of arbitrary arrests, denial of fair trials, torture and degrading treatment of prisoners. Report discusses numerous laws restricting free speech, the press, freedom of movement, and political rights. "There remained no effective judicial remedy against the denationalization of blacks into 'independent' tribal homelands or against forced resettlements."

15   In a major speech to the World Affairs Council of Boston, Secretary of State George Shultz claims US role in southern Africa is "a force for constructive, positive change," despite the fact that since Reagan took power, Pretoria has mounted more numerous and more destructive attacks on its neighbors than ever before.

23   USG announces it is setting up a mission in Windhoek, the capital of Namibia, to help monitor the disengagement of South African forces from southern Angola. The move follows a 16 February cease-fire accord between Luanda and Pretoria.

March

2 *South Africa Digest* reports that American Chamber of Commerce in SA has sent a booklet to all US State Governors and members of Congress arguing that US corporations in SA are a progressive force for change.

5 In an article titled "U.S. Policy Seen Having Little Impact Inside S. Africa," *The Washington Post* cites critics in SA who claim that Reagan's policy "has actually encouraged Pretoria to be aggressive militarily with its neighbors and obdurate domestically." The piece also says SAG leaders are hoping for Reagan's reelection.

6 Washington-based Lawyers Committee for Civil Rights Under Law initiates suit in SA courts for release of 37 Namibians captured in a May 1978 SADF raid on Cassinga, Angola. Suit is intended to highlight plight of some 150 Angolans and Namibians held captive by SA army in Namibia. SAG will deny visa to US lawyer/activist Gay McDougall and in early May will dismiss case with no explanation and no right to appeal.

7 *The New York Times* reports that "a number of prominent trustees" of the city's enormous pension system are seeking to reduce their investments in firms doing business with SA. The New York City pension fund has nearly $20b in total assets, making it the fourth largest in the US. Mayor Koch opposes the move.

19 Ciskei President Lennox Sebe appoints an American, Dr. Robert Munro, to 5-year contract as chief advisor. Munro will resign after three weeks for "personal reasons."

20 In a meeting with US State Department officials, a delegation of 7 SA church leaders criticizes recent peace accords between SAG and neighboring states due to negative impact on SA blacks. Church leaders call on USG to pressure SAG for dialogue with SA blacks.

20 United Freedom Front, an underground US group, sets off bomb in Purchase, NY office of IBM in protest of that company's involvement in SA.

21 Student antiapartheid activists begin two weeks of nationwide protest focusing on US investment in SA, and seeking divestment of college funds linked to apartheid. Campaign is coordinated by American Committee on Africa, based on planning at October 1983 National Student Conference in New York.

29 Addressing a Washington luncheon for chief executive officers of US firms in SA, Secretary of State George Shultz claims that

"misperception and frustration are feeding public pressure for disinvestment." Pleading for more companies to sign the Sullivan Principles, he warns: "if U.S. business is seen to favor the status quo in South Africa, that sets powerful forces in motion—forces of immobility in segments of the white community, forces of resentment in the non-white communities—that will contribute to instability and tension."

April

4   Amnesty International issues report, *Torture in the Eighties*, finding "considerable evidence to show that political detainees were commonly tortured and ill-treated during interrogation by security police in South Africa."

15   Bomb explosion in northern Namibia kills two US diplomats involved in monitoring ceasefire between SA and Angola. They are the first Americans reported killed in the 17-year struggle for Namibian independence.

22   *The Washington Post* reports on a "major new study of poverty" in SA sponsored by the Carnegie Corp. of NY. The study began 2 years ago, involving over 400 researchers and 20 SA universities. Key finding is growing class division in black community: as the economy becomes more capital-intensive, requiring a smaller but more skilled workforce, some blacks benefit but the vast majority suffer growing impoverishment.

25   On the tenth anniversary of the Portuguese coup, a key turning point for southern Africa, the Washington Office on Africa sponsors a Capitol Hill briefing attended by 200 Africa experts. Among those criticizing Reagan's constructive engagement policy, Maj. Gen. Joseph Garba, Nigerian representative to UN and head of UN Special Committee Against Apartheid, says he believes USG is aiding UNITA in Angola.

26   Former National Security Advisor Zbigniew Brzezinski arrives in SA for 1-week tour organized by the South Africa Foundation, a public relations firm which generally supports Pretoria. Brzezinski gives speech on state security to SADF.

27   CBS Evening News reports that Miami-based international arms dealer Peter Mulak several years ago purchased Soviet-made weapons (AK-47s, grenades, rocket launchers, mines) from the Bulgarian export agency Kintex and resold them to SAG, which in turn passed them on to UNITA in Angola.

27   Reginald E. Petty, vice president of the African Development Foundation, resigns in protest over Reagan administration's failure to appoint a board of directors with African experience. The

Foundation, established by Congress in December 1980 to fund grass-roots projects in Africa, has not yet made any grants. The Reagan administration twice sought to kill the agency by rescinding its funding. When that failed, the Administration appointed an all-Republican board with no experience in Africa or development issues.

May

11   During a visit to the US that includes a meeting with President Reagan, Botswana's President Quett K.J. Masire claims SA is trying to force his landlocked country into signing a "nonaggression pact" that would harm Botswana's relations with fellow black African nations.

13   ANC guerrillas fire rocket-propelled grenades into a Mobil Oil Corp. refinery in Durban, SA, causing damaged estimated at less than $25,000.

26-27   At their 13th annual convention in Cincinnati, the Coalition of Black Trade Unionists criticizes the AFL-CIO-sponsored African-American Labor Center for its support of industrialization in SA. CBTU convention declares that such support fails to confront apartheid and encourages multinational corporations to build runaway shops using oppressed workers.

June

2   Some 25,000 people march in the largest antiapartheid demonstration in Britain's history to protest visit of SA Prime Minister P.W. Botha. The trip to London and other Western European capitals is the first for a SA prime minister since 1963. Although pro-apartheid forces claim this helps overcome Pretoria's international isolation, Botha wins no important concessions from Western leaders.

8   Addressing the seventh annual TransAfrica dinner in Washington, SWAPO president Sam Nujoma says that Reagan's "constructive engagement" policy is "the most pro-apartheid U.S. Africa policy ever." In addition to his detailed attack on US policy, Nujoma praises groups like TransAfrica for mobilizing support for Namibian independence.

11   Pope John Paul II meets with Prime Minister P.W. Botha and Foreign Minister Roelof Botha for 28 minutes in the Vatican. Following the meeting, the Vatican issues statement saying the Roman Catholic Church considers apartheid contrary to Christian principles and human dignity. Statement also affirms Vatican support for independence of Namibia. Bishop Desmond Tutu, Secretary General of the SA Council of Churches, criticizes the Pope's meeting with Botha as a "slap in the face to all the victims of apartheid."

18   Rev. Jesse Jackson and Senator Edward Kennedy (D-MA) address meeting of the UN Special Committee Against Apartheid. Jackson calls Reagan administration policy toward SA "an act of barbarism," and points to Reagan's "double standard" on human rights by punishing Poland with economic boycott while expanding economic, political and military ties to SA. Kennedy calls for greater restrictions on US trade with SA, and says: "Not since Nazi Germany has a government tried to do what South Africa is doing today with its uprooting of people and the forced relocation of its homelands policy."

July

7   Addressing members of the UN Special Committee Against Apartheid at the Vatican, Pope John Paul II condemns the forced displacement of black South Africans from their homes, and demands independence for Namibia.

26   Latest round of talks aimed at bringing independence to Namibia break down due to disagreements between SAG and SWAPO. Following several months of intense negotiations, this failure is severe blow to Chester Crocker and Reagan administration who were seeking a diplomatic success before November elections. Talks broke down over SAG efforts to circumvent UN plan for independence contained in Security Council Resolution 435.

October

16   Bishop Desmond Tutu, General Secretary of the South African Council of Churches, is awarded the 1984 Nobel Peace Prize for his outspoken opposition to apartheid. Tutu says his minimum demands are equal civil rights for all South Africans, abolition of the pass laws, an integrated education system, and an end to the forced removal of Africans to the "homelands." Tutu accuses the Reagan administration of "aligning itself with the perpetrators of the most vicious system since Nazism." He calls on outsiders to put political and especially economic pressure on SAG to end apartheid. The Nobel Peace Prize has been awarded to a South African once before, in 1960, to President of the African National Congress, Albert Luthuli.

Bibliography

Index

1. ADAM, Heribert, "Minority Monopoly in Transition: Recent Policy Shifts of the South African State," *The Journal of Modern African Studies*, 18, 4, 1980.

   Broad-ranging, insightful analysis of political trends within the state and opposition. "The most immediately significant shift" is emerging unity of Afrikaner and English bourgeoisies on a policy of "growth at any cost." But this "must not exclude an emerging black middle class" if it is to succeed. Discusses potential cooptability of different black groups, and the "Americanization of South Africa," i.e., the increasing importance of class, rather than race, divisions. 16 pp.

2. AFRICA COMMITTEE, National Council of Churches, et al., *Namibia: The Crisis in United States Policy Toward Southern Africa* (Washington, DC: 1983).

   A coalition of over 20 trade unions, church and civic groups produced this overview of the situation in Namibia and the failure of US policy to facilitate independence. Recommends Reagan administration drop its linkage of the Namibia issue with Cuban presence in Angola, and urges Congress and the Administration to press SA harder on granting independence to Namibia. 49 pp., several appended documents.

3. AFRICA FUND, "Fluor: Building Energy Self-Sufficiency in South Africa" (New York: Africa Fund, 1979).

   Concise overview of California engineering/construction company providing strategic services to the apartheid regime. Covers Fluor's worldwide operations, their Washington lobbying in favor of Pretoria, their role in SA energy development (especially SASOL), employee relations, list of stockholders, and antiapartheid actions against Fluor. 6 pp.

4. AFRICA FUND, "U.S. Business in South Africa: Voices for Withdrawal" (New York: Africa Fund, 1980).

   Useful resource for organizing opposition to US companies in SA. Reprints statements by South African, American, and international progressives calling for withdrawal of investment. 6 pp.

5. "Africa in the U.S. Elections, 1980," *African Index*, 4 October 1980.

   Reprints the Africa policy planks of the three major presidential candidates (Reagan, Carter, Anderson). 2 pp.

6. AFRICAN NATIONAL CONGRESS OF SOUTH AFRICA (ANC), *Fuelling Apartheid* (New York: UN Centre Against Apartheid, April 1980).

   Well-informed look at SA's oil needs, the search for self-sufficiency, collaborating regimes and companies, and potential for sanctions. Available free on request. 14 pp.

7. AFRICA REPORT, November/December 1980.

Special issue with 4 articles on SA-Israel relations. "The Club of Pariahs" by Kenneth Adelman covers the "pariah state network" of Israel/SA/Taiwan/S.Korea but discounts importance of growing SA-Israel ties. "The Special Relationship" by Alfred T. Moleah gives a more critical view of historical development of SA-Israel relations. "A View From Jerusalem" by Yosef Goell discusses conflict between Israel's need for economic/military ties and its "abhorrence of the racist philosophy" of apartheid. "Isolation and Cooperation" by Willie J. Breytenbach discusses similarities/differences between SA and Israel. 19 pp., numerous photos.

8. ALBRIGHT, David E., "Soviet Policy in Southern Africa," *African Index*, 3 November 1980.

Noted authority lists Soviet interests but cautions: "Southern Africa occupies a position well down the list of Soviet geopolitical priorities." Puts Soviet policy in context of military, economic, and political capabilities in the region, as well as global strategy. References. 4 pp.

9. AMERICAN COMMITTEE ON AFRICA, *ACOA Action News*, 10, Fall 1981.

This special edition of the quarterly newsletter reports on the first-of-its-kind conference on public investment and SA held in New York 12-13 June. (Conference brought together activists and legislators to plan divestment strategy.) Contains overview of conference, speech by Julian Bond, and basic facts/logic behind divestment campaign. 4 pp., many photos.

10. AMERICAN FRIENDS SERVICE COMMITTEE, *Namibia* (Philadelphia: AFSC, 1981).

Concise sections on history, current structure of Namibian society, SA domination, international diplomacy, and US policy. Lists resources. 44 pp., map, numerous photos, chronology.

11. AMERICAN FRIENDS SERVICE COMMITTEE, *Automating Apartheid: U.S. Computer Exports to South Africa and the Arms Embargo* (Philadelphia: AFSC, 1982).

Best single document on US computer firms' involvement in SA. Extensive data on SA police/military uses of US computer technology, and evidence showing lax US enforcement of export control laws. Secret documents reveal US firms' plans to beat sanctions. 107 pp., numerous tables and graphics.

12. AMERICAN FRIENDS SERVICE COMMITTEE, *South Africa: Challenge and Hope* (Philadelphia: AFSC, 1982).

Popular overview/introduction to subject. Covers historical background, various aspects of apartheid, geopolitical context, international opposition, and proposals for antiapartheid action by Americans. Discusses relevance of nonviolent strategies. 146 pp., 3 tables, chronology, glossary, 2 maps, bibliography.

13. AMNESTY INTERNATIONAL, *Political Imprisonment in South Africa* (London: Amnesty International Publications, 1978)

Discusses historical background, legal structures, treatment of prisoners (torture/deaths in detention), death penalty, civilian killings and banning. Gives profiles of 7 prisoners of conscience. Amnesty also published a 35-page update of this report in 1979. 108 pp., numerous photos.

14. ANDERSON, David, "America in Africa, 1981," *Foreign Affairs*, special edition, "America and the World, 1981."

Overview of Reagan policy on continent with subsection on southern Africa. "During the year the tilt by the Reagan administration toward South Africa has been reflected in a tilt toward the Right in Prime Minister Botha's internal policies and a more activist hard line toward neighboring countries." 27 pp.

15. ANDERSON, Jack, "Embargo on South Africa Called Farce," *The Washington Post*, 30 May 1981.

Enumerates cases of US corporate violations of the embargo on sale of computers and other sophisticated technology to SA police and military. "Slipshod or non-existent enforcement by the Commerce Department permits U.S. companies to ignore the ban with impunity." Cites confidential cables from US embassy in SA explaining how "most firms have been able to continue sales." Offending companies include IBM, Control Data, General Electric, and RCA. Reprints available from American Friends Service Committee.

16. ANDERSON, Jack, "CIA Said to Plan New Links With Anticommunists," *The Washington Post*, 26 August 1981.

Details "a top-secret planning document" by CIA Director William J. Casey. Recognizing that many authoritarian 'free-enterprise' regimes are threatened by popular rebellions, Casey argues for "improving the capability of the agency to rapidly escalate existing aid to anticommunist forces." Casey argues that this is a "critical need...especially in Angola." Document targets other regimes for covert destabilization (Cuba, Iran, Libya).

17. ANDERSON, Jack, "CIA Gearing Up for Operations with Foreigners," *The Washington Post*, 27 August 1981.

Follow-up on previous day's column reporting on classified documents. CIA is reverting to its old interventionist ways but due to limited capabilities "the CIA is using foreign forces, some of them of dubious reliability, to carry out its clandestine activity." The Agency is "actively planning undercover operations in cooperation with such countries as Egypt, Israel, Turkey, Pakistan, Guatemala, South Africa, South Korea and the People's Republic of China."

18. ANDERSON, Jack, "U.S. Understates Business Stake in South Africa," *The Washington Post*, 30 July 1983.

Reports on contents of classified cable from US consulate in Johannesburg, showing that total US investment ($14.6b) is much greater than figure usually cited (direct investment only—$2.6b). "...the administration's business-as-usual apologists have been seriously understating the total financial investment by U.S. banks and business firms...thus playing down the potential impact of 'disinvestment,' which is being urged by human rights advocates."

19. BAILEY, Martin, *Oil Sanctions: South Africa's Weak Link* (New York: UN Centre Against Apartheid, April 1980).

Detailed answers to some basic questions: How long could SA survive an oil cut-off? What impact would this have on the international community? What impact would it have on SA's neighbors? Would it in fact be possible to cut off SA's oil? 26 pp., 4 tables.

20. BAILEY, Martin, and Bernard Rivers, *Oil Sanctions Against South Africa* (New York: UN Centre Against Apartheid, 1978).

Comprehensive examination of SA's oil industry, impact of an oil embargo on SA and its neighbors, historical attempts to impose sanctions, and strategy for "an effective embargo." Free on request. 88 pp., 28 tables, map.

21. BAKER, Donald G., "South African Policy and US Responses," *International Affairs Bulletin* (SA) 3, 2, September 1979.

Review of Carter policy and relation to SAG strategies of change. "South Africa's Achille's heel" is paucity of cooptable black leaders. However, "South Africa will not make substantive changes" necessary to rectify this "unless considerable pressure is exerted by the outside world." Although programs to coopt a black elite are needed, the history of Rhodesian and US society shows that "unless the government itself mandates and enforces these changes, the private sector will not of its own volition implement such programs." 19 pp.

22. BAKER, James E., J. Daniel O'Flaherty, and John de St. Jorre, *Public Opinion Poll on American Attitudes Toward South Africa* (Washington, DC: Carnegie Endowment for International Peace, 1979).

Contains interesting information: "in response to a general description of the situation in South Africa, an overwhelming majority of the public (86%) condemned the present system"; majority support for the US 'doing something' about the situation; plurality support for "a range of activities including supporting black organizations...seeking peaceful change"; and a clear 'no involvement' response to possible developments such as "increased internal violence" and "increased Soviet activity in the area." Includes breakdown by race, education, and political affiliation. 42 pp., numerous tables.

23. BAKER, Pauline H., "South Africa's Strategic Vulnerabilities: The Citadel Assumption Reconsidered," *The African Studies Review*, xx, 2, September 1977.

Informed academic with years of government experience presents evidence that questions the ability of the white minority regime to survive without continued support from major capitalist powers. Insightful analysis in light of threats from Botha to "go it alone." 10 pp.

24. BALL, George W., "Asking for Trouble in South Africa," *The Atlantic*, October 1977.

Former Undersecretary of State and partner in Lehman Brothers investment firm criticizes many liberal precepts of US policy toward SA, but fails to come up with a fresh approach. His strategy for gaining "the confidence of both sides" is to show "sympathy for the blacks and sensitivity to the problems of the whites...we should quietly urge the prompt elimination of 'petty apartheid' and the progressive correction of more fundamental abuses...." 18 pp.

25. BARBER, James, and Michael Spicer, "Sanctions Against South Africa: Options for the West," *International Affairs*, July 1979.

Somewhat abstract discussion of "five broad lines of approach for the West" vis-a-vis sanctions: increased economic involvement, "communication," "disengagement," "graduated pressure," and "comprehensive sanctions." "The interests to be served by active pressure against South Africa are many." Admits that "the situation on the ground in Southern Africa" is the "most important factor," yet fails to discuss it. 16 pp.

26. BARRATT, John, "Changing Patterns in US-SA Relations," *International Affairs Bulletin* (SA) 4, 1, 1980.

Schematic overview of 1) interests in SA of various sections of US state and public, 2) US policy trends, 3) SA policy trends, and 4) recent developments in SA and the US that will affect future relations. 18 pp.

27. BARRON, Deborah Durfee, and John Immerwahr, "The Public Views South Africa: Pathways Through a Gathering Storm," *Public Opinion*, January/February 1979.

"...by almost a two-to-one margin (46-26 percent), Americans favor the United States and other nations putting pressure on the South African government to give blacks more freedom." Actions such as arms embargo and halting new investment are supported by "large segments of the public." Cautions that relative to other issues (e.g., protecting US jobs, securing energy supplies, etc.) opposition to dictatorships ranks low. The public "appears reluctant to sacrifice economic interests to the cause of human rights." 6 pp.

28. BATES, Timothy, "The Impact of Multinational Corporations on Power Relations in South Africa," *The Review of Black Political Economy*, 12, 2, Winter 1983.

Concise critique of thesis that US corporate involvement is a force for progressive change. Compares the "micro" reforms (e.g., integrated washrooms, and more training for some black workers) with "macro" obstacles such as capital-intensive nature of US firms, SAG's policies of tight labor control and inferior education for blacks, etc. 11 pp.

29. BEAUBIEN, Michael C., "The Cultural Boycott of South Africa," *Africa Today*, 29, 4, 1982.

Good overview of the various South African, US and international organizations pressing for cultural boycott of SA. Lists US athletes and entertainers who have been lured by Pretoria's big paychecks. Criticizes US voting record in UN. 12 pp.

30. BEIT-HALLAHMI, Benjamin, "Israel and South Africa, 1977-1982: Business as Usual—And More," *New Outlook*, March/April 1983.

Based on Israeli and foreign press, provides numerous details on cooperation in the military, nuclear, diplomatic and economic fields. Documents Israeli collaboration in SAG's policy of regional destabilization. Difference between Labor and Likud governments has been one of style, not substance. Predicts alliance between SA and Israel will grow. 5 pp.

31. BENDER, Gerald J., "Angola: Left, Right and Wrong," *Foreign Policy*, 43, Summer 1981.

Respected US expert on Angola gives tightly-argued overview of US policy. Discredits Savimbi and supporters such as de Borchgrave and Ledeen. Shows that Reagan policy is throwback to failed Nixon/Kissinger strategy. Argues that in response to Reagan overtures Pretoria has taken "a harder line internally and externally than it had taken in the Carter years." 17 pp.

32. BERMAN, Edward H., "Foundations, United States Foreign Policy, and African Education, 1945-1975," *Harvard Educational Review*, 49, 2, May 1979.

Examines "the way in which the relationship between US foreign policy and the major American foundations has helped to shape African educational policy." Concludes that "American philanthropy" (particularly Ford, Carnegie, and Rockefeller) "was at least partially motivated by the need to promote a sympathetic view of American political and corporate activity" which was considered necessary "to ensure both continuing access to African mineral resources and the continued cultural dependence of the newly independent nations on the western bloc." 35 pp.

33. BETTS, Richard K., "A Diplomatic Bomb for South Africa?" *International Security*, 4, 2, Fall 1979.

Overview of SAG's motives and capabilities for building nuclear weapons. Discusses US and Israeli involvement, and diplomatic implications of SA's nuclear capability. "If the moral and political aim of most of the rest of the world—genuine majority rule in South Africa—comes close to realization, so also will the nuclear threat." 25 pp.

34. BIERMANN, Werner, "US Policy Towards Southern Africa in the Framework of Global Empire," *Review of African Political Economy*, 17, January–April 1980.

Broad-ranging discussion puts US policy toward southern Africa in context of global strategy in the post-war period. Collapse of Portuguese colonialism necessitated US intervention to protect corporate and security interests. Shift in US policy was only tactical. "The utmost aim of US policy-making. . . is to prevent the emergence of socialist countries" possessing relative autonomy from the capitalist world market. Author is pessimistic regarding the ability of revolutionary regimes to break free of western domination. 15 pp.

35. BIKO, Steve, "Memorandum to Senator Dick Clark on American Policy Towards Azania (South Africa)," *African Affairs*, 77, 306, January 1978.

Criticizes US for failure to back up antiapartheid rhetoric with action. Lists "a few minimum requirements" for US policy: "cease showing any form of tolerance to Bantustan leaders," press for release of Mandela and other political prisoners, apply economic pressure through trade boycotts and withdrawal of investment, etc. 3 pp.

36. BISSELL, Richard E., *South Africa and the United States: The Erosion of an Influence Relationship* (New York: Praeger, 1982).

Conservative effort, utilizing limited sources, to argue that US lack of leverage on SA is due to objective conditions rather than lack of political will by US leaders. Curious omissions: "remarkably few 'facts' available" regarding US intervention in Angolan civil war, CIA aid to Angolan factions "did not involve South Africa," and SA's 5,000 troop invasion portrayed as "small number of commando units." 147 pp., index.

37. BISSELL, Richard E., and Chester A. Crocker, eds., *South Africa Into the 1980s* (Boulder, CO: Westview Press, 1979).

Ten essays treating various internal and international aspects, including: American views, SA's strategic value to the West, SA in Soviet strategy, African states as a source of change, and regional military situation. 254 pp., index, bibliography, tables.

38. BOSTON ORGANIZING COMMITTEE, *The Fight for Freedom in South Africa: and what it means for workers in the United States* (Boston, MA: BOC, 1979)

Primer on the connections beween anti-imperialist politics and the struggle for full democracy here in the US. Non-academic language used to explain apartheid as a part of world capitalism. Overviews US corporate/government support for apartheid, and the role of racism in both countries. Discusses the peoples' fight-back and warns: "We cannot separate our fight against apartheid in South Africa from the fight for equality in the United States. Both struggles must be part of a movement against the wealthy few who run this country and the whole imperialist system." 40 pp., numerous photos, maps, bibliography.

39. BOWMAN, Larry W., "The Strategic Importance of South Africa To The United States: An Appraisal and Policy Analysis," *African Affairs*, 81, 323, April 1982.

Comprehensive review and critique of the strategic arguments used to support friendly US ties to SAG (e.g., Cape Sea Route, minerals, Soviet threat). Successfully undermines these arguments both empirically and logically. Argues that Cold War approach will backfire because "support for South Africa, and visible ties with South Africa, is the one thing that will surely turn African opinion against the West and open opportunities for the Soviet Union." 33 pp., 2 tables.

40. BOYER, Sandy, "Divesting from Apartheid: A Summary of State and Municipal Legislative Action on South Africa" (New York: Africa Fund, 1983).

Details efforts in 26 states and 18 cities to withdraw public funds from companies doing business with SA. In 1982, "Massachusetts, Michigan, Connecticut and the cities of Philadelphia, Wilmington, and Grand Rapids all enacted legislation that will force the divestment of up to $300 million." 4 pp.

41. BRANAMAN, Brenda M., "South African–Israeli Relations," Congressional Research Service, Report No. 81-174 F, 30 July 1981.

Brings together extant sources, and focuses on implications for US policy. Discusses legal basis for US aid cutoff based on nuclear proliferation. "South African–Israeli relations have strained the relations of American Jews with American blacks. . . ." 19 pp.

42. BRANAMAN, Brenda M., "U.S. Relations with Black Africa: The Impact of a Close U.S.–South African Relationship," Congressional Research Service, 1 June 1982.

Enumerates actions by Reagan administration that have engendered "African dissatisfaction with the new U.S.-South African policy. . ." Discusses "possible African reprisals" against US. 27 pp.

43. BRANAMAN, Brenda M., "South Africa: Issues for U.S. Policy," Congressional Research Service, Issue Brief #IB80032, 6 April 1983.

Overview of recent developments in SA and various aspects of US policy. Deals with questions such as the arms embargo, nuclear cooperation, and divestment/economic embargo. Lists Reagan administration actions. Discusses relevant legislation. 30 pp., chronology.

44. BRATTON, Camille A., "A Matter of Record: The History of the United States Voting Pattern in the United Nations Regarding Racism, Colonialism and Apartheid, 1946-1976," *Freedomways*, 17, 3, 1977.

Critical analysis of USG's pro-SA voting record. Argues that USG has supported colonialism and white minority rule. 9 pp.

45. BUNTING, Brian, *The Rise of the South African Reich* (Harmondsworth, England: Penguin, 1964).

The definitive work on SA's ruling Nationalist Party's roots in Nazism. Well-documented history of the ideology and action of Afrikaner variant of fascism. Reveals that current rulers were actively opposed to Allied war effort in WWII. Good antidote to SAG/USG propaganda regarding need to support 'loyal allies.' 332 pp.

46. BURCHETT, Wilfred, and Derek Roebuck, *The Whores of War: Mercenaries Today* (Middlesex, England: Penguin, 1977).

Based on revelations of the Angola war-crime trials, this book argues that the current resurgence in the use of mercenaries by western powers "is caused by the need of governments to carry on military operations, without the support or even sometimes the knowledge of their electorates, against those who have taken up arms to free themselves from colonial and other oppression." Emphasis on Angola and the failure of British and US authorities to halt this illegal practice. 240 pp., 1 map.

47. BURCHETT, Wilfred, *Southern Africa Stands Up* (New York: Urizen Books, 1978).

Sympathetic account of liberation struggles in Angola, Mozambique, "Rhodesia," Namibia and SA by veteran left journalist. Provides needed insight into ideology and functioning of the nationalist movements. Especially good on Angolan civil war. 321 pp., several maps, chronology, index.

48. BURGESS, Julian, *Interdependence in Southern Africa* (London: Economist Intelligence Unit, 1976).

Dated but well-informed overview of infrastructural linkages (railroads, electricity, roads, etc.) throughout the southern Africa region. Provides useful and sobering insight into the problems of economic dependency confronting the liberation movements and independent black states of southern Africa. 98 pp., 29 tables.

49. BURGESS, Julian, et al., *The Great White Hoax: South Africa's International Propaganda Machine* (London: Africa Bureau, 1977).

Good introduction to how the white-minority regime attempts to clean up its image worldwide. Slightly dated (written before the Information Department scandal came to light). Includes section on SA's propaganda operations in the US. 119 pp., photos, tables, index.

50. BURNETT, Nicholas R., "The Israel–South Africa Connection," *The Nation*, 20 May 1978.

Competent overview. Touches on the history of the relationship, military and economic ties, foreign investment, and implications for US policy. 4 pp.

51. CABELLY, Robert J., "Solarz and South Africa," *African Index*, 10 June 1980.

Discusses congressional and executive positions on proposed legislation that would restrict US–SA economic relations. Useful list of reasons why such legislation doesn't stand much chance. Asserts that no antiapartheid legislation has ever been produced by either Africa subcommittee. 2 pp.

52. CAMPAIGN AGAINST INVESTMENT IN SOUTH AFRICA, "Summary of State and Municipal Legislative Action on South Africa," January 1981.

Provides details of efforts in 12 states to prohibit investment of public monies in companies profiting from apartheid. Public employee pension funds and government investments total hundreds of *billions* of dollars and are accessible to democratic control. Member groups of the Campaign include ACOA, AFSC, Clergy and Laity Concerned, ICCR, TransAfrica, United Methodists, and Washington Office on Africa. 6 pp.

53. CARTER, Gwendolen M., and Patrick O'Meara, eds., *Southern Africa: The Continuing Crisis* (Bloomington, IN: Indiana University Press, 1979).

Fourteen non-theoretical essays treat each country of the region, as well as international context, from liberal to left-liberal academic perspectives. 404 pp., maps, tables, bibliography, index.

54. CARTER, Gwendolen, M., and Patrick O'Meara, eds., *International Politics in Southern Africa* (Bloomington, IN: Indiana University Press, 1982).

Nine essays of uneven quality on topics including US policy (Robert Price), the communist states and southern Africa (David Albright), Western Europe and southern Africa (Christopher Hill), the role of donor agencies (Richard Horovitz), and the international moral protest (Colin Legum). 270 pp., index, bibliography, 2 maps, 6 tables.

55. CASON, James, and Michael Fleshman, "Dollars for Apartheid," *Multinational Monitor*, November 1983.

Reports on leaked State Department document, *U.S. Investment in South Africa: The Hidden Pieces*, which puts total US investment in SA at $14.6b, much higher than the $2.6b of dire'ct investment usually cited. Total includes $3.6b in short-term bank loans and over $8b in stocks. US investors account for 57 percent of shareholdings in SA mining firms (mostly gold). Document suggests that cutoff in US investment would be much more damaging than previously admitted. 3 pp.

56. CATHOLIC INSTITUTE FOR INTERNATIONAL RELATIONS, et al., *Torture in South Africa: Recent Documents* (London: CIIR/British Council of Churches/International Commission of Jurists, 1982).

Three human rights groups present documentary evidence of systematic torture of political prisoners. Describes numerous types of physical and psychological abuse regularly utilized by SA police. List of deaths in detention, 1963-1982. 46 pp.

57. CELL, John W., *The Highest Stage of White Supremacy: The Origins of Segregation in South Africa and the American South* (Cambridge: Cambridge University Press, 1982).

Interesting historical comparison set in 19th and early 20th centuries, illuminating race/class relationship. Segregation more a product of liberal modernizers than reactionary racists. Racial oppression strengthened, not undermined, by capitalist development. "Under segregation what was really a system of labor control would be disguised by the language of physical distance and removal." 320 pp., index.

58. CENTER FOR NATIONAL SECURITY STUDIES, "CIA's Secret War in Angola," *Intelligence Report*, 1, 1, 1975.

Well-informed, concise overview of Angolan civil war, foreign intervention, and details of CIA involvement. For more in-depth coverage see STOCKWELL, and BENDER. 12 pp., map, chart, bibliography.

59. CENTER FOR SOCIAL ACTION OF THE UNITED CHURCH OF CHRIST, *The Oil Conspiracy* (New York: C.S.A., 1976).

Investigation into how multinational oil companies provided the illegal Rhodesian regime with oil and gas. Includes many internal documents of Mobil Oil Corporation and others, showing how these companies planned their evasion of international sanctions. 49 pp., many reproduced documents, photographs, map.

60. CHEMICAL WORKERS INDUSTRIAL UNION, "Workers' Struggle at Colgate," *South African Labour Bulletin*, 6, 8, July 1981.

Interesting document that details "a blatantly anti-union stand" by Colgate-Palmolive of South Africa. Although a signer of the Sullivan Principles and claiming that transnational corporations "can play an important role in eliminating petty apartheid in business," Colgate refused to accept worker demands for union rights. Article includes extensive documentation of management and union positions. 16 pp.

61. CHICAGO COMMITTEE FOR A FREE AFRICA, *Sell the Stock: The Divestiture Struggle at Northwestern University and Building the Anti-Imperialist Movement* (Chicago, IL: Peoples College Press, 1978).

Argues for withdrawal of US investment from SA and divestiture of university funds as a means of pressuring US companies. Discusses reasons for opposing investments and supporting liberation struggles. 146 pp.

62. *CHRISTIANITY AND CRISIS*, "Toward Disengagement from South Africa," (special issue) 38, 3, 13 March 1978.

Numerous articles on: the liberation struggle (Ben Magubane); US policy (Thomas Karis); US investment (Tami Hultman and Reed Kramer); the divestment campaign (Tim Smith and Prexy Nesbitt), among others. 29 pp., numerous photos.

63. CHURCHILL, Ward, "U.S. Mercenaries in Southern Africa: The Recruiting Network and U.S. Policy," *Africa Today*, Second Quarter, 1980.

Former employee of *Soldier of Fortune* magazine discusses its role in recruitment of US mercenaries. Non-enforcement of Neutrality Act and evasion of arms embargo "imply at least tacit acceptance, if not outright underwriting, of mercenaries" by USG. Author views this as new counterinsurgency method for the 1970s and 80s. 25 pp.

64. CLARK, Senator Dick, *U.S. Corporate Interests in Africa*, Report to the Committee on Foreign Relations, U.S. Senate (Washington, DC: Government Printing Office, 1978).

Argues that US corporations in SA "have made no significant impact on either relaxing apartheid or in establishing company policies which would offer a limited but nevertheless important model of multinational responsibility." Includes study of US loans to SA from 1974-1976 ($2.2b), roughly the equivalent of SA's military and oil expenditures. Lists US corporations in SA. 232 pp., numerous tables.

65. CLIFFORD-VAUGHAN, F. McA., ed., *International Pressures and Political Change in South Africa* (Cape Town: Oxford University Press, 1978).

Seven essays by (primarily) white South African academics. Two focus on US–SA relations and others look at internal changes in SA and international isolation of the apartheid regime. 109 pp., index.

66. CLOUGH, Michael, "Why Carrots Alone Won't Work," *African Index*, 30 June 1981.

Insightful analysis of Reagan's and Pretoria's strategy on Namibia.

Provides evidence that Botha has too much at stake to allow elections which would surely be won by SWAPO. SAG was moving toward settlement due to international pressure but Reagan's election "encouraged the Botha government to shift to a 'wait-and-see' strategy." Contains much useful information. Includes statements on Namibia by Chester Crocker. 4 pp.

67. CLOUGH, Michael, ed., *Changing Realities in Southern Africa: Implications for American Policy* (Berkeley, CA: Institue of International Studies, 1982).

Seven articles of uneven quality on Zimbabwe, Namibia, SADCC, Soviet policy, SA's regional policy, and US aid policy. Piece on SA's regional policy fails to discuss destabilization efforts. Some useful facts but not much new material. 318 pp., index, appendix on minerals.

68. COHEN, Barry, *The Black and White Minstrel Show: Carter, Young and Africa* (Nottingham, England: Spokesman Books, 1977).

Left critique of Carter's foreign policy as traditional imperialist goals wrapped in new 'human rights' ideology. Attacks Carter/Young belief in corporations as a progressive force in southern Africa. 22 pp.

69. COHEN, Barry, "U.S. Imperialism and Southern Africa," *Review of African Political Economy*, 9, May–August 1978.

Criticizes Carter administration's tendency to equate the problems of southern Africa with the civil rights struggle in the US. Views the Andrew Young position on Africa as the most sophisticated brand of imperialist thinking. Some useful insights into US strategy through 1977. 4 pp.

70. COKER, Christopher, "The United States and National Liberation in Southern Africa," *African Affairs*, 78, 312, July 1979.

Interesting discussion of "the uneasy relationship between American liberalism and African radicalism." Argues that the USG "continues to see its multinational corporations and their marketing operations to be vital in linking the region into the international economy," and thus "it is still attempting to prevent national liberation from undermining the economic infrastructure of southern Africa." 11 pp.

71. COKER, Christopher, "Retreat into the Future: The United States, South Africa, and Human Rights, 1976–78," *The Journal of Modern African Studies*, 18, 3, 1980.

Article is "an attempt to see why the human-rights policy has fared so badly" and why SAG reforms are due to changes in the region rather than US policy. Argues that "America's failure. . .was one of perception": narrowly viewing the problem as strictly racial, and lacking a grasp of the subtleties of SA politics. 16 pp.

72. COKER, Christopher, "Collective Bargaining as an Internal Sanction: The Role of U.S. Corporations in South Africa," *The Journal of Modern African Studies*, 19, 4, 1981.

Examines the record of US investment and employment codes such as the Sullivan Principles to assess the limits and possibilities for using these as lever for change. Criticizes assertion that methods used in US civil rights movement will work in SA. US corporations have great power but are unlikely to threaten apartheid in fundamental ways. 19 pp.

73. COKER, Christopher, "The United States and South Africa: Can Constructive Engagement Succeed?" *Millenium: Journal of International Studies*, 11, 3, Autumn 1982.

Traces the historical roots of US policy notion that continued involvement with the white minority will facilitate reform while preserving US economic and strategic interests. Discusses the constraints "which will almost certainly prevent political change in South Africa from being managed or controlled." 18 pp.

74. "Cold War Cripples Africa Policy," *Washington Notes on Africa*, Summer 1978.

Brief but insightful piece on rightward drift of Carter policy. International incidents such as the second Shaba invasion, and domestic attack by Republicans in 1978 congressional elections, push Carter into Cold War stance. 2 pp.

75. COLON, Dominique, and Truman Dunn, "South Africa: Taking Stock of Divestment," (New York: American Committee on Africa, October 1979).

Provides solid introduction to the issue of selling stock of companies profiting from apartheid. Reviews the logic of arguments for and against divestment. Lists six organizations specializing in alternative investments. 4 pp.

76. "Confidential Diplomatic Cable Reveals Black Hostility to US Investment in South Africa," *Southern Africa*, April 1978.

Detailed analysis by US ambassador to SA, William Bowdler, examines attitudes of different sectors of black population. Finds support for US investment only among "older working blacks," "some black businessmen," and well-known conservatives such as Chief Sebe and Lucy Mvubelo. Opposition is much broader based. "With radicalization of black attitudes, tendency to call for disinvestment grows stronger. . . .role of American firms here will become increasingly controversial and rationale for continued presence will seem less and less persuasive to growing numbers of blacks." Cites reasoning of SA blacks in opposition to foreign investment. 4 pp.

77. CONGRESSIONAL BLACK CAUCUS, "The African-American Manifesto on Southern Africa," *The Black Scholar*, January/February 1977.

Enlightening policy document from September 1976 Black Leadership Conference on southern Africa. Eleven point program for US policy is still relevant. Scathing critique of traditional US policy: nationalism, not communism, is main motivating force of SA revolution; SA majority has right to seek change by whatever means necessary and take assistance from any source. 6 pp.

78. CONGRESSIONAL RESEARCH SERVICE, *Imports of Minerals from South Africa by the United States and the OECD Countries,* prepared for the Subcommittee on African Affairs, Committee on Foreign Relations, US Senate (Washington, DC: Government Printing Office, 1980).

This report finds that contrary to right-wing assertions, "South African minerals are of significant, but not critical, importance to the West. . . in the case of each of the critical minerals imported from South Africa, means are available for dealing with an interruption without depending on the Soviet Union as an alternative supplier." Reviews possible conditions under which SA supplies may be cut. Much data on wide array of minerals. 46 pp., numerous charts and tables.

79. CONRAD, Thomas, "U.S. data processing corporations are supplying South Africa with the brains of its military and police services," *Multinational Monitor,* April 1982.

Main author of AFSC book on US computer firms in SA gives overview of key role played by US technology in SA's repressive apparatus. Special section on how Reagan opened loopholes in export restrictions. 4 pp.

80. CONRAD, Thomas, "Legal Arms for South Africa," *The Nation,* 21 January 1984.

Examines how the Reagan administration gutted US restrictions on trade with SA, and facilitated contacts between police/military leaders of US and SA. "The volume of arms trade between the two countries is greater than it has ever been." In Reagan's first three years he authorized over $28.3m worth of exports of Munitions List commodities—"one and a half times the total value of commercial military equipment exported to Pretoria during the previous thirty years." Concludes that there is little hope for enforcement of arms embargo under Reagan. 5 pp.

81. COOPER, Allan D., *U.S. Economic Power and Political Influence in Namibia, 1700–1982* (Boulder, CO: Westview Press, 1982).

Unique resource. Massive compendium of data on US involvement in Namibia. Analyzes US commercial interests in various sectors of the economy, and the overlap of these commercial interests with US policy elite. US policy is contradictory: "active participation in establishing and maintaining the subordination of Namibia to South Africa and . . . rhetorical protests against South Africa's violation of human rights in Namibia." 222 pp., 18 tables, 9 charts, bibliography, index.

82. COPSON, Raymond W., *South Africa: Reform Proposals/U.S. Policy*, Congressional Research Service, Report No. 83-132F, 1983.

Brief discussion of constitutional reforms within context of various pressures on SAG (demographic, international, white and black political pressure, etc.). Gives pro and con arguments for SAG reforms and Reagan's 'constructive engagement' policy. 75 pp.

83. CORNEVIN, Marianne, *Apartheid Power and Historical Falsification* (Paris: UNESCO, 1980).

Following a general introduction to apartheid, the author critiques ten myths perpetrated by the white minority: that whites and blacks arrived in SA at the same time, that the Voortrekkers advanced into an uninhabited land that belonged to no one, that the homelands correspond to the areas historically occupied by each black 'nation,' etc. 144 pp., bibliography, 3 tables, 5 maps.

84. CORPORATE DATA EXCHANGE, *Pension Investments: A Social Audit* (New York: CDE, 1979).

Examines 142 major private and public pension plans and their stock holdings in 99 'target' companies to show who has how much invested in SA. Companies are checked by other criteria such as union/nonunion, OSHA violators, equal employment violators. "At $500 billion and growing by 10 percent a year, pension funds already own between 20 and 25 percent of the stock of companies listed on the New York and American exchanges." 115 pp., mostly charts.

85. COTTER, William R., and Thomas Karis, "'We Have Nothing to Hide': Contacts Between South Africa and the U.S." *Social Dynamics*, 3, 2, 1977.

Traces the history and politics of how USG and SAG regulate their visa policies. Reveals that USG has been more open to visits from pro-apartheid than anti-apartheid citizens of SA. Includes list of Americans on SA's "black list." 12 pp.

86. CROCKER, Chester, "A Mid-Term Assessment of the Carter Administration's Policies in Africa," *International Affairs Bulletin*, 3, 1, June 1979.

Admits that "we had in the past seen little reason to take Southern African problems seriously, preferring to live off the status quo and the European colonial legacy." Hence when Portuguese colonialism collapsed and the US wanted to intervene, there was not much of a "diplomatic base" for US efforts. Indirectly admits that Kissinger gave green light for 1975 SA invasion of Angola. Warns white South Africans that "in a bloodbath, we cannot take sides." Argues that Americans are polarized regarding US Africa policy: "there is simply no solid domestic base" for "a durable and moderate policy." 12 pp.

87. CROCKER, Chester, "South Africa: Strategy for Change," *Foreign Affairs*, Winter 1980/81.

Main architect of Reagan's Africa policy asserts that "white politics are demonstrating a degree of fluidity and pragmatism that is without precedent in the past generation." Crocker sees great potential for evolution away from apartheid, if only the whites are given more time. Elaborates his notion of "constructive engagement" (i.e., all carrots, no sticks) in US diplomacy. Essential reading for understanding failure of Reagan policy in SA. 29 pp.

88. CROCKER, Chester, "Regional Strategy for Southern Africa," 29 August 1981 address to American Legion in Honolulu, Current Policy series, 308, Bureau of Public Affairs, US Department of State.

Standard litany: "Soviet Union and its surrogates" are causing trouble, we need the minerals, the Cape Sea Route is endangered, etc. Defends Reagan administration attempts "to build a more constructive relationship with South Africa." That nation "is an integral and important element of the global economic system" and Reagan's team "has no intention of destabilizing South Africa to curry favor elsewhere." Available free on request. 4 pp.

89. "CRUSADE OF TOKENISM," *Financial Mail*, 20 October 1978.

Criticizes Carter's policy toward SA: "despite the stronger antiapartheid rhetoric...in practical terms his policy amounts to little more than wait and see." Although Carter's stand made it "difficult for SA to tap the important American capital market," the Administration lobbied against three pieces of legislation aimed at curtailing US investment in SA. Illuminates the contradictory nature of US policy toward SA. 5 pp.

90. CURRY, Robert L., "U.S.–AID's Southern Africa Program," *Journal of Southern African Affairs*, 5, 2, April 1980.

Scrutinizes the political nature of AID's program increases. Funding shift toward Economic Support Fund (formerly "Security Supporting Assistance") furthers tradition of putting US political-military interests before development needs. 14 pp., 3 tables.

91. DAG HAMMARSKJOLD LIBRARY, *Sanctions Against South Africa: A Selective Bibliography* (New York: UN, 1981).

Lists hundreds of (mostly English-language) sources, broken down into various categories: general, trade, arms, oil, sports, nuclear weapons capability, investments, loans, etc. 28 pp.

92. DANAHER, Kevin, "U.S. Policy Options Toward South Africa: A Bibliographic Essay," *A Current Bibliography on African Affairs*, 13, 1, 1980-81.

Discusses literature on three basic options for US policy: friendly relations with SAG, verbal/symbolic criticism, and material pressure.

Only the latter strategy, advocated by antiapartheid movement, has never been tried by USG. 24 pp., bibliography.

93. DANAHER, Kevin, "Sanctions Against South Africa: Strategy for the Anti-Apartheid Movement in the 1980s," *UFAHAMU: Journal of the African Activist Association*, X, 1 and 2, Fall/Winter 1980-81.

Critique of US policy toward sanctions. Examines US public opinion toward SA and suggests organizing strategies for the antiapartheid movement. 14 pp.

94. DANAHER, Kevin, "Secret Documents: Reagan Leans Right, SWAPO Left Out," *Southern Africa*, July–August, 1981.

Discusses contents of secret State Department documents leaked in late May, relating them to overall Reagan strategy in the region. Provides evidence that Reagan administration is more interested in propping up white-supremacy than fostering democracy in Namibia and South Africa. 4 pp.

95. DANAHER, Kevin, *The Political Economy of U.S. Policy Toward South Africa* (PhD Dissertation, University of California/Santa Cruz, 1982).

Traces US involvement from late 1800s, focusing on relationship between economic interests and US policy. Emphasis on policy in the post-war period, arguing that US policy represents class interests rather than national interest. 676 pp., bibliography, 30 tables.

96. DAVIS, Jennifer, "U.S. Dollars in South Africa: Context and Consequence" (New York: Africa Fund, February 1978).

Concise examination of the importance of US foreign investment to rapid growth and structural transformation of SA economy. Also points to crucial role played by US banks in rescuing SA economy from severe crisis. 6 pp., 4 tables.

97. DAY, Samuel H., Jr., "The Afrikaner Bomb: Pretoria marches toward Doomsday," *The Progressive*, September 1982.

Based on an extensive investigation, concludes that SAG tested nuclear device on 22 September 1979, and that both SAG and USG have attempted to obscure this fact. 10 pp.

98. DE ST. JORRE, John, "South Africa: Is Change Coming?" *Foreign Affairs*, Fall 1981.

Informed critique of "the basic premise of the Reagan administration's 'tilt' toward South Africa," namely that "P.W. Botha's government represents a unique opportunity for change." Shows that Pretoria is not able or willing to make fundamental changes in apartheid. Concludes that "the new U.S. policy toward South Africa seems likely to create more liabilities than assets for the United States." 16 pp.

99. DEUTSCH, Richard, "Carter's African Record," *Africa Report*, March–April 1978.

Traces first year of Carter administration's policy toward southern Africa. Even-handed account which calls attention to the importance of NATO allies in the formation of US policy. Discussion of congressional forces and brief treatment of conflict in Horn of Africa. 5 pp., photos.

100. DEUTSCH, Richard, "Carter's Congressional Rift," *Africa Report*, November–December 1978.

Traces development of conflict between the Administration and various forces in the House and Senate during Carter's first year. Provides details on certain members of Congress and pieces of legislation. 4 pp.

101. DEUTSCH, Richard, "The Republican Challenge on Africa," *Africa Report*, May–June 1979.

Review of Republican attacks on Carter administration for being 'soft' on the Soviet Union with regard to Africa and elsewhere. Although "appeasement of white supremacy in southern African and the refrain 'the Russians are coming' are not new tunes for the Republican rightwing," the article warns of an impending conservative offensive as the 1980 election draws near. 3 pp.

102. DEUTSCH, Richard, "Reagan's African Perspectives," *Africa Report*, July–August 1980.

"The African problem is a Russian weapon aimed at us" is Reagan's simplistic formula for this diverse continent. Author explores the views of Reagan's top advisors as well. Dominant themes: competition with Moscow very important, emphasis on strategic matters (military, minerals) rather than economic development, sympathy for white SA and Savimbi in Angola. 4 pp.

103. DEUTSCH, Richard, "Building an Africa Policy," *Africa Report*, July–August 1981.

Projected Reagan policy in Africa based on statements of Chester Crocker at his Senate confirmation hearings, his fact-finding mission to Africa, and the UN Security Council debate on Namibia. Claims US must "walk tightrope" between SA and the rest of Africa, and not choose between them. 4 pp.

104. DIGGS, Charles C., Jr., "Action Manifesto," *Issue*, 11, 1, Spring 1972.

Fifty-five recommendations for US severance of ties to Portugal and SA and active support for the liberation movements. Diggs' very progressive stand is particularly interesting in light of his eventual ouster as Chairman of the House Subcommittee on Africa. 8 pp.

105. "Doing Business With A Blacker Africa," *Business Week*, 14 February 1977.

A "Special Report" on southern Africa subtitled "At stake are billions in U.S. investments and one of the world's great storehouses of oil and vital materials." Full of ideological assumptions about the source of black oppression, the nature of the struggle against it, the 'progressive' role US corporations can play. 13 pp.

106. DONNELLY, Warren H., and William N. Raiford, "U.S. Foreign Policy Towards South Africa: The Case of Nuclear Cooperation," Congressional Research Service, Report No. 82-24S-F, 26 January 1981.

Broad overview of SA's nuclear program and US involvement in its development. "The Reagan administration...is in active pursuit of nuclear cooperation" even though SAG refuses to sign the Non-Proliferation Treaty. Surveys possible UN action and future issues for US–SA nuclear collaboration. 41 pp.

107. DOWNEY, Congressman Tom, "Congressional Ad Hoc Monitoring Group on Southern Africa," *Journal of Southern African Affairs*, 5, 2, April 1980.

Moved by the murder of Steve Biko, congressional liberals set up this group "to oversee the fate of other political prisoners in South Africa." Downey traces development of this loose-knit body, details its activities/accomplishments, and reveals SA spying on the group. Includes list of members and guest speakers. 10 pp.

108. DUFFY, David L., "Survey of the United States Government's Investments in Africa," *ISSUE* (special number) VIII, 2/3, Summer/Fall 1978.

Dated but interesting overview of 29 departments and agencies, including NASA, AID, various State Department bureaus, Commerce, Defense. References to southern Africa scattered throughout text. Based on government documents. 111 pp., numerous tables, bibliography.

109. DUNN, Truman, "U.S. Corporations in South Africa: A Summary of Strategic Investments," (New York: American Committee on Africa, 1980).

Provides concise overview of US investments in strategic sectors such as energy, computers, transportation, nuclear, military, and bank loans. Criticizes companies for their labor practices. 6 pp.

110. DU TOIT, Darcy, *Capital and Labour in South Africa: Class Struggles in the 1970s* (London, and Boston, MA: Kegan Paul International Ltd., 1981).

Radical analysis of "the class nature of the social struggle in South Africa." Covers historical development of the working class, various political tendencies, government regulations, evolution of the mass movement of the 1970s, and efforts to build black trade unions. Useful antidote to mainstream analyses that focus solely on race. 495 pp., 24 tables, bibliography, index.

111. "Election 1980: Carter and Reagan on Southern Africa," *Washington Notes on Africa*, Summer 1980.

Critical look at both candidates' positions. "Aside from some of the public rhetoric during 1977/78, the Carter policies have meant business as usual with South Africa." Background data on many Reagan aides shows they are favorably disposed to apartheid. Issue also includes article: "Will the CIA Intervene Again in Angola?" 4 pp.

112. EL-KHAWAS, Mohamed, A., "Southern Africa: A Challenge to the OAU," *Africa Today*, 24, 3, July– September 1977.

Assessment of the broad range of assistance given by OAU to various liberation movements in southern Africa, and analysis of the increasingly important role played by "front-line" states since withdrawal of Portugal from Africa. 16 pp, 2 tables.

113. EL-KHAWAS, Mohamed A., *Angola: The American–South African Connection* (Washington, DC: African Bibliographic Center, 1978).

Documents the cooperation between the US and SA in attempts to keep the MPLA from coming to power in Angolan civil war, and continuing efforts to destabilize the left-leaning regime. 15 pp.

114. EL-KHAWAS, Mohamed A., "Reagan's Policy Toward South Africa: Constructive or Destructive Engagement?" *The International Journal of World Studies*, 1, 1, Winter 1984.

Argues that Reagan's friendly policy toward the white regime has facilitated Pretoria's regional aggression, done nothing to encourage internal reform, assisted Pretoria in its search for nuclear weapons capability, and reduced US credibility in Africa to its lowest ebb since 1977. 19 pp.

115. EL-KHAWAS, Mohamed A., and Francis A. Kornegay, Jr., eds., *American–Southern African Relations: Bibliographic Essays* (Westport, CT: Greenwood Press, 1975).

Somewhat dated pieces on "American Involvement in Angola and Mozambique," US policy toward Zimbabwe, Namibia, "United States Investments in Southern Africa," "Black America and U.S.–Southern African Relations," "American–Southern African Relations at the Crossroads." 188 pp.

116. EL-KHAWAS, Mohamed A., and Constance Morris Hope, "A Bibliographical Essay on U.S. Diplomatic Relations with South Africa," *Journal of Southern African Affairs*, 4, 1, January 1979.

Useful survey of literature on US policy from Kennedy to Carter. Extensive bibliography through 1978. Argues against continuing ties to the white minority, stating that "a decade of dialogue accompanied with a substantial increase in American investment in South Africa did not bring about any change in the apartheid system but to the contrary the oppressive laws were increased in number and vigorously enforced." 34 pp.

117. EMMANUEL, Arghiri, "White-Settler Colonialism and the Myth of Investment Imperialism," *New Left Review*, 73, May–June 1972.

Important theoretical piece criticizing traditional theories of imperialism for "their failure to recognize a third factor that intervenes between imperialist capitalism and the peoples of the exploited countries," namely, settlers who develop interests different from home country and indigenous population. In settler states where natives were harnessed as labor force (e.g., southern Africa, Israel, northern Ireland) political development is more problematic than settler states where indigenes were destroyed (e.g., USA, Australia). 22 pp., tables.

118. FERGUSON, Clyde C., "The United States, the United Nations and the Struggle Against Racial Apartheid," in Natalie Kaufman Hevener, ed., *The Dynamics of Human Rights in U.S. Foreign Policy* (New Brunswick, NJ: Transaction Books, 1981).

Brief analysis of US position on SA in UN. Main reasons for US blocking sanctions: it would hurt US corporate interests, and set precedent for UN action against Israel. "More than any other single factor, the U.S. position on issues of South African racial policies has been a proximate cause of the decline of U.S. prestige, and hence influence, in international organizations." 11 pp.

119. FERGUSON, Clyde, and William R. Cotter, "South Africa: What Is To Be Done?" *Foreign Affairs*, January 1978.

Interesting appraisal of US/SA relations from a left-liberal perspective. Aimed at government audience, concludes with long list of possible actions USG could take to put pressure on the white minority. 21 pp.

120. FEUSTEL, Sandy, "African Minerals and American Foreign Policy," *Africa Report*, September–October 1978.

Detailed discussion of US dependence on various minerals produced in Africa (with emphasis on southern Africa). Includes brief analysis of each mineral. 6 pp., photos, 4 tables.

121. FIERCE, Milfred C., "Black and White American Opinions Towards South Africa," *The Journal of Modern African Studies*, 20, 4, 1982.

Reviews findings of major opinion polls to illuminate US attitudes on SA and US policy. Americans generally agree apartheid is wrong but much confusion and contradiction over what to do about it. Highlights differences between whites and blacks, elites and masses, Democrats and Republicans. 18 pp., 7 tables.

122. FIRST, Ruth, Jonathan Steele, and Christabel Gurney, *The South African Connection: Western Investment in Apartheid* (Middlesex, England: Penguin, 1973).

Somewhat dated but well documented critique of British (and other western) corporate investment in SA. Amasses considerable data to show that this investment strengthens apartheid and that "Britain and the West profit from apartheid." 352 pp., index, numerous tables and appendices.

123. FISHER, Scott, *Coping With Change: United States Policy Toward South Africa* (Washington, DC: National Defense University, 1982).

Brief but interesting analysis by US Air Force Colonel. Recommends stockpiling minerals, restricting US exports, nonexpansion of US investment, increased contacts with black leadership including ANC and PAC, more attention to human rights, mandatory adoption of Sullivan Principles. 83 pp., 7 tables, 1 map.

124. FOLTZ, William J., *Elite Opinion on United States Policy Toward Africa* (New York: Council on Foreign Relations, 1979).

Survey of members of CFR and Committees affiliated with CFR. "Like other categories of American leadership, (Congress and senior corporate executives, for example) both groups are overwhelmingly white and male." The elites surveyed are much less isolationist than the general public. "Most respondents saw accommodation with black African opinion as a prerequisite for any effective policy." Includes special section on SA. 25 pp., numerous tables.

125. FOREIGN POLICY ASSOCIATION, "South Africa: Can U.S. Policies Influence Change?" in *Great Decisions '84* (New York: Foreign Policy Association, 1984).

Summarizes key aspects of apartheid and recent developments in SA. Briefly examines role of foreign investment, the African opposition, SAG's regional policy, and US interests and policy options. Designed for classroom use, concludes with questions for discussion. 11 pp., 7 photos, 1 map, bibliography.

126. FOREIGN POLICY STUDY FOUNDATION, *South Africa: Time Running Out* (Berkeley and Los Angeles, CA: University of California Press, 1981).

Rockefeller-funded study of SA and US policy options. Many strong points but weak on corporate connection. Debunks some conservative propaganda regarding mineral dependency, 'strategic Cape route,' and recent SA reforms. Fails to take liberation movement seriously, and is opposed to measures that would harm profits (divestment, sanctions). Recommends ending nuclear collaboration, expanding arms embargo, non-recognition of bantustans, more aid to neighboring states, and increased contact with black leaders. 517 pp., many tables, photos, maps, bibliography.

127. FREDERICKSON, George M., *White Supremacy: A Comparative Study in American and South African History* (New York: Oxford University Press, 1981).

Ambitious undertaking that generally succeeds. Guided by "persistent focus on the attitudes, beliefs, and policies of the dominant whites." Weak on black resistance as causal factor. Sound scholarship in readable form. Provides evidence on relationship between racialism and capitalist development. 356 pp.

128. GAETSEWE, John, *Life and Labour in Transnational Corporations in South Africa* (New York: UN Centre Against Apartheid, December 1980).

Documents labor practices in TNCs, alleging collaboration with the regime. Criticizes the misleading and cosmetic nature of reforms. Covers regulation of unions, migrant worker status, wages, industrial health, covert supply of western weaponry, and significance of the National Supplies Procurement Act. 27 pp.

129. GANN, L.H., and Peter Duignan, *South Africa: War, Revolution, or Peace?* (Stanford, CA: Hoover Institution Press, 1978).

Classic restatement of the right-wing position by friends of Reagan: blacks in SA are better off than in rest of Africa, "white fears are not unreasonable and should be treated with respect," "sanctions won't work," "we should press for minor reforms in the hope that piecemeal changes will have a multiplying effect," if blacks insist on fighting for power "the ultimate result can only be disaster." 85 pp., 11 tables, index.

130. GELB, Leslie, "U.S. Seeks Angola Compromise As Price for Accord on Namibia," *The New York Times*, 1 June 1981.

Based on secret State Department memo, article exposes Reagan strategy on Namibia, SA, Angola. Reagan's plan is to 1) win Pretoria's trust by easing export restrictions, moving ahead on nuclear relations, upgrading military ties, etc.; 2) make demands on Angola—"recognition is out unless the Cubans leave and they cut a deal with Savimbi . . .if they won't play we have other options"; 3) obtain African backing for this linkage, "African leaders would have no basis for resisting the Namibia–Angola linkage once they are made to realize that they can only get a Namibia settlement through us." The document suggests lying about the Namibia–Angola linkage: "We would insist that these are unrelated, but in fact they would be mutually reinforcing, parallel tracks of an overall strategy." 2 pp.

131. GERVASI, Sean, "Under the NATO Umbrella," *Africa Report*, September-October 1976.

Criticizes efforts by major capitalist countries "to build a global system of defense...by bringing strong regional powers into the western alliance" to act as "surrogate colonial powers" in their respective regions. Documents western military support for SA. 5 pp., map, photos.

132. GERVASI, Sean, *The United States and the Arms Embargo Against South Africa: Evidence, Denial, and Refutation* (Binghampton, NY: Braudel Center/S.U.N.Y., 1978).

Detailed account of how western corporations and governments have circumvented the UN arms embargo against SA. Contains: Gervasi's testimony before the House Subcommittee on Africa; the Administration's position on the embargo; and further evidence on US arms transfers to South Africa from a paper Gervasi presented to the UN, 20 May 1978. 49 pp.

133. GERVASI, Sean, "Caesar's Planners Look at Africa," *Africa Report*, January-February 1980.

Sharp critique of Pentagon-backed study by SAMUELS, et al., of Soviet/Cuban activity in Africa. Attacks their overriding emphasis on East–West competition, and failure to understand the West's economic exploitation of Africa. Argues that "there is no prospect, within the present international economic order, that Africa can escape from poverty." Hence the liberation movements struggle for economic, as well as political, sovereignty. 2 pp., 2 photos.

134. GIBSON, Urath, *Marketing in South Africa*, Overseas Business Report, US Department of Commerce, March 1981.

Paid for with your tax money to help businessmen profit from apartheid, this booklet gives a good overview of the SA economy and business conditions. Sections on distribution and sales, transportation and utilities, taxation, employment regulations, advertising, investment laws, "notes for business travellers," and more. 36 pp., 8 tables.

135. GILLARD, Michael, and E.S. Ely, "Mobil and Rhodesia: A Scandal That Won't Go Away," *The Village Voice*, 6-12 May 1981.

Discusses documents recently received by Treasury Department which provide "indisputable evidence that subsidiaries of Mobil US supplied oil and petroleum products to the white supremacist regime of former prime minister Ian Smith in Rhodesia, now Zimbabwe, in violation of UN sanctions and possibly US law." Inaction by Reagan administration will be another slap in the face to black Africa.

136. GISSELQUIST, David, "The IMF and South Africa," Washington, DC: Center for International Policy, May 1982.

Discusses history of IMF support for SAG, the political issues and impact of IMF loans to SAG, UN investigation of IMF–SAG relationship, and efforts to curtail this lending. 5 pp., 2 tables.

137. GOLDBERG, Glenn S., *IRRC Directory of U.S. Corporations in South Africa* (Washington, DC: Investor Responsibility Research Center, 1982).

Provides basic data on some 400 US-owned subsidiaries operating in SA. For each firm gives name, US address, subsidiary in SA, percent equity held by US parent company, whether or not a Sullivan signatory, etc. 49 pp., index.

138. GOLDSTEIN, Myra S., *The Genesis of Modern American Relations with South Africa, 1895–1914* (PhD Dissertation, State University of New York at Buffalo, 1972).

Details the early importance of US equipment and technicians to SA's industrial development, especially mining. Particular US companies and mining engineers played key roles. Examines politics of official US support for British in Boer War. 266 pp., bibliography.

139. GOSHEN, Carolyn J., and Philip Musser, *Southern Africa: A Select Guide to U.S. Organizational Interests* (Washington, DC: African Bibliographic Center, 1979).

Reference work listing over 300 organizations concerned with, or operating in, southern Africa. Cross-indexing and brief descriptions of each organization (including churches, businesses, liberation movements, etc.). 74 pp., index.

140. GREENBERG, Stanley B., *Race and State in Capitalist Development* (New Haven, CT: Yale University Press, 1980).

Important work which deserves more attention. Comparative study of white supremacy in US and SA. Focuses on white labor, large-scale farmers and industrialists. "Capitalist development brought, along with wage labor, factories, and cities, the intensification of racial discrimination." Includes sections on Israel and N. Ireland. Puts SA racism in broader theoretical context. 489 pp., maps, tables, bibliography.

141. GREENBERG, Stanley B., "Economic Growth and Political Change: the South African Case," *The Journal of Modern African Studies*, 19, 4, 1981.

Solid, scholarly refutation of the thesis that capitalist economic growth necessarily undermines racial oppression. Presents abundant data and sound logic to argue that "there is little prospect that economic growth, even under the most optimistic assumptions, will fundamentally alter the economic inequalities characteristic of South Africa." Undermines claim that foreign investment speeds progressive change. 38 pp., 6 tables.

142. GROESBECK, Wesley, "The Transkei: Key to U.S. Naval Strategy in the Indian Ocean," *Military Review*, LVI, 6, June 1976.

US Army Major outlines the economic, strategic and political advantages to US establishing a naval base at Port St. James in the "independent" Transkei. Groesbeck argues that such an action would provide strategic advantage in southern Africa "without breaking the US arms embargo against the Republic of South Africa or supporting apartheid." 6 pp.

143. HANKS, Robert J., *Southern Africa and Western Security* (Cambridge, MA and Washington, DC: Institute for Foreign Policy Analysis, 1983).

Restatement of the right-wing position, stressing SA's value as a strategic asset in East–West competition. In addition to Cape Sea route and minerals, SA is important because it "is a potential bulwark standing in the way of ultimate Soviet hegemony over all of Southern Africa." Evils of apartheid receive scant attention and only as impediment to full embrace of SA by the West. 74 pp., 1 map, 1 table.

144. HARSCH, Ernest, and Tony Thomas, *Angola: The Hidden History of Washington's War* (New York: Pathfinder Press, 1976).

Scathing critique of US government support for SA and other antisocialist forces in Angola's civil war from a Fourth International perspective. 157 pp., maps, bibliography.

145. HARVEY, Charles, et al., *Foreign Investment in South Africa: The Policy Debate* (Uppsala, Sweden: Africa Publications Trust, 1975).

Number 5 in a series of books on SA and its international context. Eleven articles by as many different authors cover the main arguments (pro and con) in the debate over multinational corporate involvement in SA. 250 pp.

146. HAUCK, David, Meg Voorhes, and Glenn Goldberg, *Two Decades of Debate: The Controversy Over U.S. Companies in South Africa* (Washington, DC: Investor Responsibility Reserch Center, 1983).

Overviews history of 1) efforts by antiapartheid activists to force US banks and corporations to end involvement in SA, 2) response of the corporations, and 3) involvement of US government in the debate. Useful for understanding this crucial aspect of the struggle against apartheid. 163 pp.

147. HECATHORN, Miloanne, Karen Johnson, and Samuel Ragent, *Our Town Out Of South Africa* (San Francisco, CA: American Friends Service Committee, 1982).

Excellent citizens' guide on how to pass local legislation taking public funds out of banks and corporations that profit from apartheid. Packed with practical step-by-step information on how to establish and win a campaign for divestment. Based on California cases but most information is generally applicable. 125 pp., numerous graphics, documents.

148. HERO, Alfred O., Jr., and John Barratt, eds., *The American People and South Africa* (Lexington, MA: Lexington Books, 1981).

Twelve authors, including Chester Crocker, present as many essays on subjects such as: public opinion, economic relations, black Americans, churches, and universities. 228 pp., index.

149. HILBERT, Roger, and Christiane Oehlmann, *Foreign Direct Investments and Multinational Corporations in Sub-Saharan Africa: A Bibliography* (Frankfurt and New York: Campus Verlag, 1980).

Slightly dated, massive compilation of sources, mostly in English but some in German and French. Sections include: general (many go beyond Africa), company information sources, research methodology, theory, history, quantitative, as well as separate sections on each country—35 pages on SA. 699 pp., author index.

150. HOOGENDIJK, Dr. Ferry A., "Muldergate: The Eschel Rhoodie Story," *Elseviers Magazine* (Netherlands), August 1979. (also reprinted in *Facts and Reports*, 31 August 1979).

Based on extensive interviews with former SA minister of information, this article reveals: covert operations to produce pro-apartheid propaganda in numerous countries were approved by the highest levels of SAG, including current Prime Minister Botha; John McGoff, a right-wing US newspaper magnate with ties to Nixon, Ford, etc., received $10m from SA in attempt to buy *The Washington Star*; McGoff also used SA money to purchase the second-largest paper in California's capitol, *The Sacramento Union;* Gerald Ford and former Secretary of the Treasury, William Simon, were paid $10,000 each to give pro-SA lectures; SA's military intelligence service encouraged the secession of Biafra from Nigeria. Also documents SA's attempts to influence elections in Zimbabwe and Namibia. 14 pp. *(Facts and Reports)*

151. HOUSER, George, "Contingency Planning by General Motors, South Africa," (New York: UN Centre Against Apartheid, 1978).

Reports on internal GM documents outlining the company's contingency plans "in the event of civil unrest." Houser concludes that the memos "reveal clearly the close identity of interests between the Government of South Africa and a major United States investor." 8 pp.

152. HOUSER, George, "Carter's African Policy," (New York: Africa Fund, 1979).

Surveys the changes in Africa that resulted in "a new style in African-related tactics" by the Carter administration, but persuasively argues that "there has been no fundamental change in overall US attitudes and policy toward Africa." 6 pp.

153. HOVEY, Gail, "South Africa: Questions and Answers on Divestment," (New York: Africa Fund, 1981).

Useful data and logic for answering the 12 most frequently asked questions regarding efforts to convince institutional investors to sell holdings in companies investing in SA. 4 pp.

154. HOVEY, Gail, *Namibia's Stolen Wealth: North American Investment and South African Occupation* (New York: Africa Fund, 1982).

Good primer on Namibia and US involvement. Brief profiles of individual companies and key sectors of the Namibian economy. 52 pp., several maps, tables, bibliography.

155. HULL, Galen, "South African Propaganda in the U.S.: A Bibliographic Essay," *African Studies Review*, XXII, 3, December 1979.

History and structure of Pretoria's political manipulations in US. Lists relevant organizations and periodicals, as well as specific books/articles. Fascinating reading, but needs updating since the "Infogate" scandal. 32 pp.

156. HULL, Galen Spencer, *Pawns on a Chessboard: The Resource War in Southern Africa* (Washington, DC: University Press of America, 1981).

Extensive data on the mineral sectors of Zaire, Zambia, Zimbabwe, and SA. A comprehensive source on this issue. Includes background political and economic information, as well as critique of Reagan administration's Cold War approach to southern Africa. 236 pp., 49 tables, bibliography.

157. "I.C.A. Enlightens South Africa," *Washington Notes On Africa*, Summer 1979.

One of very few articles available on International Communication Agency's South Africa program. The various cultural and educational exchanges of the program "are intended to speed reform and protect US corporate interests by aiding moderate blacks and liberal whites to construct a non-violent solution." Names many names in a blistering attack on this aspect of US policy. Issue also contains articles on Rhodesia, AID study of southern Africa, and US ties to SASOL development. 3 pp.

158. "The Indian Ocean: The US Responds," *Africa Confidential*, 9 May 1979.

Overview of US military buildup and its relation to African nations. "In 1970 a research team at the US School of Naval Warfare had concluded that cooperation with South Africa for regional defence would be necessary." Cites 1974 quote of US Navy Admiral John McCain: "What has happened in Angola and Mozambique makes our possession of Diego Garcia more important than ever. But it also means that we absolutely need access to Simonstown and Durban." 2 pp.

159. INTERNATIONAL CONFEDERATION OF FREE TRADE UNIONS, "Investment in Apartheid: List of Companies with investment and interests in South Africa," (New York: UN Centre Against Apartheid, June 1978).

Gives the name and nationality of 1,883 transnational corporations from 14 countries, including the US. 26 pp.

160. INTERNATIONAL DEFENCE AND AID FUND, *The Apartheid War Machine* (London: IDAF, 1980).

Excellent source on the SA military. Covers organizational structure, strategy, weapons, economic and political ramifications, paramilitary forces, regional attacks, and more. Useful reference from reliable organization. 74 pp., 11 tables, maps.

161. "Israel Joins SA Nuclear Sub Project," *8 Days*, 28 February 1981.

Claims that "Israeli and South African scientists and engineers are secretly building a nuclear submarine at Simonstown." This is part of "the expanding Israeli–South African military partnership." Also, SA is secretly providing financial support for Israel's new Lavi fighter-bomber which will be produced under license in SA. Claims that in 1975 "the Israelis, with discreet encouragement from Dr. Henry Kissinger, supplied equipment, technicians and military intelligence to help the South Africans when they invaded Angola."

162. "Israel: The growing link with South Africa," *Business Week*, 22 May 1978.

Provides details on burgeoning economic ties. Israel provides "a stepping-stone into the Common Market" for SA goods. Weaponry sales. "For businessmen it is a natural alliance, and they expect it to grow." 2 pp.

163. *ISSUE: A Quarterly Journal of Opinion*, (special issue on USG activity in Africa), VIII, 2/3, Summer/Fall 1978.

Catalogues the activities of 29 USG agencies which "carry on various activities in or concerning Africa" for fiscal years 1976-1978. Very specialized resource. 111 pp., numerous tables.

164. *ISSUE: A Quarterly Journal of Opinion*, (special issue on southern Africa), IX, 1/2, Spring/Summer 1979.

This double issue contains 16 essays, including: "How the US Arms South Africa and Rhodesia," Michael Klare and Eric Prokosch; "The Case Against the CIA," John Stockwell; "Socialist State Strategy and Arms in Southern Africa," George Shepherd; "Why US Corporations Should Get Out of South Africa," Ann Seidman; "Imperialism and the Liberation Struggle in Southern Africa," Nzongola Ntalaja; and congressional testimony by Randall Robinson; among others. 82 pp., several tables, bibliography.

165. *ISSUE: A Quarterly Journal of Opinion*, XII, 3/4, Fall/Winter 1982.

Contains several articles on SA and US involvement, including: three critiques of Reagan's "constructive engagement" policy by Sam Nolutshungu, Bernard Magubane, and Deborah Toler; an African Studies Association roundtable on US policy toward Africa featuring critics and supporters of Reagan's policy; an analysis of SADCC and US foreign aid by Ed Brown; and two updates on recent changes in SA by Gwendolen Carter and Pearl-Alice Marsh. 75 pp., 4 tables.

166. JACKSON, Deborah A., "Mercenaries and Southern Africa," (New York: UN Centre Against Apartheid, April 1980).

Statement of National Conference of Black Lawyers urging adoption of an international convention against mercenaries. Condemns US in particular for not prosecuting clear cases of recruitment.

167. JACKSON, Henry F., "Reagan's Policy Rupture," *Africa Report*, September/October 1981.

Concise overview of postwar US policy regarding strategic/military cooperation with SAG. Reagan broke the trend by moving into closest collaboration since 1950s. Calls for reduction of US governmental and corporate ties to the white minority regime. 5 pp.

168. JACKSON, Henry F., *From The Congo to Soweto: U.S. Foreign Policy Toward Africa Since 1960* (New York: William Morrow and Co., 1982).

Clearly written overview with chapters on US policy toward the Congo crisis, Angola, Egypt, SA, strategic minerals, and the role of black Americans. Criticizes Cold War myopia of US policy, recommends disengagement from SA. 324 pp., 5 tables, 2 maps, index.

169. JINADU, L.A., *Human Rights and US–African Policy Under President Carter* (Lagos, Nigeria: Nigerian Institute of International Affairs, 1980).

Well documented critique of the liberal interventionist strain in US foreign policy. Focusing on southern Africa, Jinadu compares the Carter rhetoric with reality and finds the actual policy very similar to Kissinger's. Useful criticism of policy themes regarding SA such as "peaceful change," and assertion that SA struggle is same as civil rights struggle in US. 120 pp.

170. JOHNSON, David Lawther, "Sanctions and South Africa," *Harvard International Law Journal*, 19, 3, Fall 1978.

Detailed analysis of relevant provisions of UN Charter, history of Security Council action regarding sanctions, whether UN could apply additional sanctions, in what ways the SA situation qualifies as a threat to international peace and security, and chances for success of UN sanctions. 43 pp.

171. KAPLAN, Ruth, *Anglo American Corporation of South Africa Ltd.: Investments in North America* (New York: Africa Fund, 1982).

Revealing look at the holdings of "the largest foreign investor in the United States in 1980 and again in 1981." In addition to its "dominant economic influence in southern Africa," the Anglo group's North American operations include Minorco, an investment firm with assets over $2b, Philbro, "the world's largest publicly owned commodity trader" (50 percent of revenues come from marketing oil), and Newmont Mining, involved in Namibia. North American directors include Felix Rohatyn and Walter Wriston. 36 pp., numerous tables and charts.

172. KARIS, Thomas, "United States Policy Toward South Africa," in Carter and O'Meara *Southern Africa: The Continuing Crisis* (Bloomington, IN: Indiana University Press, 1979).

Detailed description of US policy from Truman to Carter by former employee of State Department and Rockefeller Foundation. Negotiated settlement in SA "is surely an unrealistic prospect if white South Africa faces only moderate and not overwhelming pressures from outside to reinforce the black struggle inside the country for radical change." 49 pp.

173. KARIS, Thomas G., "Revolution in the Making: Black Politics in South Africa," *Foreign Affairs*, Winter 1983/84.

Well-informed analysis by noted expert on SA black politics. Focuses mainly on ANC, its ideology and operations. Criticizes US policy for rhetorically supporting peaceful change while depending on "unilateral change by a minority government based upon institutionalized violence." Urges greater US contact with ANC. 28 pp.

174. KEITA, Maghan, "African–American Interactions with South Africa," *OMOWE* (Howard University Student Assembly) 4, 1, 1980.

Critical account of certain black elites internationally, their role in the "management of Africa and the diaspora on behalf of world capitalism." Details the failure of pro-capitalist black leaders to further the cause of black liberation in SA. 5 pp.

175. KELLER, Major Gerald J., "Israeli–South African Trade: An Analysis of Recent Developments," *Naval War College Review*, Spring 1978.

Well-informed assessment by US Marine Corps officer of why the Jewish state would ally itself with former Nazi sympathizers. Key reasons include: "the South African market for Israeli-manufactured weapons," and Israel's "desire to acquire material necessary to manufacture nuclear weapons." For SA the benefits include access to Israeli military hardware and training, and "transfer of Israeli industrial and agricultural technology." 6 pp.

176. KELLY, John, "Intimate Embraces: The IMF and South Africa," *Counterspy*, September-November 1983.

Based on confidential IMF documents, discusses political and economic conditions surrounding IMF's 1982 decision to grant over $1b in credit to SAG. Shows how IMF has consistently supported SAG even though conditions for SA's black majority grow worse. 9 pp.

177. KITCHEN, Helen, ed., *Options for U.S. Policy Toward Africa* (Washington, DC: American Enterprise Institute for Public Policy Research, 1979).

Former editor of *Africa Report* serves up a smorgasbord of primarily conservative and liberal views on US Africa policy. Short pieces are grouped into policy option categories (e.g., "The Geostrategic Option," "The 'Afro-Centric' Perspective," "Tempered Idealism," etc.). Provides brief sample of numerous authors' work. 76 pp., 1 table.

178. KLARE, Michael T., "U.S. Arms Deliveries to South Africa: The Italian Connection," Transnational Institute Special Report (Washington, DC: Institute for Policy Studies, 1977).

Brief case study of how US firms circumvent arms embargo. Examines the links between US aircraft firms, Italian aircraft firms, and SA Air Force. 4 pp., 1 chart.

179. KLARE, Michael, "The Corporate Gunrunners: South Africa's U.S. Weapons Connections," *The Nation*, 28 July-4 August 1979.

Documents efforts by corporations to channel guns, ammunition, computers, helicopters, etc., to the apartheid regime. Concludes that "U.S. officials have been inexcusably negligent in their enforcement of the embargo on South Africa," and advocates "a full-scale investigation by Congress or the Justice Department." Available from Institute for Policy Studies. 4 pp.

180. KLARE, Michael T., "Evading the Embargo: Illicit U.S. Arms Transfers to South Africa," *Journal of International Affairs*, 35, 1, Spring/Summer 1981.

Detailed examination of lax US enforcement of UN arms embargo. Three main ways to transfer US arms to SA: illegal corporate transfers, third country transfers, and "gray area" sales (i.e., equipment such as planes and helicopters that can be designated civilian but also have military uses). 14 pp.

181. KLARE, Michael T., and Eric Prokosch, "Getting Arms to South Africa," *The Nation*, 8-15 July 1978.

Examines the various means—"legal and illegal, direct and indirect, overt and covert"—by which US corporations, with tacit or explicit US government support, have circumvented the UN embargo on arms deliveries to SA. Available from Institute for Policy Studies.

182. KLEIN, Beate, "The Banks Say—On South Africa," (New York: Interfaith Center on Corporate Responsibility, 1978).

Numerous statements by bank officials regarding their loans to SA. Useful resource for divestment work. 15 pp.

183. KLEIN, Beate, *Bricks in the Wall: An Update on Foreign Bank Involvement in South Africa* (Geneva: World Council of Churches/ Programme to Combat Racism, March 1981), also pub. by UN Centre Against Apartheid, May 1981.

Comprehensive treatment of the subject. Well documented and clearly written. Demystifies technical aspects; reveals political content of 'economic' bank practices. 62 pp., numerous charts, tables and documents.

184. KORNEGAY, Francis A., Jr., "Southern Africa and the Emerging Constituency for Africa in the United States: A Selected Survey of Periodical Literature," *A Current Bibliography on African Affairs*, 5, 1, January 1972.

Analysis of African nationalism in southern Africa in the late 1960s and its relation to American race struggles and increased black involvement in African affairs. Contains valuable (if somewhat dated) survey of pro-Africa organizations and periodicals in the US, as well as a look at formidable media apparatus constructed by SAG to improve its image abroad. 10 pp.

185. KORNEGAY, Francis A., Jr., *Washington and Africa: Reagan, Congress, and an African Affairs Constituency in Transition* (Washington, DC: African Bibliographic Center, 1982).

Critical review of literature from early Reagan period. Examines Reagan's critics and supporters in Congress and the public. Criticizes US groups on Left and Right involved in African affairs. Information on US domestic struggle over apartheid. 64 pp., 3 appended documents.

186. LAKE, Anthony, *Caution and Concern: The Making of American Policy Toward South Africa, 1946-1971* (PhD Dissertation, Princeton University, 1974).

Former head of Policy Planning at State Department under Carter describes domestic political forces shaping US policy. Provides insight into bureaucratic politics on this issue. Change must come from top level of government or from outside. Says black community is key to antiapartheid effectiveness. Lists ten ways interested groups can influence policy. 498 pp.

187. LANNING, Greg, "Role of Transnational Mining Corporations in the Plunder of South Africa's Mineral Resources," (New York: UN Centre Against Apartheid, November 1979).

Provides historical background as well as closer look at 13 British and US companies. The US firms are Newmont, Amax, Phelps Dodge, US Steel, Union Carbide, Kennecott, and Engelhard. 22 p., 12 charts and tables.

188. LAURENCE, John C., *Race Propaganda and South Africa* (London: Victor Gollancz Ltd., 1979).

A very important book which has received little attention. Provides a forceful critique of the major themes of SA propaganda (whites and blacks arrived at the same time historically, the wage gap is narrowing, apartheid is being phased out, SA is a staunch ally of the West, etc.). Well-researched. 215 pp.

189. LAWRENCE, Robert, "Reagan's Africa Arsenal," *Southern Africa*, November–December 1980.

Traces the backgrounds of Reagan's top foreign policy (esp. Africa) advisors. Most are linked to right-wing think-tanks and are supporters of SA's white minority. 3 pp.

190. LEGUM, Colin, *The Western Crisis Over Southern Africa* (New York: Africana Publishing Co., 1979).

Detailed discussion of SA, Namibia, and Zimbabwe with useful insights into international diplomacy. Written before Vorster's replacement as Prime Minister by P.W. Botha, the book documents the intensification of struggle and attempts by the National Party to carry out reforms needed to maintain its grip on power. 260 pp., numerous tables.

191. LEMARCHAND, Rene, ed., *American Policy in Southern Africa* (Washington, DC: University Press of America, 1981).

Thirteen essays of generally high quality, including: policy toward Mozambique, Allen Isaacman and Jennifer Davis; Kissinger in Angola, Gerald Bender; Zimbabwe, Edgar Lockwood; Namibia, William Johnston; 2 essays on CIA involvement; 2 on US blacks and Africa policy; and several on policy toward SA. 500 pp.

192. LEOGRANDE, William M., *Cuba's Policy in Africa, 1959–1980* (Berkeley, CA: Institute of International Studies, 1980).

Probably the best single source on the subject. Chapters on Angola and Ethiopia as well as general sections on future prospects and Cuban policy in the global context. Well-informed section on Angolan war is antidote to distortions of USG and press accounts. 82 pp., 4 tables.

193. LEONARD, Richard, "Computers in South Africa: A Survey of U.S. Companies" (New York: Africa Fund, November 1978).

Examines role of US computer companies in SA, the ways that computers strengthen apartheid, and critically analyzes the claims made by companies in justifying their SA operations. Mini-profiles of 12 computer companies. 15 pp.

194. LEONARD, Richard, "A Review of Current U.S. Actions on Enforcement of the Arms Embargo Against South Africa," (New York: American Committee on Africa, 1983).

Details the Reagan record of relaxing enforcement of the arms embargo. Legal restrictions on export of technology to SA police/ military have been either overturned or ignored, thus providing SA's repressive apparatus with crucial high-technology items. Also provides evidence that those caught making illegal shipments to SA have not been vigorously prosecuted. 13 pp.

195. LEONARD, Richard, *South Africa At War* (Westport, CT: Lawrence Hill and Co., 1983).

Readable and comprehensive source on SA's police/military apparatus, black forces (especially ANC), the war in Namibia, foreign arms transfers to SA, "the propaganda war," "total strategy," and "the crisis in American policy." Appended documents include Freedom Charter, list of SAG propaganda projects, and secret USG documents leaked in 1981. 280 pp., 8 tables, index.

196. LIBBY, Ronald T., *Toward An Africanized U.S. Policy for Southern Africa: A Strategy for Increasing Political Leverage* (Berkeley, CA: Institute of International Studies, 1980).

Intelligent discussion of the white power structure of SA and its regional dominance, the liberation movements, and US policy in the post-1975 period. Title is somewhat misleading: the "strategy for increasing leverage" refers to US government leverage over the SA government, not African or Afro-American influence on US policy. However, the book details how Carter administration worked closely with Nigeria and Frontline States "because through them they could exert pressure upon the liberation movements without precipitating a further involvement in the region of the Soviet Union or other socialist countries." 120 pp., numerous tables.

197. LITVAK, Lawrence, Robert DeGrasse, and Kathleen McTigue, *South Africa: Foreign Investment and Apartheid* (Washington, DC: Institute for Policy Studies, 1978).

Produced as an organizing tool for the divestment movement, a thorough critique of the 'progressive force' thesis. Contents include: concise introduction to the institutional structure of apartheid and how it functions to supply a 'cheap' labor force for domestic and foreign capital; data on US investment and its role in maintaining the military/policy apparatus; critique of US policy and arguments for complete withdrawal of US investment. Appendices: US banks and corporations doing business with SA. 100 pp.

198. LOBBAN, Richard, "American Mercenaries in Rhodesia," *Journal of Southern African Affairs*, 3, 3, July 1978.

Background data on numerous Americans involved in recruiting mercenaries. Contrasts US laws against mercenary recruitment with government inaction and is "forced to conclude that the presence of American mercenaries in Rhodesia is simply an unacknowledged portion of the American policy for that nation." 6 pp.

199. "Making the most of a pullout from South Africa," *Business Week*, 20 October 1980.

"Growing numbers of U.S. and foreign multinational corporations are exploiting loopholes in South Africa's stringent foreign-exchange controls to withdraw capital from the country." Brief discussion of manipulations of 'financial rand' and 'commercial rand.' "Since January, 1979, alone, direct foreign investment in manufacturing totalled 319.3 million rands—but disinvestment in the same sector was 315.7 million rands." Details on ITT pullout. 1 p.

200. MANNING, Robert, and Stephen Talbot, "American Cover-Up on Israeli Bomb," *The Middle East*, June 1980.

Presents evidence that USG aided Israel and SA in developing and testing a nuclear weapon. Carter administration covered up because the revelation would be "a major embarrassment" and "would torpedo Carter's nonproliferation campaign, which is one of his major foreign policy concerns." 5 pp.

201. MARCHINO, Michael, and Robert K. Musil, "Guns of Bitterness: The American Mercenaries," *The Nation*, 10 April 1976.

Points to "postwar recession, inflation and unemployment" as causes which "have set adrift a small army of veterans from Vietnam who must sell their skills." Briefly looks at mercenary politics ("Unemployment as well as bitterness, right-wing ideology, sexism and a love of adventure, is a constant motif in mercenary literature.") 3 pp.

202. MARTIN, David C., and John Walcott, "Smuggling Arms to South Africa," *The Washington Post*, 5 August 1979.

Traces the intricate connections through which "an American–Canadian munitions firm with close Pentagon ties has illegally supplied the apartheid government of South Africa with special 155-mm shells that have 20 percent greater range than standard ammunition and no less accuracy." Points to possible USG collaboration in the smuggling operation.

203. MARTIN, Patrick Henry, *American Views on South Africa, 1948-1972* (PhD Dissertation, Louisiana State University, 1974).

Documents efforts by SAG and conservative allies in US to influence American opinion. Touches on the importance of cross-national political linkages for understanding the failure of US government to actively oppose apartheid. 314 pp., bibliography.

204. MAZRUI, Ali A., "Zionism and Apartheid: Strange Bedfellows or Natural Allies?" *Alternatives: A Journal of World Policy*, IX, 1983.

Examines historical similarities based on parallel efforts to implement culturally separatist ideologies. Traces the political impact of religion, the "martyrdom complex," labor policies, militarization, etc. Concludes that "a joint military-industrial complex between Israel and South Africa is in the making." 25 pp.

205. McKEE, Clarence, "A Black American Visits South Africa," *Lincoln Review*, 3, 2, Fall 1982.

Originally published by this conservative black journal but reprinted and distributed freely by SAG's propaganda apparatus in the US. This plea for more US investment in SA hits several familiar themes: SA blacks would suffer most from divestment, US corporations can stimulate reform, the Soviets are bigger threat than apartheid, etc. 7 pp.

206. MEHLMAN, Maxwell J., Thomas H. Milch, and Michael V. Toumanoff, "United States Restrictions on Exports to South Africa," *American Journal of International Law*, October 1979.

Traces history of US embargo policy and gives detailed legal examination of restrictions then in effect (since, relaxed by Reagan). Finds that "the South African security forces continue to be able to obtain a substantial amount of logistical support from U.S. sources." Recommends specific changes in US export policy. 23 pp.

207. MEZGER, Dorothea, "How the Mining Companies Undermine Liberation," *Review of African Political Economy*, 12, May–August 1978.

Focuses on the strategies of the mining industry in SA to protect their future profits in the event of a transfer to some form of majority rule. Concludes that the industry's links to international capital and foreign governments are strong enough to accommodate the destruction of apartheid, control the effects of nationalization, and prevent a full transition to socialism. A sobering analysis that emphasizes the difficulties that lie ahead for the liberation movement. 13 pp., 2 tables.

208. MILKMAN, Ruth, "Apartheid, Economic Growth and U.S. Foreign Policy in South Africa," *Berkeley Journal of Sociology*, XXII, 1977-78.

Overview of SA's social structure and role of US corporations in supporting it. "South Africa is a unique society in which the class divisions marking it as a capitalist society have been rendered almost entirely invisible due to the intensity of racial cleavages and the degree to which skin color has become the basis of one's relationship to the means of production." 55 pp.

209. MITTELMAN, James H., "America's Investment in Apartheid," *The Nation*, 9 June 1979.

Good journalistic piece on US corporations and apartheid, SA's role as a regional, subimperialist powerhouse, and the evolution of US policy toward southern Africa. 5 pp.

210. MORRELL, Jim, *International Institutions and Economic Sanctions on South Africa* (Geneva: International University Exchange Fund, 1980).

This critical report surveys SA's various sources of foreign credit (private banks, governments, the World Bank) with emphasis on the most important source—the IMF. Provides useful details on different ways USG has supplied credit to SA. 38 pp., numerous tables and charts.

211. MORRELL, Jim, "A Billion Dollars For South Africa," (Washington, DC: Center for International Policy, June 1983).

Based on confidential documents, provides background on how IMF decided to grant $1.1b loan to SA. Despite unprecedented opposition from Congress and Third World governments, Reagan administration lobbied in favor of loan. Gives evidence that SA did not technically qualify for the loan, did not really need it, and the amount roughly equalled the cost of SA's war in Namibia and Angola for past two years. 7 pp., several tables.

212. MORRELL, James, and David Gisselquist, "How the IMF Slipped $464 Million to South Africa," (Washington, DC: Center for International Policy, January 1978.)

Detailed documentation of IMF's 1976-77 loans to the wealthiest country on the African continent. The $464m "was more than all the rest of the countries in Africa put together received during the same two years." The fact that SA's "increase in military spending in 1976/ 1977 came to $450 million—almost exactly the amount of IMF assistance," did not deter the Carter administration, which "quietly supported" the loans "even while castigating the white-supremacy government in public." 8 pp., numerous tables.

213. MUGOMBA, Agrippah T., "The Militarization of the Indian Ocean and the Liberation of Southern Africa," *Journal of Southern African Affairs*, IV, 3, July 1979.

Traces history of Western military collaboration with SAG, SA's role as militarized "sub-imperial" power of the West, and the implications of this collusion. Western support for SAG allows further entrenchment of minority power, greater frustration among blacks, thus increasing chances of violent revolution. 18 pp.

214. MURAPA, Rukudzo, "The Political Economy of United States Policy in Southern Africa," *The Review of Black Political Economy*, 7, 3, Spring 1977.

Places US policy toward SA within context of "Nixon doctrine" alignment with regional powers like Brazil, Iran, Indonesia, and Israel. Stresses importance of US corporate investment as influence on US policy. 27 pp., 4 tables.

215. MYERS, Desaix III, et al., *U.S. Business in South Africa* (Bloomington, IN: Indiana University Press, 1980).

Much useful data. Chapters include internal developments regarding business and labor, foreign capital's role, the sanctions debate, as well as case studies of 4 industries (oil, computers, minerals, motor vehicles). Substantial discussion of divestment debate in US. Useful appendices, (e.g., SA labor laws, investment policies of US colleges, etc.). 375 pp., numerous tables.

216. MYERS, Desaix III, and David M. Liff, "South Africa Under Botha: The Press of Business," *Foreign Policy*, 38, Spring 1980.

Wide-ranging discussion of the political impact of foreign and domestic business on the policies of apartheid. Looks at reform measures that "fall far short of the political and economic equality sought by blacks." Gives pros and cons of trying to use business as reform catalyst. . . general outlook is not very hopeful. 20 pp.

217. NAGORSKI, Andrew, "U.S. Policy Options vis-a-vis South Africa" in Whitaker, ed., *Africa and the United States: Vital Interests* (New York: Council on Foreign Relations/New York University Press, 1978).

Discusses pros and cons of three general strategies toward SA. Argues that "the sanctions option is inherently more flexible and more complex than is generally perceived." Points out that sanctions against SA, if enforced, could be effective because "the very size of South Africa's economy makes it in some ways more vulnerable than Rhodesia; its need for trade and investment are of a larger magnitude." 24 pp.

218. NARMIC, "Investing in Apartheid," (Philadelphia, PA: American Friends Service Committee, 1983).

Directory of the several hundred US corporations directly investing in SA. Lists for each company: US parent, SA affiliate, product/service. 12 pp.

219. NARMIC, *Military Exports to South Africa: A Research Report on the Arms Embargo* (Philadelphia, PA: American Friends Service Committee, 1984).

Based on information released under Freedom of Information Act, this critical report details US military support to SA despite the UN arms embargo. Discusses the arms embargo, loopholes, police/military cooperation between US and SA, and the Reagan record of allowing more weapons technology to be exported to SA. 23 pp., several charts and tables.

220. NEDBANK GROUP, *South Africa: An Appraisal* (Johannesburg: The Nedbank Group, 1983).

Extensive statistical data on SA's domestic and international economic situation. Includes data on employment, investment, trade, balance of payments, etc. Available free on request from: Nedbank Limited, 535 Madison Avenue, N.Y., N.Y. 10022. 280 pp., 120 tables, bibliography.

221. NESBITT, Prexy, "New Strategies for International Action Against Transnational Corporate Collaboration with Apartheid," (New York: UN Centre Against Apartheid, 1979).

Emphasizes need for coordination of different tactics (mass demonstrations, divestment work, legislative strategies, etc.). Discusses need for linking antiapartheid work with other political struggles, and connecting various national antiapartheid movements. 15 pp.

222. "New U.S. Policy on South Africa," *TransAfrica News Report* (special edition) August 1981.

Reprints leaked State Department documents detailing views of USG and SAG regarding situation in southern Africa. The two regimes share basic objectives such as blocking USSR and other left forces in region, and bringing SA deeper into the western alliance. Key disagreement, however, on how to proceed on Namibia: USG needs internationally accepted settlement, but SAG knows SWAPO would win free elections. 8 pp.

223. NICKEL, Herman, "The Case for Doing Business in South Africa" (Washington, DC: Ethics and Public Policy Center, 1978).

Article reprinted from *Fortune* magazine which helped Nickel get post as Reagan's ambassador to SA. Argues that US corporate presence in SA is beneficial to blacks. 10 pp., photos.

224. NOER, Thomas J., *Briton, Boer, and Yankee: The United States and South Africa, 1870-1914* (Kent, OH: Kent State University Press, 1978).

US policy during this period "reflected prevailing concepts of economic expansion, evangelism, and racism." Covers early economic penetration, US support for Britain in Boer War, USG attempts to regulate black American ties to black South Africans, etc. Helps reveal that US support for racism in SA has deep roots. 192 pp., bibliography.

225. NYANGONI, Wellington, W., *The O.E.C.D. and Western Mining Multinational Corporations in the Republic of South Africa* (Washington, DC: University Press of America, 1982).

Detailed look at key SA industries—gold, diamonds, metals, uranium—and the role of western corporations and governments. Argues that the "complicated interlocking structures of Western conglomerates and the South African mining houses...provide financial and military stability to the apartheid state." 228 pp., 27 tables, 3 appendices, bibliography.

226. NYERERE, Julius K., "America and Southern Africa," *Foreign Affairs*, July 1977.

President of Tanzania delivers eloquent appeal to early Carter administration for America to "carry its declared support for human equality and dignity into policies which will weaken the forces of racialism and colonialism in southern Africa, so that the peoples of those areas can triumph more quickly and with less bloodshed." "The South African economy needs to be weakened, not strengthened, if apartheid is to be overthrown. South Africa therefore needs to be isolated economically, politically, and socially by the rest of the world until there has been a change in political direction." An excellent critique of western involvement in southern Africa by a highly respected African statesman. 14 pp.

227. NYERERE, Julius, "The Role and Responsibility of the United States in South Africa and Rhodesia," *The Black Scholar*, October 1977.

Somewhat dated but still relevant. Criticizes US policy for being "prompted more by super-power competition than by a genuine concern for equality and justice in Southern Africa." Argues that "the conflict in Southern Africa is not a capitalist versus communist struggle at all. It is a nationalist struggle for political freedom and for human equality." 7 p.

228. NZUWAH, Mariyawanda, "A Bibliography of Contemporary Publications on Southern Africa from 1970," *Journal of Southern African Affairs*, April 1978.

Extensive compilation of English-language books and pamphlets. More useful for scholars than activists. 13 pp.

229. NZUWAH, Mariyawanda, "A Guide to Contemporary Resources and Reference Materials on Southern Africa (1961–1978): A Selected Bibliography," *Journal of Southern African Affairs*, 3, 3, July 1978.

Massive compilation of books, pamphlets, and government documents covering Angola, Mozambique, Zimbabwe, SA, etc. Includes addresses of important antiapartheid organizations. 48 pp.

230. NZUWAH, Mariyawanda, "An Index of Selected Resolutions, Documents, and Declarations of the United Nations on Southern Africa," *Journal of Southern African Affairs*, 4, 2, April 1979.

Lists UN actions on Angola, Mozambique, Zimbabwe, Namibia, and SA, from 1946 to 1978. Includes brief annotations for most items. 60 pp.

231. NZUWAH, Mariyawanda, and William King, "Afro-Americans and U.S. Policy Toward Africa," *Journal of Southern African Affairs*, 2, 2, April 1977.

"The thrust of this essay" is "that Afro-Americans have historically been deprived of a role in the formulation of U.S. policy towards Africa." Traces the history of US relations with Africa to reveal a basic contradiction between US humanitarian and commercial interests. The failure of "the largest ethnic minority group in the United States" to significantly affect policy is attributed to lack of economic resources. 9 pp.

232. OFUATEY-KODJOE, W., "The United States, Southern Africa and International Order," *Journal of Southern African Affairs*, 1, (special issue) October 1976.

Analyzes the "substantive diplomatic behavior of the United States" in order to illuminate "the contradictions between U.S. declarations in support of the principles of self-determination and human rights, and U.S. actions which have seemed to consistently favor the white minority regimes." Posits the armed struggle as a major determinant of US policy ("if the Africans had not started fighting the US would have continued its policy of increasing support for the white regime and colonial regimes in Southern Africa"). 14 pp.

233. OTTAWAY, David, "Africa: U.S. Policy Eclipse," *Foreign Affairs*, special annual, "America and the World—1979," 1980.

Argues that although the Carter administration "had begun by explicitly rejecting Kissinger's globalist approach. . .in favor of an African regional perspective," during 1979 Carter's policy was lapsing into a Cold War mode. Warns that an East–West emphasis "would serve to alienate most of Africa, including those countries the United States has relied on most closely in furthering its economic and political interests." 22 pp.

234. OUDES, Bruce, "The United States' Year in Africa: Reinventing the Wheel," in Colin Legum, ed., *Africa Contemporary Record* (New York and London: Africana Publishing Co., 1979).

Well-informed discussion of 1977 "Carter reorientation" of policy toward Africa. "Having no major civil rights initiative to push, and being unwilling to embark on LBJ-type spending programmes so popular with many black Americans, Carter apparently saw his Africa initiative as not only wise on foreign policy grounds but also politically advantageous in relation to black Americans." 15 pp.

235. OUDES, Bruce, with Michael Clough, "The United States' Year in Africa: From Confidence to Caution," in Colin Legum, ed., *Africa Contemporary Record* (New York & London: Africana Publishing Co., 1980).

Broad-ranging article touches on policy toward Rhodesia, CIA activity, relations with SA, arms sales, "the Black Lobby," changes in Congress, and more. Lacks coherence but contains interesting tidbits: e.g., on 4 May 1978, as Carter was saying "We have no intention to intercede in any war in Angola," Brzezinski and CIA Director Turner were trying to get Senator Clark's approval for covert aid to UNITA. 12 pp.

236. OZGUR, Ozdemir A., *Apartheid: The United Nations and Peaceful Change in South Africa* (Dobbs Ferry, NY: Transnational Publishers, 1982).

Traces efforts by UN to pressure SAG away from apartheid. These efforts at inducing "internal peaceful change" have been rebuffed by SAG. Concludes that while outside pressure is helpful, internal forces—including armed struggle—will be decisive. Appends list of General Assembly and Security Council resolutions. 220 pp., bibliography, index, 1 map, 8 photos.

237. PAYNE, Richard J., "The Soviet/Cuban Factor in the New United States Policy Toward Southern Africa," *Africa Today*, 25, 2, April–June 1978.

Analyzes Carter administration policy within "the context of Soviet/ Cuban activities." While touching on US economic interests, he argues that "the primary political interest of the United States appears to be checking Soviet/Cuban advances." 19 pp.

238. PAYNE, Richard J., "Southern Africa and the Law of the Sea: Economic and Political Implications," *Journal of Southern African Affairs*, 4, 2, April 1979.

General introduction to the international negotiations over seabed mining, with rich countries favoring corporate exploitation and poor countries pushing for an equal distribution of seabed wealth. Good overview of various nations' positions but fails to examine US efforts to oppose the poor nations. 11 pp.

239. PAYNE, Richard J., and Eddie Ganaway, "The Influence of Black Americans on US Policy Towards Southern Africa," *African Affairs*, 79, 317, October 1980.

Gives special attention to black role in 1976 presidential election and to growing black political power generally as it relates to US Africa policy. 8 pp., 1 table.

240. PETRAS, James F., and Morris H. Morley, "Development and Revolution: Contradictions in the Advanced Third World Countries—Brazil, South Africa, and Iran," *Studies in Comparative International Development*, Spring 1981.

Compares "the conditions under which the process of capital accumulation takes place and its impact on class structure" in three "sub-imperialist" nations. Rejects concepts such as "national interest," to argue that "class cleavages are not confined to national boundaries but they involve international class units." Key goal is to "identify the location of core capital within the class structure of peripheral societies and its relationship to the peripheral state and dominant classes." 40 pp., bibliography.

241. PHILLIPS, Lindsey, "South Africa's Future: 'No Easy Walk to Free-dom'," *Working Papers for a New Society*, March-April 1979.

Sobering assessment of Pretoria's ability to resist demands for funda-mental changes in apartheid but includes tactical suggestions for antiapartheid forces. Good introduction aimed at general readership. 19 pp.

242. PILLAY, Vella, *The Role of Gold in the Economy of Apartheid South Africa* (New York: UN Centre Against Apartheid, March 1981).

Executive member of British Anti-Apartheid Movement discusses the history, labor relations, and international role of the SA gold industry. 29 pp., 15 tables.

243. "Pretoria in New Moves to Get US Nuclear Fuel," *Africa Economic Digest*, 3 July 1981.

Discusses secret US government documents showing SA has attempt-ed to circumvent US restrictions on sale of enriched uranium. 2 pp.

244. PRICE, Robert M., *U.S. Foreign Policy in Sub-Saharan Africa: National Interest and Global Strategy* (Berkeley, CA: Institute of International Studies, 1978).

Excellent critique of "globalist" approach to US policy. Analyzes "U.S. interests in sub-Saharan Africa" and "what effective options are available to the U.S. to counter increased Cuban and Soviet involve-ment." Argues that "the 'danger' of radicalization and concomitant Soviet involvement have come to dominate U.S. policy concerns regarding sub-Saharan Africa," even though "the political assumptions underlying the automatic equation of radical regimes with a Soviet security threat are seriously flawed." Recommends "humanitarian" aid to the liberation movements and economic pressure on the apartheid regime. 69 pp.

245. PRICE, Robert M., and Carl G. Rosberg, eds., *The Apartheid Regime: Political Power and Racial Domination* (Berkeley, CA: Institute of International Studies, 1980).

Thirteen informative, scholarly articles on Afrikaner politics, the liber-ation movements, the black trade union movement, Buthelezi/In-katha, government reform programs, and international context. Much useful information, generally from a liberal to left-liberal perspective. 376 pp., index, bibliography, numerous tables.

246. "Racism or Reason: The Corporations That Refuse to Sign the Sullivan Principles," *Business and Society Review*, 46, Summer 1983.

Responses from nine corporations to survey asking why they hadn't signed the Sullivan Principles. Varied responses: never heard of them, too much paperwork, we already do more than Sullivan requires, we were never asked to sign, it's none of your business, etc. Also gives data on top ten US banks lending to SA, 1979-1982. 4 pp., 1 table.

247. RAIFORD, William, "South Africa: Foreign Investment and Separate Development," *Issue*, IX, 1/2, Spring/Summer 1979.

Discusses role of foreign capital (direct investment and bank loans) in SA economy. Overview of US policy and SAG response. Describes 14 bills in Congress that would affect US investment in SA. 6 pp.

248. RAIFORD, William N., Barbara J. Bascle, and Allen F. Agnew, *South African Mineral Resources: Importance to the United States and the OECD Countries* (Washington, DC: Congressional Research Service, 1978).

Useful document designed "to examine the dependence of the United States upon South African mineral supplies and...the principal United States–South African corporate relationships that characterize the mining industry." Reveals that the US would be "capable of making satisfactory adjustments to a denial by the Republic of South Africa of its mineral supplies" but that NATO allies would be put under greater strain, thus indirectly affecting the US. Emphasizes the dependence of SA on the North Atlantic countries and downplays the potential for a SA denial of minerals to the West. 64 pp., numerous tables.

249. RAY, Ellen, William Schaap, Karl Van Meter, and Louis Wolf, eds., *Dirty Work 2: The CIA in Africa* (Secaucus, NJ: Lyle Stuart Inc., 1979).

Over 30 essays on various aspects of CIA activity in Africa. Topics include: media manipulation, mercenaries, covert intervention in Angola, CIA/BOSS collaboration, nuclear relations, and illegal arms traffic to SA. Large appendix with details on CIA officers in Africa. 523 pp., index.

250. "Reagan's Choice," *Africa*, 117, May 1981.

Overview of early Reagan policy in southern Africa. Cites "pressure within the administration" to "supply enriched uranium to South Africa." Reagan's "officials seriously and excitedly talk about giving military assistance to the UNITA movement." Suggests that Reagan will funnel aid through Savimbi's external headquarters, Morocco. Useful information on pro-apartheid lobbyists in Washington. 6 pp.

251. RIELLY, John E., "The American Mood: A Foreign Policy of Self-Interest," *Foreign Policy*, 34, Spring 1979.

Culled from an opinion survey by the Chicago Council on Foreign Relations, finds that "forty per cent of the public favors the United States taking an active stance in opposing apartheid in South Africa." Reveals strong sentiment opposed to US military intervention abroad. 12 pp., 7 tables.

252. RIVERS, Bernard, "Fuelling Apartheid," special issue of the *Newsletter: Council on Economic Priorities*, December 1978.

CEP research director documents how just 2 US oil corporations: 1) own a third of all US assets in SA, 2) "control nearly 40% of the South African oil market," 3) "supply the South African armed forces," and 4) "have provided oil for Rhodesia, in defiance of United Nations sanctions." Concludes that "progressive" hiring and wage policies by these firms are deceptive "when compared with their overall impact—which is to act as virtual extensions of the South African state, whose central object is to maintain the status quo." 6 pp., 1 table, 2 photos.

253. ROBINSON, Randall, *The Emancipation of Wakefield Clay* (London: Bogle-L'Ouverture Publishers, 1978).

Relevant novel that has not received attention it deserves. Black American soldier, part of US force in SA to combat liberation movement, receives education from freedom fighters/"terrorists." Raises important issues. 106 pp.

254. ROBINSON, Randall, "South Africa Under Botha: Investments in Tokenism," *Foreign Policy*, 38, Spring 1980.

Executive Director of TransAfrica criticizes "the familiar litany" of liberal views on SA as presented in Rotberg and Myer/Liff articles in same issue of *Foreign Policy*. Attacks two underlying assumptions of liberal/conservative positions: 1) that the corporate sector, "which thrives on the cheap labor guaranteed by repression," can be pushed to take a stand against apartheid, and 2) that white South Africa will respond to polite pressure from business. A US policy of gentle persuasion is "meaningless." US interests "lie in accommodation and identification with the black majority that will inevitably inherit South African society." 4 pp.

255. ROGALY, Gail Lynda, *South Africa's Foreign Relations, 1961–1979: A select and partially annotated bibliography* (Braamfontein, SA: South African Institute of International Affairs, 1980).

Cites 2,656 sources on various aspects of SA's foreign policy. Most entries have brief descriptions and many are relevant to US–SA relations. Includes list of bibliographic sources, subject index, and author index. 462 pp.

256. ROGERS, Barbara, *White Wealth and Black Poverty: American Investment in Southern Africa* (Westport, CT: Greenwood Press, 1976).

A largely empirical investigation into the complex and controversial role of US corporations in southern Africa. Primary emphasis is on SA but some material on Rhodesia and on the former Portuguese colonies. 331 pp., index.

257. ROGERS, Barbara, "Sunny South Africa: A World-wide Propaganda Machine," *Africa Report*, September-October 1977.

Short but useful rundown of what was known about SA's propaganda network in the US prior to the Information Department scandal. 6 pp.

258. ROGERS, Barbara, "South Africa's Fifth Column in the United States," *Africa Report*, November-December 1977.

A brief examination of SA's effort to build a network of Americans prepared to promote the apartheid regime. Much additional information has since become available. 3 pp.

259. ROGERS, Barbara, *Divide and Rule: South Africa's Bantustans* (London: International Defence and Aid, 1980).

Revised, expanded edition. Best single source on this subject. Sound scholarship with much detail but clearly written. 136 pp., tables, photos, map.

260. ROGERS, Barbara, and Brain Bolton, *Sanctions Against South Africa: Exploding the Myths* (Manchester, England: Manchester Free Press, 1981).

Sophisticated effort to undermine the standard arguments against sanctions, e.g., the West is too dependent on SA's minerals, sanctions would cause too much unemployment (especially in England), sanctions would hurt black South Africans the most. Much useful data on western mining companies and limits of mineral dependence. 104 pp., numerous tables.

261. ROGERS, Barbara, and Zdenek Cervenka, *The Nuclear Axis: The Secret Collaboration Between West Germany and South Africa* (New York: Times Books, 1978).

"Today there is virtually no doubt that the white racist minority in Pretoria has—or shortly will have—its finger on the nuclear button." Provides meticulous documentation of how the major capitalist powers (including US and Israel) helped SA develop nuclear potential. Includes hitherto secret government documents. Excellent 60-page chapter on US policy. Numerous tables document the extent of US collaboration. 464 pp., maps, photos, numerous tables, index.

262. ROTBERG, Robert I., "South Africa Under Botha: How Deep a Change?" *Foreign Policy*, 38, Spring 1980.

Believes that "the oligarchy ruling South Africa still thinks that black political demands can be dismissed." Yet the author still argues that polite US diplomacy can liberalize the Afrikaners. Advocates a policy somewhere between Carter and Reagan: "temper withdrawal and denial with inducement, bargain using the more savory Kissinger ploys." 18 pp.

263. ROTHMYER, Karen, "The McGoff Grab," *Columbia Journalism Review*, November/December 1979.

Detailed report on activities of right-wing US publisher and his SA ties. McGoff allegedly tried to buy US newspapers with South African government money. McGoff is personal friend of Gerald Ford (who received $10,000 for delivering a speech favoring US investment in

SA). Also involved is Richard Mellon Scaife, right-wing millionaire and backer of the Heritage Foundation. Extensive details on SA propaganda operations in the US. 7 pp., 4 photos.

264. ROTHMYER, Karen, *U.S. Motor Companies in South Africa: Ford, General Motors, and Chrysler* (New York: Africa Fund, 1979).

Brief but insightful analysis of the strategic role played by the 'big three' in insuring the industrial and military might of the apartheid regime. Much useful information. 19 pp.

265. ROTHMYER, Karen, "The South Africa Lobby," *The Nation*, 19 April 1980.

Documents SAG operations in US which range "from wining and dining Congressmen to secretly bankrolling the purchase of American newspapers, underwriting phony academic conferences and sponsoring golfing junkets for businessmen." Cites confessions of SA Information Minister: $250,000 given to aid 1978 defeat of Senator Dick Clark, "$3.9 million was channeled into the Ford Presidential campaign in 1976," and more. 4 pp.

266. RUDD, Andrew, "Divestment of South African equities: How risky?" *The Journal of Portfolio Management*, Spring 1983.

Tests the portfolio implications of divesting from US firms with subsidiaries in SA. Finds that "the effect on portfolio risk of excluding the companies operating in South Africa, the 150 to 200 major US companies, is, contrary to intuition, not particularly important." 6 pp., 6 tables.

267. SAMOFF, Joel, "Transnationals, Industrialization, and Black Consciousness: Change in South Africa," *Journal of Southern African Affairs*, 3, 4, October 1978.

Useful theoretical formulation "concerned with identifying the underlying relationships and orientations that will condition change over the next decade or so." Provides an overview of SA development within the context of world capitalism in order to illuminate "two major tensions": 1) "competition between foreign and local capital and between different forms of capital within South Africa," and 2) "that between owners and producers in South Africa." 31 pp., extensive bibliography.

268. SAMUELS, Michael A., et al., *Implications of Soviet and Cuban Activities in Africa for U.S. Policy* (Washington, DC: Georgetown Center for Strategic and International Studies, 1979).

Pentagon-sponsored study by 5 leading conservatives, including Chester Crocker. Standard recommendations: increase military aid; more training for Africans, especially civil administrators; create "an environment conducive to expanded private investment." Regarding white minority rule "U.S. diplomacy has a delicate task: on the one hand, to disassociate Washington from racist practices in Africa; and, on the other, to discourage the inclination to seek solutions through force and sanctions." 73 pp.

269. SAUL, John S., and Stephen Gelb, "The Crisis in South Africa: Class Defense, Class Revolution," *Monthly Review*, (special double issue), July-August 1981.

Good overview. Theoretical but highly readable. Gives 1) historical background, 2) aspects of the economic and political crises, 3) the state's strategy (especially Riekert and Wiehahn), 4) problems and opportunities for organized labor and the liberation movement. Concludes with (weakest) section on US policy. Authors display an impressive knowledge of subject matter. 156 pp.

270. SCHMIDT, Elizabeth, *Decoding Corporate Camouflage: U.S. Business Support for Apartheid* (Washington, DC: Institute for Policy Studies, 1980).

Devastating critique of Sullivan Principles, racial guidelines for US companies developed by GM board member Leon Sullivan. Shows that even if all suggested reforms were implemented, effect on black masses would be miniscule. Includes concise overview of apartheid economy, strategic role of US firms, and recent SAG reforms. Much useful data. 127 pp., numerous tables, graphs, photos.

271. SCHMIDT, Elizabeth, *One Step In the Wrong Direction: An Analysis of the Sullivan Principles* (New York: Episcopal Churchmen for South Africa, 1983).

Concise critique of Sullivan code and most recent report on company compliance. (Dismal results caused Leon Sullivan to criticize US firms for not doing enough.) Findings: roughly half US firms in SA won't sign on, dwindling number of signatories willing to report on activities, one-third of those reporting received lowest rating, and data suggesting that pay scales and training for blacks are not improving rapidly. 24 pp.

272. SCHOEMAN, Elna, *South West Africa/Namibia—An International Issue, 1920-1977: A Select Bibliography* (Braamfontein, SA: South African Institute of International Affairs, 1978).

Somewhat dated but still useful compilation of 1,098 mostly English sources, some relevant to US-SA relations. Many UN documents. Some citations have brief annotations. Includes chronology, subject index and author index. 161 pp.

273. SCHOEMAN, Elna, *South Africa and the United Nations: A select and annotated bibliography* (Braamfontein, SA: South African Institute of International Affairs, 1981).

Cites 1,007 sources, mainly from the 1960s and 1970s, regarding SA, Namibia and the UN. Many UN documents. Some sources relevant to US-SA relations. Includes author index and subject index. 244 pp.

274. SCHOMER, Howard, "South Africa: beyond fair employment," *Harvard Business Review*, May-June 1983.

A protestant minister and director of a consulting firm specializing in social policy advice to investment portfolio managers, Schomer details the "climate of renewed repression" in SA. Foreign companies invest there because "the return on direct investment since 1970 has been in the 14% to 16% (of assets) range, with occasional bonanza years (like 1980) in which after-tax profits soar as high as 30%." SAG reforms "have done more to placate world opinion than to improve the lot of Africans." American and other foreign banks "have buttressed the reign of white supremacy." Warns that major changes are needed urgently to avoid upheaval. 12 pp., map, several tables.

275. "The Secret State Department Documents," *Covert Action Information Bulletin*, 13, July-August 1981.

Reproduces in full several Reagan administration strategy documents. They include: detailed memo on Crocker meetings April 1981 with SA leaders, memo on Crocker's meetings with other African and European leaders, and long "scope paper" from Crocker to Haig on what US strategy should be vis-a-vis SA. Interesting reading. 5 pp.

276. SEIDMAN, Ann and Neva, *South Africa and U.S. Multinational Corporations* (Westport, CT: Lawrence Hill and Co., 1977).

Documents how the corporations that dominate the US economy are also crucial for the perpetuation of inequality in SA. Extensive data on minerals, manufacturing, oil, finance, etc. 251 pp., 2 maps, numerous tables and charts.

277. SEIDMAN, Ann W., and Neva Makgetla, *Activities of Transnational Corporations in South Africa* (New York: UN Centre Against Apartheid, 1978).

Extensive data compiled to "identify by national origin the main transnational and parastatal companies and banks with investments in the major sectors of the South African economy." Stresses the strategic importance of corporate capital and technology-transfer in key sectors like iron/steel, autos, petroleum, nuclear, and electrical equipment. 93 pp., numerous tables.

278. SEIDMAN, Ann, and Neva Seidman Makgetla, *Outposts of Monopoly Capitalism: Southern Africa in the Changing Global Economy* (Westport, CT: Lawrence Hill and Co., 1980).

Examination of western corporate penetration of southern Africa (especially SA) in post-war period. Useful data on numerous industries: mining, oil, agriculture, and banking. Illuminates how western capital aided SA in dominating the region for mutual benefit of South African and western ruling classes. 370 pp., numerous tables and charts, index.

279. SEILER, John, *The Formulation of U.S. Policy Toward Southern Africa, 1957-1976: The Failure of Good Intentions* (PhD Dissertation, University of Connecticut, 1976).

Former USG official gives extensive details on US policy toward the white minority regimes. Documents the ineffectiveness of liberal and left critics to move US policy against apartheid. Concludes that "the net effect of US regional policy sustained the white regimes." 613 pp., 7 tables, bibliography.

280. SEILER, John, "Has Constructive Engagement Failed?" *Orbis*, Winter 1982.

Criticizes early Reagan policy for giving Pretoria "too many incentives too soon with no apparent indication of any political cost, thus giving at least tacit encouragement to preemptive raids and economic destabilization against black regional states..." 7 pp.

281. SHAPIRO, Harvey D., "South Africa: The turn of the screw," *Institutional Investor*, January 1979.

Discusses lending policies of western (mainly US) banks in response to deteriorating political and economic conditions in SA. Also views impact of US divestment activism. Probability of further decline in SA's creditworthiness. 4 pp.

282. SHEPHERD, George W., Jr., *Anti-Apartheid: Transnational Conflict and Western Policy in the Liberation of South Africa* (Westport, CT: Greenwood Press, 1977).

Dated yet useful overview of causal factors in the international arena: non-government organizations, the UN, various boycotts, blacks in Britain and the US, church groups, arms embargo. 246 pp., index.

283. SHEPHERD, George W., Jr., "Clues to Reagan's Africa Policy," *Africa Today*, 27, 4, 1980.

Veteran Africanist reviews two recent books by top Reagan advisors and provides useful insights into the details of their Cold War perspective. In criticizing the works of Kenneth Adelman, Richard Bissell, and Chester Crocker, Shepherd points out that any increase in Soviet influence in Africa is due more to the increasing independence of Africa from western domination, not from a basic change in Soviet policy. Criticizes the notion "that superior Western military and counter-insurgent intervention is the ultimate basis for preserving Western interests." 5 pp.

284. SHIPPING RESEARCH BUREAU, *Oil Tankers To South Africa*, March 1981, S.R.B., P.O. Box 11898, 1001 GW Amsterdam, The Netherlands.

Dutch antiapartheid activists list details of oil tankers supplying SA. Many are US-owned. This in violation of OPEC and OAU regula-

tions. Book is part of ongoing effort to stop oil to SA. 90+ pp.,
numerous tables, bibliography.

285. SJOLLEMA, Baldwin, *Isolating Apartheid* (Geneva: World Council of
Churches, 1982).

In keeping with WCC's long-standing opposition to white minority
rule, then-head of their Programme to Combat Racism presents
concise overview of western collaboration with Pretoria and what to
do about it. Explains what various church groups have done to
combat apartheid. 136 pp., 6 appendices.

286. SMITH, Tim, and Craig Howard, "The Campaign for Withdrawal,"
Africa Report, July-August 1978.

An overview of US banks' involvement in the financing of apartheid
and their response to pressure from labor, church, and student organizations. 4 pp.

287. SOLARZ, Stephen J., "A Rapprochement with Racism?" *Orbis*, Winter 1982.

Former Chair of House Africa Subcommittee (D–NY) argues that
Reagan's policy toward SA "serves neither the interests nor the ideals
of the United States." Reagan refused to support aid to SA students
studying in US. We are losing goodwill around the world due to
"America's refusal to match our ritualistic and rhetorical opposition to
apartheid with even the smallest steps to make that opposition effective." 7 pp.

288. *South Africa and Sanctions: Genesis and Prospects.* Papers and com-
ments delivered at a symposium jointly organized by the South
African Institute of Race Relations and the South African Institute of
International Affairs, Johannesburg, 24 February 1979.

Four academic papers discuss the history of sanctions efforts, the
political prospects for sanctions, and various types of sanctions (economic, diplomatic, cultural, etc.). Generally sympathetic to the white
minority but contains useful information. 95 pp.

289. SOUTH AFRICA CATALYST PROJECT, *Anti-Apartheid Organizing
On Campus and Beyond* (Palo Alto, CA: SA Catalyst Project, 1979).

A how-to book. Includes useful material on antiapartheid struggles,
US foreign policy, the Krugerrand, using the media for political ends,
and lists organizations, films and periodicals relevant to antiapartheid
work. 77 pp., bibliography, numerous photos and graphics.

290. "South Africa: Embargoes and the USA," *Africa Confidential*, 20
October 1978.

Reviews US policy regarding the arms embargo and US sales (particularly aircraft). US planes used in 1975 invasion of Angola. "South
Africa is the US's tenth largest customer for light planes and helicop-

ters." Transfer of US arms via third parties such as W. Germany and Italy. Concludes that militarily, "Pretoria is still strikingly dependent on foreign suppliers for key components and for essential design technologies." 2 pp.

291. "South Africa's foot-dragging vexes U.S. companies," *Business Week*, 20 October 1980.

"Caught between apartheid critics at home and increasingly militant black workers in South Africa itself, U.S. multinationals find Pretoria's racial reforms virtually non-existent." Despite gold-based growth, "net foreign investment in manufacturing has been virtually flat since the start of 1979." Discusses Sullivan Principles, labor struggles, and skilled labor shortage. Lists recent US investments and divestments. Concludes: "political consciousness among South African blacks has reached a point where economic gains will not cool demands for full black citizenship and voting rights." 3 pp., 2 charts, 2 photos.

292. "South Africa's need for more black managers," *Business Week*, 8 June 1981.

Discusses contradictions between apartheid restrictions and economy's need for supervisors. "There are simply not enough white managers" to fill all positions. Education system is main problem: "The country spends 90% less on the education of a black child than it does on a white child." Although US companies "have the added impetus of pressure from 'liberal' groups at home," their programs have little impact; managing director of General Motors South Africa admits: "We will be lucky if we have several nonwhites in genuine managers' posts even by 1990." 2 pp.

293. SPECIAL COMMITTEE AGAINST APARTHEID, *Recent Developments in Relations Between Israel and South Africa*, Report by the Sub-Committee on the Implementation of United Nations Resolutions on Collaboration with South Africa, 31 October 1978.

Covers visits of government officials, military and nuclear cooperation, economic ties, cultural ties, tourism, etc. Concludes with recommendations for breaking this alliance. 40 pp.

294. SPOONER, Ward Anthony, *United States Policy Toward South Africa, 1919–1941, Political and Economic Aspects* (PhD Dissertation, St. John's University, 1979).

No theory but plenty of historical facts to show that "the United States played a significant role in South African development." Early South African prosperity "was inexorably linked and dependent upon American gold requirements." Documents early corporate involvement. USG presence was concerned mostly with facilitating trade/investment. 374 pp., 3 tables, bibliography.

295. STEVENS, Richard P., and Abdelwahab M. Elmessiri, *Israel and South Africa: The Progression of a Relationship* (New Brunswick, NJ: North American, 1977).

Several articles criticizing the historical, political, economic, and cultural linkages between the two settler states. Generally well-researched and includes dozens of reprinted articles and documents relevant to the theme. 228 pp., index, maps.

296. STOCKWELL, John, *In Search of Enemies: A CIA Story* (New York: W.W. Norton & Co. Inc., 1978).

Unique account by former chief of CIA Angola task force during the 1975-76 civil war. Numerous important revelations: CIA stepped up its activities *before* the Soviets made their major commitment; Kissinger and CIA personnel systematically lied to Congress and the American people; the CIA, in alliance with foreign mercenaries, helped kill thousands of Angolans even though their overall strategy was to *not* win the war; CIA covert operations are rife with corruption (e.g., ties to the Mafia) and ineffectiveness; the CIA systematically collaborates with the SA secret police. Argues persuasively for abolishing the CIA's covert operations branch. 285 pp., maps, photos, index.

297. STONE, Peter H., "Muldergate on Madison Avenue," *The Nation*, 14 April 1979.

Discusses SAG Information Department scandal and various propaganda operations in US. Focuses on role played by SAG friends such as Gerald Ford, John McGoff, and public relations firm Sydney S. Baron and Co. 3 pp.

298. SUCKLING, John, Ruth Weiss, and Duncan Innes, *Foreign Investment in South Africa: The Economic Factor* (Uppsala, Sweden: Africa Publications Trust, 1975).

Six insightful articles dealing with the role of foreign investment, trade, and bank loans; the structure of the parastatals; and SA's role in regional development. 198 pp., statistical appendix, numerous tables.

299. "The Sullivan Principles After Six Years: Compliance and Noncompliance," *Business and Society Review*, 44, Winter 1983.

Lists over 100 US companies operating subsidiaries or affiliates in SA which have refused to sign the Sullivan Principles. Also lists those signatory firms that have been judged "flagrant violators" of the principles, and those which "need to make better progress." 3 pp.

300. TANZER, Michael, et al., *Oil—A Weapon Against Apartheid: Proposals for Action to Cut Off South Africa's Supply of Oil* (New York: Sanctions Working Group, 1980).

Four oil experts analyze SA's vulnerability to an oil embargo. Explains forms of action that either have been taken or could be taken by governments, the UN, oil workers and activists. 81 pp., several appendices.

301. TAYLOR, David, "Israel–South Africa Nuclear Link Exposed," *The Middle East*, April 1981.

Traces intricate collaboration between Israel, SA, sections of USG, and Space Research Corporation of Vermont in testing nuclear artillery shell off SA's coast in September 1979. Carter administration "was relatively successful" in its cover-up, despite abundant evidence that SA tested nuclear device. 4 pp., several photos.

302. THOBHANI, Akbarali H., "The Mercenary Menace," *Africa Today*, 23, 3, July-September 1976.

Quotes US Federal Code statutes that outlaw mercenarism. Cites evidence that "mercenaries received training at Fort Benning, Georgia." Documents government foot-dragging on the mercenary problem and warns policymakers that the triumph of African nationalism in southern Africa is inevitable. "Mercenaries only delay this victory causing, in the process, a lot of unnecessary loss of lives and property." 8 pp.

303. TOMEH, George J., *Israel and South Africa: The Unholy Alliance* (New York: New World Press, 1973).

Compares apartheid to the system of control in Israel. Includes examination of economic ties, political-military cooperation, cultural ties, comparative ideology, and more. 76 pp., several tables.

304. "Trade Unions: America Steps In," *Work In Progress*, 24, 1982.

Critical assessment of AFL-CIO involvement in SA. Covers September 1982 visit to SA by AFL delegation, background on AFL's African American Labor Center and its controversial director, Irving Brown (veteran anticommunist alleged to have ties to CIA), and background of Nelson "Nana" Mahomo, director of AALC's southern Africa program. 8 pp., 3 photos.

305. TUTU, Desmond, "Black South African Perspectives and the Reagan Administration," *TransAfrica Forum*, 1, 1, Summer 1982.

General Secretary of SA Council of Churches reports that black South Africans "knew they were in trouble when their white compatriots went into expressions of ecstatic delight and joy when Ronald Reagan won the U.S. presidential elections." Judges Crocker's "constructive engagement" policy a total failure: SAG has grown more aggressive throughout the region, and internal "reforms" are aimed at furthering minority rule. "When we are free...we will remember who helped us get free. The Reagan administration is certainly not on that list." 12 pp.

306. UNITED NATIONS, "Resolutions Adopted by the United Nations General Assembly and Security Council on the Question of *Apartheid*, 1960–1980" (New York: UN, 1981).

Reproduces 36 resolutions detailing UN positions on SA. Most comprehensive resource of its kind. 112 pp.

307. UNITED NATIONS ECONOMIC AND SOCIAL COUNCIL, *Activities of Transnational Corporations in Southern Africa: Impact on Financial and Social Structures* (New York: UN, March 1978).

Covers SA, Namibia, and Zimbabwe: internal conditions as related to foreign investment. Discusses bank and corporate policies, wages, employment practices, union rights. Much useful data. 80 pp., numerous charts and tables.

308. UNITED NATIONS ECONOMIC AND SOCIAL COUNCIL, "Activities of Transnational Corporations in Southern Africa and Their Collaboration with Racist Minority Regimes in That Area" (New York: UN, 2 April 1980).

Details the role of foreign capital and technology in supplying SA's industrial, military and nuclear sectors. Criticizes the labor practices of transnational corporations (TNCs) vis-a-vis African workers and their trade unions. 44 pp., numerous tables.

309. UNITED NATIONS GENERAL ASSEMBLY, *Consideration of All Aspects of Sanctions Against South Africa*, report submitted by the Organization of African Unity to International Conference on Sanctions Against South Africa, 20-27 May 1981.

Includes OAU decisions on sanctions, analysis of possible sanctions (economic and military), impact of sanctions on neighboring states, and lessons from the Rhodesia sanctions experience. Reprints numerous OAU resolutions. 108 pp., 9 tables.

310. UNITED NATIONS GENERAL ASSEMBLY, *Developments in South Africa Since the Uprising of 1976*, Report submitted by the International Defence and Aid Fund for Southern Africa (New York: UNGA, 1981).

Detailed, reliable account of popular resistance, armed struggle, and government response. Includes chronology of armed struggle incidents, and overview of Pretoria's aggression on neighboring states. 56 pp., 4 tables, chronology.

311. UPPER VALLEY COMMITTEE FOR A FREE SOUTH AFRICA, *Dartmouth and Southern African Investments: The Case for Divestiture* (Hanover, NH: Upper Valley Committee, 1979).

Critical of corporate and university profit-making from investments in SA. Focuses on tactics used by university bosses when confronted by antiapartheid activists. 130 pp.

312. "USA: Strategic minerals and Africa," *Africa Confidential*, 22, 13, 17 June 1981.

Underlines Reagan team's obsession with this issue (hence refusal to sign Law of Sea Treaty requiring sharing of sea-bed minerals). Lists personnel and recommendations of Reagan's Strategic Minerals Task Force; it all bodes ill for US policy vis-a-vis SA. Also discusses stockpiling efforts of US and major allies. 3 pp.

313. US CONGRESS, House, Committee on International Relations, *Resource Development in South Africa and U.S. Policy* (Washington, DC: Government Printing Office, 1976).

Testimony of 19 witnesses (mostly government officials) and reproduction of numerous documents regarding US involvement in SA resource development, especially its nuclear program. Gives much information on US transfers of nuclear material and technology to SA. Information on various policy questions regarding US trade/investment in SA. 442 pp., numerous tables.

314. US CONGRESS, House, Committee on International Relations, *United States-Angolan Relations* (Washington, DC: Government Printing Office, 1978).

Testimony by former CIA case officer (John Stockwell), academic expert (Gerald Bender), and two companies (Boeing and Gulf), all arguing for recognition of MPLA government. Stockwell's account of the CIA intervention is concise and revealing. Reprints Bender's *Foreign Policy* article. 55 pp.

315. US CONGRESS, House, Committee on International Relations, *United States Private Investment in South Africa* (Washington, DC: Government Printing Office, 1978).

Dozens of academics, corporate and government officials submit evidence on the implications of US investments in SA. Critics argue that US corporate presence strengthens regime; defenders stress importance of fair employment codes. Touches on sanctions, Sullivan principles, US policy, and pending legislation to restrict US investment. 641 pp., numerous tables and documents.

316. US CONGRESS, House, Committee on International Relations, *United States-South Africa Relations: Nuclear Cooperation* (Washington, DC: Government Printing Office, 1978).

Seven government officials and 2 academics testify on SA's weapons potential, international trade in nuclear materials and technology, legal issues, safeguards, and US policy. 83 pp., numerous tables.

317. US CONGRESS, House, Committee on Foreign Affairs, *U.S. Policy Toward South Africa* (Washington, DC: Government Printing Office, 1980).

Large compendium of testimony by scholars, businessmen and government officials on topics such as: Sullivan Code, "homelands," "reform," US corporations, and government policy. 912 pp., numerous tables.

318. US CONGRESS, House, Committee on Foreign Affairs, *The Possibility of a Resource War in Southern Africa* (Washington, DC: Government Printing Office, 1981).

Testimony by four experts sheds doubt on USSR's ability/desire to deny West the mineral resources of southern Africa. Includes information on substitutes, alternatives sources, etc. for certain strategic minerals. 120 pp.

319. US CONGRESS, House, Committee on Foreign Affairs, *South Africa: Change and Confrontation* (Washington, DC: Government Printing Office, 1981).

Critical assessment of the limitations of government-initiated change. Reports "a universal feeling among black leaders that Prime Minister Botha has failed to live up to his early promises about initiating extensive reforms." Includes section on US role (Sullivan Code, bank loans, Krugerrand sales, etc.). 29 pp.

320. US CONGRESS, House, Committee on Foreign Affairs, *U.S. Educational Assistance in South Africa: Critical Policy Issues,* Report of a Staff Study Mission to South Africa (Washington, DC: Government Printing Office, 1982).

Concise overview of problems in SA education system with suggestions for US assistance. Despite minor reforms, "there is precious little to indicate that SAG has changed its view of the role of education in perpetuating the social and political disenfranchisement of its black population." 36 pp.

321. US CONGRESS, House, Committee on Foreign Affairs, *Enforcement of the United States Arms Embargo Against South Africa* (Washington, DC: Government Printing Office, 1982).

Testimony by two State Department officials, and a staff report by the Africa Subcommittee that concludes: "...while there has been an official *policy* of embargoing arms to South Africa...the relevant U.S. Government agencies have thus far failed to adopt *procedures* to effectively implement the embargo." Also provides evidence of CIA collaboration with SA to procure arms. 92 pp.

322. US CONGRESS, House, Committee on Foreign Affairs, *Controls on Exports to South Africa* (Washington, DC: Government Printing Office, 1983).

Eight government witnesses and 6 other experts testify on US trade restrictions vis-a-vis SA. Despite denials by Reagan officials, evidence suggests Reagan has loosened restrictions on trade with SA police/military. 321 pp.

323. US CONGRESS, House, Committee on Foreign Affairs, *Regional Destabilization in Southern Africa* (Washington, DC: Government Printing Office, 1983).

Ten scholars testify on SA's efforts to impede economic development and support for ANC in neighboring states. Conservatives downplay SA's role but others provide details of SA's aggression in region. 175 pp.

324. US CONGRESS, House, Committee on Foreign Affairs, *U.S. Corporate Activities in South Africa* (Washington, DC: Government Printing Office, 1983).

Submissions by numerous government and private witnesses regarding 3 pieces of legislation pending in the House. One introduced by Solarz (D-NY) would require all US firms in SA to adopt Sullivan code, prohibit sales in US of Krugerrands, and bar US banks from lending to SAG. The second, introduced by Gray (D-PA) would require US to ban any new US investment in SA (profits generated in SA could be reinvested there). Third, introduced by Bingham (D-NY), would reimpose export restrictions of Carter era that were dumped by Reagan. Reagan officials oppose the bills. 327 pp., 2 tables, 11 appendices.

325. US CONGRESS, Senate, Committee on Foreign Relations, *U.S. Policy Toward Southern Africa* (Washington, DC: Government Printing Office, 1975).

Interesting historical document with testimony and data from a variety of sources. Contains dozens of entries on Mozambique, Angola, Rhodesia, SA, and Namibia. 527 pp., 6 maps (poor quality), numerous tables.

326. US CONGRESS, Senate, Committee on Foreign Relations, *South Africa* (Washington, DC: Government Printing Office, 1976).

Massive compendium of testimony by scholars, businessmen and government officials. Dated but useful as historical document. 792 pp., numerous tables.

327. US CONGRESS, Senate, Committee on Foreign Relations, *Imports of Minerals From South Africa By The United States And The OECD Countries* (Washington, DC: Government Printing Office, 1980).

Useful data on key SA minerals, extent of western dependence, supply disruption scenarios, and corporate structure in mining industry. Concludes that supply disruption of long duration is highly unlikely, US is far less vulnerable than OECD, and all could take steps to decrease vulnerability. 46 pp., numerous tables.

328. US CONGRESS, Senate, Committee on Foreign Relations, *Nomination of Chester Crocker* (Washington, DC: Government Printing Office, 1981).

Detailed look at background and thinking of Reagan's Assistant Secretary of State for Africa. Includes texts of radio programs by pre-presidential Reagan denouncing "terrorists" Mugabe, Nkomo, and Nujoma; the even farther-right line of Sen. Jesse Helms (R-NC); as well as Crocker's responses to Committee questions. 49 pp., 7 tables.

329. US DEPARTMENT OF STATE, *Country Reports on Human Rights Practices* (Washington, DC: Government Printing Office, 1981).

Issued annually in February, includes section on SA. Subjects covered include torture, disappearances, arbitrary arrest, cruel or degrading treatment of prisoners, denial of fair trial, invasion of the home, economic deprivation, inequalities in education, restrictions on freedom of speech/press/religion/assembly/movement/political participation, etc. 19 pp.

330. "U.S./South Africa," *Africa News*, (special report) 25 May 1979.

Several pieces: divestment campaign, book reviews, and overview of US policy after Carter took over. Useful survey of Carter's shift toward quieter stance on apartheid, as well as details on trade, arms sales, etc. 10 pp.

331. VARYRNEN, Raimo, "Transnational Corporations in the Military Sector of South Africa," *Journal of Southern African Affairs*, V, 2, April 1980.

Extensive discussion of SA's arms procurement, R&D, computers, weapons production, and how western companies fit into this scheme. "U.S. transnationals active in the military sector of South Africa are production—rather than research—intensive." Also discusses military aspects of strategic minerals, oil, nuclear power, and bank loans. Contains interesting tidbits: "A third of the sales by the local IBM subsidiary are to the South African government, including the Department of Defence and the Atomic Energy Board." 56 pp.

332. WALTERS, Ronald W., "Uranium Politics and U.S. Foreign Policy in Southern Africa," *Journal of Southern African Affairs*, IV, 3, July 1979.

One of the top experts on SA's nuclear program and US role provides concise historical overview. US and SA elites have developed mutually-beneficial ties regarding uranium and nuclear technology, which inhibit a tougher Washington policy against apartheid. 19 pp., 1 table.

333. WALTERS, Ronald W., "The United States and the South African–Namibian Uranium Option," *Africa Today*, 30, 1/2, 1983.

Provides evidence of growing US dependence on SA/Namibian uranium. Makes several recommendations for antiapartheid action against this development. 9 pp., 3 tables.

334. WEISS, Ted, "American Policy and African Refugees," *Africa Report*, January-February 1984.

US congressman (D-NY) criticizes Reagan's "constructive engagement" policy because it "implies tacit approval of a system of brutal repression that has sent thousands of refugees fleeing from South Africa and Namibia into the surrounding states." The policy has not only damaged our relations with black Africa, but has "utterly failed to achieve its intentions. Since it was initiated, persecution of blacks in South Africa has actually intensified, and Namibia is no closer to independence now than it was in the late 1970s." 2 pp.

335. "We shot this young girl. She must have been about five..." *The Guardian* (Br.) 29 January 1981.

Former SA military commander describes SA operations against southern Angola. "Our main job is to take an area and clear it. We sweep through it and we kill everything in front of us, cattle, goats, people, everything." "...half the time the locals don't know what's going on. We're just fucking them up and it gets out of hand...SWAPO still get by us...it's not as if we are stopping them." Discredits UNITA. Reveals how SA troops do UNITA's fighting for them.

336. WESTERN MASSACHUSETTS ASSOCIATION OF CONCERNED AFRICAN SCHOLARS, *U.S. Military Involvement in Southern Africa* (Boston, MA: South End Press, 1978).

Documents strategic significance for apartheid of corporate investment in oil, electronics, and motor industry. Twelve chapters on mercenaries, nuclear cooperation, CIA, arms embargo, US Indian Ocean strategy, among other topics. Several documents appended. 276 pp., numerous tables, bibliography, index.

337. WHALEN, Eileen, and Ken Lawrence, "American Workers and Liberation Struggles in Southern Africa," *Radical America*, May–June 1975.

Somewhat dated description of efforts by sections of organized labor to combat racism and block US corporate and government support for white minority rule. 15 pp.

338. WHITAKER, Jennifer Seymour, ed., *Africa and the United States: Vital Interests* (New York: Council on Foreign Relations/New York University Press, 1978).

Eight essays by 7 policy analysts associated with the Council on Foreign Relations, a major business-oriented think-tank. Focusing on US economic and strategic interests, as well as competition with the Soviets, the book includes: "US Policy Toward Africa," Whitaker; "US Economic Interests in Africa," Bertolin; and "US Policy Options vis-a-vis South Africa," Nagorski. 255 pp., 2 maps, 9 tables, index.

339. "Will the CIA Intervene Again in Angola?" *Washington Notes on Africa*, Summer 1980.

Concise overview of US covert policy. Provides details on the legislative and military struggles. Discusses UNITA propaganda efforts in the US and future prospects for US–Angola relations. 4 pp.

340. WINTER, Gordon, *Inside BOSS: South Africa's Secret Police* (Harmondsworth, England: Penguin Books, 1981).

Detailed account by former SA secret police operative, including sections on CIA cooperation, SA's destabilization against neighbors, and covert operations against antiapartheid elements in SA. Numerous allegations regarding CIA: they helped foment split between ANC/PAC, channeled money to various groups and individuals, and encouraged the 1975/76 SA invasion of Angola. 640 pp., index.

341. WITHERELL, Julian W., *United States and Africa, 1785-1975* (Washington, DC: Government Printing Office, 1978).

Head of the African and Middle Eastern Division of the Library of Congress lists 8,827 official US documents and government-sponsored publications covering all of Africa except Egypt. Specialized book which includes congressional and presidential documents, diplomatic papers, treaties, commercial reports, etc. Of those on SA, most are aimed at helping US business. 949 pp.

342. YOUNG, Andrew, "The United States and Africa: Victory for Diplomacy," *Foreign Affairs* (special issue, "America and the World, 1980").

Self-congratulatory view of Carter administration's final year in Africa. Light treatment of other regions with major emphasis on southern Africa. Mugabe's victory in Zimbabwe is seen as vindication for a regionalist (as opposed to Cold War) approach to US policy. Readable overview but contains no new information for serious Africa-watchers. 18 pp.

343. ZINN, Kenneth S., "Reagan and Southern Africa," *Coalition Close-Up* (Newsletter of the Coalition for a New Foreign and Military Policy) July 1981.

Views Reagan's "constructive engagement" policy toward SA as "first step towards a full-fledged alliance with that regime." Reviews 1) Reagan's early gestures to SA, 2) what Pretoria wants from US, 3) SA attacks on Angola and Mozambique, and 4) stalled diplomacy on Namibia. "By actively siding with apartheid, the U.S. is once again on the wrong side of history." 3 pp., graphics.

Directory of
Information Sources

Periodicals

AF Press Clips
  Bureau of African Affairs
  Department of State
  Washington, DC 20520

  Weekly collection of clippings on Africa from mainstream US press. Available free on request to organizations.

Africa Confidential
  5/33 Rutland Gate
  London SW7
  England

  Eight-page bi-weekly often carries information on
  southern Africa not available elsewhere. Airmail to US
  $70/year.

The African Communist
  Inkululeko Publications
  39 Goodge Street
  London W1P 1FD
  England

  Quarterly journal of the South African Communist
  Party. Airmail to US $15/year.

Africa News
P.O. Box 3851
Durham, NC 27702

Best weekly news and analysis available in US. Much on southern Africa. $25/year.

Africa Today
Graduate School of International Studies
University of Denver
Denver, CO 80208

Quarterly journal often carries information useful to antiapartheid movement. $12/year.

ANC Weekly News Briefing
801 Second Avenue
New York, NY 10017

Weekly collection of news stories from the South African and international press.

Anti-Apartheid News
13 Mandela Street
London NW1 ODW
England

Monthly newspaper covers British antiapartheid movement, and situation in South Africa and Namibia. $10/year.

Facts and Reports
Holland Committee on Southern Africa
O.Z. Achterburgwal 173
1012 DJ Amsterdam
The Netherlands

Bi-weekly collection of news stories from the southern African and European press and radio. Airmail to US $53/year.

Focus on Political Repression in Southern Africa
International Defence and Aid Fund
64 Essex Road
London N1 8LR
England

Bi-monthly news and analysis of SA courts, police, military, and resistance movement. Airmail to US $10/year, includes three Briefing Papers per year on particular subjects.

Objective: Justice
United Nations Information Center
1889 F Street, NW
Washington, DC 20006

Bi-annual magazine covering UN support for struggles against racism and apartheid. Free on request.

Resister
COSAWR
B.M. Box 2190
London WC1N 3XX
England

Journal of the Committee of South African War Resistance (COSAWR), issued bi-monthly, covering military aspects of apartheid, and the draft resistance movement. Airmail to US $8/year.

SECHABA
African National Congress
801 Second Avenue
New York, NY 10017

Monthly journal of the ANC containing articles, interviews, and book reviews relating to the struggle against apartheid. $10/year.

South Africa/Namibia Update

African-American Institute
833 UN Plaza
New York, NY 10017

Monthly news and analysis culled from the South
African and international press. $24/year.

Washington Notes on Africa

110 Maryland Avenue, NE
Washington, DC 20002

Quarterly news and analysis from the Washington
Office on Africa. $10/year brings the quarterly and
occasional legislative alerts on southern Africa.

Organizations

Africa Resource Center
464 19th Street
Oakland, CA 94612
(415) 763-8011

Information center with extensive material on southern Africa.

American Committee on Africa/Africa Fund
198 Broadway, Suite 401
New York, NY 10038
(212) 962-1210

Researches and publishes literature on southern Africa, provides speakers, films, etc., on apartheid and the struggle against it. Provides material assistance (medical, agricultural supplies) to victims of white minority rule.

American Friends Service Committee
Peace Education Division, Southern Africa Program
1501 Cherry Street
Philadelphia, PA 19102
(215) 241-7169

Based on Quaker nonviolent philosophy, educates and mobilizes citizens in support of the oppressed majority in SA and against US policies that aid minority rule.

Artists and Athletes Against Apartheid
545 8th Street, SE, Suite 200
Washington, DC 20003
(202) 547-2550

Headed by Arthur Ashe and Harry Belafonte, this group brings together entertainers and organizations to encourage a cultural boycott of SA.

Association of Concerned Africa Scholars (ACAS)
P.O. Box 791
East Lansing, MI 48823

Organization of progressive Africanists in US. Consistent supporters of liberation struggles in southern Africa.

Episcopal Churchpeople for a Free Southern Africa (ECSA)
339 Lafayette Street
New York, NY 10012
(212) 477-0066

Monitors human rights situation in southern Africa and publishes newsletter, "For A Free Southern Africa."

Interfaith Center on Corporate Responsibility
475 Riverside Drive
New York, NY 10115
(212) 870-2294

Monitors US corporate involvement in SA and supports shareholder resolutions calling for workplace reform.

International Defense and Aid Fund for Southern Africa
P.O. Box 17
Cambridge, MA 02138
(617) 491-8343

International organization with home base in London provides legal and material aid to victims of apartheid. Produces high-quality books, newsletters, and photo exhibits.

Lawyers' Committee for Civil Rights Under Law

Southern Africa Project
1400 Eye Street, NW
Washington, DC 20005
(202) 371-1212

Aids SA political detainees, initiates legal action in US to discourage support of SA, and provides information on legal battles in SA.

New World Resource Center

1476 West Irving Park Road
Chicago, IL 60613
(312) 348-3370

Long-time supporter of liberation movements, with large selection of material on southern Africa.

Southern Africa Media Center

630 Natoma Street
San Francisco, CA 94103
(415) 621-6196

Distributes numerous films on SA and the struggle against apartheid.

Toronto Committee for the Liberation of Southern Africa

427 Bloor Street West
Toronto, Ontario, Canada
(413) 967-5562

Veteran support group provides material aid and education. Publishes bi-monthly newsletter.

TransAfrica

545 8th Street, SE
Washington, DC 20003
(202) 547-2550

Black lobbying group focusing on US policy in Africa and the Caribbean. Publishes newsletter and journal with useful information on legislation and policy.

United Nations Centre Against Apartheid

UN Secretariat
New York, NY 10017
(212) 754-6674

Publishes numerous free studies on all aspects of apartheid and the struggle against it. Most documents also
available from UN Information Center, 1889 F Street,
NW, Washington, DC 20006

Washington Office on Africa

110 Maryland Avenue, NE
Washington, DC 20002
(202) 546-7961

Lobbying and information center focusing on US
policy in southern Africa. Quarterly newsletter, "Washington Notes on Africa," is a dependable source.

Liberation Movements

African National Congress of South Africa (ANC)
Suite 405
801 Second Avenue
New York, NY 10017
(212) 490-3487

Pan Africanist Congress of Azania (PAC)
Suite 703
211 East 43rd Street
New York, NY 10017
(212) 986-7378

South West Africa Peoples Organization (SWAPO)
Room 1401
801 Second Avenue
New York, NY 10017
(212) 557-2450

Index

About the Author

Kevin Danaher received his Ph.D. from the University of California. Formerly an associate fellow of the Institute for Policy Studies in Washington, D.C., he is author of *South Africa and the United States: An Annotated Bibliography* (Washington, D.C.: IPS, 1979). His articles have appeared in *Monthly Review, Harvard Educational Review, TransAfrica Forum, Politics and Society,* and *Le Monde Diplomatique.* He works for the Institute for Food and Development Policy in San Francisco.